The Securitization of Migi

The international movement of people is provoking worldwide anxiety and apprehension. Nation-states around the globe, especially Western ones, are cracking
down on migration for security reasons. International migration has become a key
security issue and is perceived, by some, as an existential security threat.

The Securitization of Migration is about the movement of people and the
system of order underpinning the movement. In undertaking a comparative study
of Canada and France, the study analyzes the process of securitizing migration.
It explores the process of discursively and institutionally integrating international migration into security frameworks that emphasize policing and defense.
Drawing upon social theory, migration studies, and Securitization Theory,
Philippe Bourbeau seeks to understand the concepts of power underlying security
frameworks and how these affect the treatment of migrants and immigrants. This
book is one of the first to systematically and comparatively examine the role of
political agents, media agents, and contextual factors in the process of securitizing
migration.

The book will be of interest to students and scholars concerned with comparative and theoretical approaches to security and migration studies.

Philippe Bourbeau is a SSHRC Postdoctoral Fellow in the Centre for International
Policy Studies at the University of Ottawa, Canada.

Security and Governance Series

Edited by Fiona B. Adamson, School of Oriental and African Studies, University of London
Roland Paris, University of Ottawa
Stefan Wolff, University of Nottingham

Editorial Board:
Mohammed Ayoob, Michigan State University
Richard Caplan, University of Oxford
Neta Crawford, Boston University
Stuart Croft, University of Warwick
Donatella della Porta, European University Institute
Michael Doyle, Columbia University
Lynn Eden, Stanford University
Takashi Inoguchi, University of Tokyo
Elizabeth Kier, University of Washington
Keith Krause, Graduate Institute of International Studies, Geneva
Bruce Russett, Yale University
Timothy Sisk, University of Denver
Janice Gross Stein, University of Toronto
Stephen Stedman, Stanford University
Mark Zacher, University of British Columbia

This series reflects the broadening conceptions of security and the growing nexus between the study of governance issues and security issues. The topics covered in the series range from issues relating to the management of terrorism and political violence, non-state actors, transnational security threats, migration, borders, and "homeland security" to questions surrounding weak and failing states, post-conflict reconstruction, the evolution of regional and international security institutions, energy and environmental security, and the proliferation of WMD. Particular emphasis is placed on publishing theoretically informed scholarship that elucidates the governance mechanisms, actors and processes available for managing issues in the new security environment.

Rethinking Japanese Security
Peter J. Katzenstein

State Building and International Intervention in Bosnia
Roberto Belloni

The UN Security Council and the Politics of International Authority
Edited by Bruce Cronin and Ian Hurd

The Dilemmas of Statebuilding
Confronting the contradictions of postwar peace perations
Edited by Roland Paris and Timothy D. Sisk

Protest, Repression and Political Regimes
An empirical analysis of Latin-America and sub-Saharan Africa
Sabine C. Carey

The International Humanitarian Order
Michael N. Barnett

The International Politics of Mass Atrocities
The case of Darfur
Edited by David R. Black and Paul D. Williams

Truth Commissions and Transitional Societies
The impact on human rights and democracy
Eric Wiebelhaus-Brahm

Emerging Transnational (In)Security Governance
A statist-transnationalist approach
Edited by Ersel Aydinli

Peacebuilding and Rule of Law in Africa
Just peace?
Edited by Chandra Lekha Sriram, Olga Martin-Ortega and Johanna Herman

Hegemony and Democracy
Bruce Russett

The Securitization of Migration
A study of movement and order
Philippe Bourbeau

The Securitization of Migration

A study of movement and order

Philippe Bourbeau

 Routledge
Taylor & Francis Group

LONDON AND NEW YORK

First published 2011
by Routledge
2 Park Square, Milton Park, Abingdon, Oxon, OX14 4RN

Simultaneously published in the USA and Canada
by Routledge
711 Third Avenue, New York, NY 10017

Routledge is an imprint of the Taylor & Francis Group, an informa business

Typeset in Times by Prepress Projects Ltd, UK

British Library Cataloguing in Publication Data
A catalogue record for this book is available from the British Library

Library of Congress Cataloging-in-Publication Data
Bourbeau, Philippe
The securitization of migration: a study of movement and order/Philippe
Bourbeau.
p. cm. – (Security and governance series)
Includes bibliographical references and index.
1. Border security–Management–Case studies. 2. Ports of entry–Security
measures–Case studies. 3. Canada–Emigration and immigration–
Government policy. 4. France–Emigration and immigration–Government
policy. I. Title.
JV6271.B58 2011
325–dc22
2010037781

ISBN: 978-0-415-73148-5 (pbk)
ISBN: 978-0-415-59451-6 (hbk)
ISBN: 978-0-203-82934-9 (ebk)

First issued in paperback 2013

To B.

Contents

x *Contents*

Figures

Tables

Acknowledgments

Writing a book always takes longer than one has imagined. At every step of this challenging yet stimulating project, I have had the chance to have fascinating conversations and delightful interactions with several colleagues and friends.

Without a doubt, this book would not have been possible without the encouragement, counsel, and support of Michael C. Williams. Mike's contagious enthusiasm and fascination for theoretical discussions have indeed been—and still are—a great source of inspiration for me. I feel privileged to have had the opportunity to work with such a committed and insightful scholar for the last two years.

I owe a special debt of gratitude to two professors in the Department of Political Science at the University of British Columbia (UBC). Brian Job has been very supportive of my research project, making himself available in difficult times as well as in more joyful times. This book is far better because of his keen eye, sensitive ear, and great sense of organization and structure. I wish to also especially thank Richard Price. On several occasions Richard has provided a much-needed razor-sharp reading of my work and he has forced me to think about my argument in novel and stimulating ways. Both Brian and Richard have shown a tremendously high level of professionalism and commitment in all my years at UBC.

Roland Paris, Director of the Centre for International Policy Studies at the University of Ottawa, has also been very supportive of this project. His dynamism has made my postdoctoral tenure in his Centre a stimulating and enriching experience that I can only strongly recommend. I would also like to thank the editors of the Security and Governance Series, Roland Paris, Fiona Adamson and Stefan Wolff, for including my book in their excellent series. The editorial team at Routledge also deserve a special mention for their patience and professionalism.

Numerous friends and colleagues have offered thoughtful comments on earlier drafts. I wish to thank in particular Ole Wæver, Andrew Geddes, Christian Joppke, Didier Bigo, Yves Tiberghien, Dan Hiebert, Jef Huysmans, Catherine Dauvergne, Marie-Claude Smouts, Patrick Weil, Martin Heisler, and Diana Lary. They also, on numerous occasions, sat down with me to chat freely over coffee, which turns out to be equally gratifying. I also want to thank the three anonymous reviewers for comments on earlier versions of the book.

I also benefited greatly from discussions with colleagues at institutions with which I have been affiliated or where I have been invited to conduct research in the past few years. The Centre for International Policy Studies at the University of Ottowa, the Department of International Politics at Aberystwyth University, the Centre of International Relations at UBC, the Robert Schuman Centre for Advanced Studies at the European University Institute (EUI), and the Centre d'études et de recherche internationale (CERI-Sciences-Po) have all provided ideal working environments. This project received generous financial support from the Social Science and Humanities Research Council of Canada, the Security and Defence Forum of the Department of National Defence of Canada, the Canadian Consortium on Human Security, and the Metropolis British Columbia Centre of Excellence for Research on Immigration and Diversity.

Un merci tout special à mes amis de toujours et à ma grande famille, particulièrement Jean et Joanne.

My deepest words of love, gratitude, and humility go to Barbara and our children, Anjara and Numa. Barbara's love, unfailing patience, and tireless support sustained me throughout the process. "The ice is thin, come on dive in."

1   Introduction

A study of movement and order

The movement of people is provoking worldwide anxiety and apprehension and casting long-established patterns of cultural identity, belonging, and security into a state of uncertainty. In this troubled context, abrasive rhetoric about migration is gaining popularity; nation-states around the globe, especially Western ones, are cracking down on migration for security reasons.

Multilateral and bilateral agreements have been signed, international and domestic institutions have been created, extradition and deportation agreements between receiving and sending states have been authorized, and conventions and protocols have been ratified with, at their core, the linkage between migration and security. A sharp increase in border control is also noticeable: by the end of the 1990s (i.e. before 9/11), the United States Immigration and Naturalization Service had more employees authorized to carry guns than any other federal law enforcement force (US Department of Justice 2000). International migration has become a key security issue and is perceived, in some eyes, as an existential security threat. Scholars have referred to this current state of affairs as *securitized migration* or as the *securitization of migration* (Wæver *et al.* 1993).

This book is about the movement of people and the system of order underpinning the movement. In undertaking a comparative study of Canada and France between 1989 and 2005, the study analyzes the process of securitizing migration. That is, it explores the process of discursively and institutionally integrating international migration into security frameworks that emphasize policing and defense (see Huysmans 2006).

To be sure, migration has been controlled through national policies and bilateral and/or multilateral agreements for a long time. Moreover, the notion that certain individuals could pose security threats has been a reality for many years. The factors that have recently begun to cause alarm, however, are (1) the notion of migration in a *collective* sense posing an existential threat to the security of the state and/or the society; (2) the prominence given to immigration as a security threat; and (3) its attendant effects in political practice, which have undergone significant and even startling changes.

Since the late 1980s, there has been a wave of academic interest in the relationship between the movement of people and world politics. Unsurprisingly, the nature and mechanisms of the securitization of migration is the subject of considerable debate.[1] In international relations (IR), scholars attuned to realist premises of anarchy and material interest argue that Western states should fear the "coming anarchy" associated with mass migration (Huntington 2004; Kaplan 1994). Another stream of theorizing that has its roots in IR is neoliberalism; Christopher Rudolph (2003, 2006) revisits the grand state strategy perspective and contends that the "structural threat environment" is the primary explanatory factor for the securitization of migration. Another model, which takes its cue from critical security studies (largely defined) and political sociology, is the governmentality of unease model. Didier Bigo, one of the most active advocates of this model, argues that the securitization process has to do above all with routinized practices of professionals of security and the transformation of technologies they use (Bigo 2002, 2008). Of these models, Securitization Theory (ST) provides the most widely applied and fully developed model for the study of the securitization process (Buzan *et al.* 1998; Wæver 1995).[2] Nonetheless, ST has difficulties finding a place within wider categories of IR theory as realists and neoliberal institutionalists treat ST with polite neglect and critical theorists find ST not critical enough (Booth 2005a; Smith 2005; Wyn Jones 2005).

This book seeks to advance both ST and its engagement with IR theory by linking ST to constructivism—an approach that ST borrows but has not yet explored to its full potential. I argue that constructivism offers sound theoretical foundations to propose refinements to ST. My argument is not that ST should find its "home" in constructivism. Nor is my objective to propose a constructivist model for the study of the securitization process that would stand in opposition to ST. Rather, I want to suggest that constructivism offers fruitful correctives that can be integrated within ST without distorting the theory. My goal is to propose a refined version of ST.

The argument

In this book I make three contributions to the securitization research literature. First, I argue that a departure from ST's analytical axioms of "conditions" toward a constructivist approach stressing the importance of multifaceted contexts and the inter-relationship between agents and structural/contextual factors is needed. A constructivist perspective underscores that linguistic utterances are always produced in particular contexts and that the social properties of these contexts endow speech acts with a differential value system. My study presents an analytical framework that understands the relationship between agents and contextual factors as mutually constituted, durable but not static, generative, and structured. My analysis also permits the inclusion of time in the analytical framework by opting for a "moving pictures" approach to the phenomenon of securitized migration, instead of taking merely a "snapshot" view of the phenomenon, to borrow a forceful image from Paul Pierson (2004).

Second, I put forward a constructivist approach that acknowledges the polymorphous character of power. Building on the work of Michael C. Williams (2007) and of Michael Barnett and Raymond Duvall (2005), my study underlines that power operates through diffuse processes embedded in the historically contingent and multifaceted cultural settings. Seen in this light, I contend that ST identifies only conditions that *facilitate* the securitization process; the theory overlooks contextual factors that *constrain* or *limit* the securitization process. In addition, I demonstrate that the power of contextual factors does not function in a binary, direct, and almost mechanical way, as is currently understood in securitization research. Rather, my study shows that the power of contextual factors works in a diffuse yet tangible way, and within a continuum of power ranging from enabling to constraining capacities.

Third, I propose a model for the study of the securitization of migration that offers guiding principles to account for the variation in levels of securitized migration. Indeed, I argue that, because ST treats security as a binary notion, it cannot explain variation in levels of securitized migration. The only variation that ST recognizes is along the spectrum of non-politicization, politicization, securitization, and de-securitization. Once an issue reaches the securitization phase, ST does not distinguish whether the issue is strongly securitized or weakly securitized. This is problematic because if variation does exist there is no theoretical space in ST, as currently organized and applied, to provide adequate guidance for the suggestion of hypotheses accounting for variations within cases across time or across cases. Contrary to this standpoint, my analytical framework will permit both an empirical measurement of levels of securitized migration and the deduction of hypotheses to account for the variation.

Methods of inquiry

In the following chapters, I explore the role of two securitizing agents (political, media) and of two contextual factors (exogenous shocks, domestic audiences) in the securitization process. For the purpose of this study, political agents are elected politicians and members of the government—those who are in power. I have focused my analysis on the leaders of the governing political party as well as the ministers in charge of foreign affairs and immigration portfolios.[3] In Canada, my political agents are Prime Ministers, Ministers of Foreign Affairs, and Ministers of Citizenship and Immigration. In France, I have chosen Presidents, Prime Ministers, Ministers of Foreign Affairs, and Ministers of Interior. For each agent I examined their complete set of speeches made between 1989 and 2005. In total, I have retrieved, collected, and quantitatively and qualitatively analyzed nearly 3,500 speeches.

In this study, media agents are editorialists of major national newspapers. In Canada, my media agents are editorialists from *The Globe and Mail* and *La Presse*. The former is generally regarded as Canada's national newspaper and the latter as the most important French-language newspaper. Taken together, they have a daily circulation of more than 500,000 copies (weekdays). In France, I have selected editorialists of *Le Monde* and *Le Figaro*; their combined daily circulation is also substantial with on average 850,000 copies (weekdays). These two newspapers are largely considered the two most important newspapers in France. For each media agent I examined the complete set of editorials written between 1989 and 2005 in which the issue of the movement of people was discussed. In total, I have systematically retrieved, collected, and quantitatively and qualitatively analyzed 900 editorials.

This selection of agents is not a theoretical statement on who constitutes a securitizing agent; in designing the study, I had to limit the range of agents under investigation. Likewise, although this research investigates *actors* involved in the securitization of migration, the emphasis is not on the *authors* of the securitization—if such a role exists. As Hannah Arendt (1958: 184–5) underscores superbly,

> the stories, the results of action and speech, reveal an agent, but this agent is not an author or producer. . . . The perplexity is that in any series of events that together form a story with a unique meaning we can at best isolate the agent who set the whole process into motion . . . we never can point unequivocally to him as the author of its eventual outcome.

On top of the quantitative and qualitative analysis of politicians' speeches and editorialists' editorials, I conducted a limited but well-targeted number of interviews in each country case using a multiple-choice questionnaire, semi-structured questions, and open-ended questions. In Canada, I interviewed eight senior bureaucrats from five departments/agencies; in France, I interviewed eight individuals from three departments. Without revealing their identities, among the interviewees were national security advisers, executive directors, an assistant deputy minister, a vice-president of an enforcement branch, and senior immigration policy advisers.

An exogenous shock refers to an event or a group of events that induce points of departure from established sociological, cultural, and political patterns. The so-called "refugee crisis of the 1990s" and the terrorist attacks of September 11, 2001 are particularly relevant exogenous shocks in the present context. This is not to say that Canadian and French larger historical contexts, the geographic location of each country, the bombing of Air India Flight 182 in 1985 in the case of Canada, or key judicial landmarks (for instance the Singh case in Canada) were not important in the securitization process. In fact, I briefly discuss these contextual factors in Chapter 2. However, I argue that the refugee crisis of the early 1990s and the terrorist attacks of 9/11 are the most important exogenous shocks in the years that this study covers (1989–2005).

With regard to domestic factors, I investigate the role of audiences for reasons that will be established in the theoretical discussion that follows. Obviously, numerous other domestic factors could be important in the securitization process. My focus on audiences is not meant to be a theoretical statement on what could be a contextual factor involved in the process. Rather, I am confining my study for purposes of feasibility to an exhaustive analysis of a particular set of contextual domestic factors that are undeniably central to the process of securitizing migration, without discounting that others play roles as well. I draw on three principal

Table 1.1 Corpus of research

	Political agents: speeches	Media agents: editorials	Contextual factors			Interviews
			Manifestos	Bills/laws	Opinion polls	
Canada	1,067	587	60	5	52	8
France	2,396	312	14	3	69	8
Total	3,463	899	74	8	121	16

sources to track down how audiences shape the securitization process. First, I have collected the political manifestos of the main federal political parties in Canada as well as the most important presidential candidates in France. In total, I have analyzed more than seventy political manifestos. Second, I examined the extent to which Parliament has allowed or constrained securitizing actors' moves by analyzing whether the most important immigration laws regarding the securitization of migration were passed, narrowly passed, or defeated in each country case. I have examined five pieces of legislation in Canada and three in France. Third, I have examined public opinion on questions related to the migration–security relationship. In total, I have collected and analyzed more than 120 public opinion polls, as Table 1.1 summarizes.

The primary research method that I employ in this study is a traditional content analysis. To give further robustness to my findings, I use the logic of triangulation of methodological approaches: I have tried throughout the study to check findings obtained with one research method against findings attained from another type. For instance, I employ a content analysis of every speech by a given agent to understand how this particular agent perceives the issue of international migration. What is he/she talking about when he/she talks about the movement of people: is it to highlight the benefits of multiculturalism, to underscore the difficulties of immigrants to integrate the job market, to celebrate the diversity and the richness that immigrants bring to the host society, to question to efficiency of the refugee determination process, and so on. In the next step, I isolate the securitizing moves, that is, when an agent argues that international migration is a security concern for the state and/or the society. Then, I use statistical analysis to provide a graphic overview of the pattern of engagement of each securitizing agent with the phenomenon of securitized migration and to further study the relationship between migration and security. To check for any discrepancy between these findings, I use interviews with senior bureaucrats of several departments/agencies. In addition, I employ survey and poll research as well as socio-historical analysis to capture the role of public opinion and contextual factors in the securitization of migration.

Boundaries, significance, and logics

For my purposes, migration is the movement of people crossing international borders; this includes the United Nations' largely accepted definition of migrants as persons living outside their country of birth or citizenship for 12 months or more, but it also includes refugees, foreign migrant workers, student migrants, border workers, denizens, and legal and "extra"-legal migrants. Because the focus of this study is on the international aspect of the movement, I have excluded internally displaced persons (IDP) from the analysis.

Employing this rather broad definition makes sense for several reasons. First, the aim of the study is to examine how the *international movement* of people has been socially constructed as a security concern in Canada and France. As such, the focus is on the deeply intertwined relationship between the *international movement of people* and the *international system of order* underpinning the movement. Second, precise distinctions between, for example, legal and illegal migrants or migrants and refugees would limit more than they would reveal, despite the fact that these distinctions render a better understanding of the term "migration." Indeed, I contend that a security framework is not applied only to refugees but rather to the entire category of the movement of people.

Critics might contend here that the object of securitization is not the movement of people in its totality but the more circumscribed aspects of the phenomenon of migration (e.g. illegal/irregular migration, refugees), therefore calling for a narrower definitional positioning. They eschew two fundamental elements. First, states' authorities define what constitutes an irregular/illegal migrant. There is no multilateral coordination between countries on what is an illegal migrant. An illegal migrant in France could well be a legal migrant in Canada. Neither theoretically nor empirically does our understanding of the illegal versus legal migrants dichotomy necessarily have to be that of a particular state. As Morice and Rodier (2005) argue, classifying migrants and refugees creates a harmful distinction in the context of a state's attempt to control migratory movement under national security concerns; the classification process is not neutral.

Second, it is the malleability of the concepts of "migration" and "security" that makes them especially useful in politics (Edelman 2001). As the following chapters demonstrate, the state's security apparatus purposively provokes an elision and confusion of migration categories. Overdrawing an analytical distinction between several categories of migration would indeed miss the "flexibility" quality that politicians have been particularly eager to exploit. Indeed, research focusing merely on "illegal" migration would miss important features of the phenomenon of securitized migration, such as in cases when legal would-be immigrants have been detained for several days before being granted permission to stay in France, or when legal tourists have been "strongly" invited to board a plane bringing them back to their country of origin the day after their plane landed in Vancouver.

The questions and answers that this study provides are timely and relevant for several reasons. First, we do not have a profound understanding of the mechanisms at play in the securitization process. The current benchmark in securitization research—that is, ST—is not without limits and flaws, as many scholars have noted in the past decade. As such, one of the objectives of this study is to take steps in providing an answer to both Hayward Alker's (2005) call for further research on whether—and to what extent—identity-specific values are severely threatened enough within particular societies to require securitization responses, and Martin Heisler's (2006) remark that a coherent and comprehensive theoretical framework making sense of the link between migration and security has yet to be produced.

Second, my study is one of the first in migration studies and security studies to offer indicators of the phenomenon of securitized migration. Despite the increasing attractiveness of the topic of securitized migration in scholarly works, our understanding of the phenomenon of securitized migration is relatively limited. Several scholars take securitized migration for granted; others strive to analyze the securitization process without aiming to isolate indicators of securitized migration or to offer "thick" description of the phenomenon. The focus has been on proposing explanations as to why migration is securitized almost at the expense of answering the question of how we have established that migration is in fact securitized. In contrast to this standpoint, my study proposes and employs a combination of indicators offering a nominal measurement, a degree measurement, and within-case analyses using two categories of indicators: institutional indicators and security practices indicators.

In a related way, a comparison of the securitizing processes in Canada and France is particularly relevant because these two country cases occupy distant positions on the migration–security continuum. As Chapter 2 will demonstrate, Canada displays a low level of securitization of migration, whereas France has a high level of securitization. Because my study involves comparing considerable variation in the phenomenon to be explained, it could act as a matrix for further research on social mechanisms involved in the process of securitizing migration and on hypotheses making sense of the variation in levels of securitized migration.

My study provides an unparalleled, comprehensive, rich, and incisive analysis of the social constituents of securitized migration in a post-Cold War era. Indeed, my study is one of the first to systematically and comparatively examine the role of several political agents, numerous media agents, and the main contextual factors in the process of securitizing migration across cases and with a relatively long time span (1989–2005).[4]

The richness of the analysis also permits the juxtaposition of the two logics emerging in constructivist security studies—that is, the logic of exception and the logic of unease. To summarize (this issue will be further discussed in the concluding chapter), the logic of exception, upon which ST relies, takes its cue from Carl Schmitt's and Giorgio Agamben's notion of the state of exception. It postulates that security is about the fight against an existential threat that necessitates exceptional measures. The logic of exception emphasizes urgency and survival in the process of securitizing an issue (Buzan *et al.* 1998; Doty 2007; Landau 2006; Wæver 2009; Williams 2003). The logic of unease, building on Michel Foucault's and Pierre Bourdieu's system of thoughts, focuses on the role of the professionals involved in the management of (in)security (and their routinized practices) in creating and reproducing a governmentality of unease (Bigo 1998a, 2002, 2008; Ceyhan and Tsoukala 2002; Doucet and de Larrinaga 2010; Walters 2002). Contrary to the current standpoint that treats these two logics as competing views, I argue that scholars should refrain from overdrawing distinctions between the two logics, for it is not clear that they are mutually exclusive.

Précis of the study

The program of work contains six chapters. Before getting into the heart of the study, Chapter 2 presents the rational for the selection of cases and the indicators that I have developed to understand whether migration has been securitized or not. Chapter 3 presents the merits of adopting a constructivist perspective in the particular context of this study. It reviews the relevant literature trying to make sense of the linkage between migration and security; thereby, it identifies the weaknesses and limits of these models. The last section of the chapter details my own approach.

I examine the agential and structural/contextual components of the social mechanisms of the securitization process in the following three chapters. Chapter 4 studies the role of political agents within and across my two country cases. Chapter 5 redirects the focus by studying editorialists. Chapter 6 considers the role of important contextual factors—exogenous shocks and domestic audiences—in the process of securitizing international migration.

As the study unfolds across chapters, I engage—sometimes on theoretical terms, sometimes on empirical ones—with several debates and hypotheses of international relations and migration studies. Among them are whether migration and security were linked simply because immigrants are more involved in criminal activities than "local" people; whether international events such as the terrorist attacks of 9/11 drive the securitization in some objective way; whether my emphasis on contextual factors as a site of potential explanations for variation in levels of securitized migration is compatible with the embedded liberalism model developed in migration studies; and whether there is a difference between politicization and securitization of migration.

These are exciting and timely debates in IR and security studies literature. The first step in tackling them starts with defining and describing the phenomenon of securitized migration, a task I undertake in the next chapter.

Part I
Developing an analytical framework

2 Securitized migration

"[I would rather] die in Nigeria for a reason than waste away in [detention in Canada] when I had done nothing wrong." A few days after having written these words to immigration officials, Michael Akhimien, a 39-year-old Nigerian who claimed refugee status in Canada on October 28, 1995, died on December 18, 1995, while in a detention center. During his detainment, Akhimien made two applications to withdraw his refugee application. He did not want to be in Canada anymore; yet that is where he died.[1]

In France, two undocumented migrants died in Roissy-Charles de Gaulle Airport during their deportations in December 2002 and January 2003 respectively. Ricardo Barrientos, a 52-year-old Argentine, and Mariam Getu Hagos, a 24-year-old Somali, both died on the airplane when French border police officers who where accompanying them forced their upper bodies on to their legs and their heads between their knees while the plane was taxiing for take-off. They had come to France to seek asylum.

These idiosyncratic events are a manifestation of a larger phenomenon that is taking place in world politics, that is, the securitization of migration. Canada and France are no exceptions.

The application of a security framework to the movement of people—what is referred to here as *securitized migration*—can be observed in both "classic countries of immigration" such as Canada and "reluctant countries of immigration" such as France (Cornelius *et al.* 2004). The similarity in behavior across cases brings to the forefront the question of social mechanisms involved in the securitization process. How does migration become securitized? What is the relative importance of material factors and ideational factors in the process? What category of agents has been particularly efficient at becoming securitizing agents in the context of migration? Are media agents undoubtedly securitizing agents? Do cultural factors have any role in the securitizing process? Trying to provide an answer to these questions is at the heart of my study.

Although migration has been securitized in both Canada and France, there is a considerable variation in the *levels* of securitization. As the following pages will demonstrate, migration is weakly securitized in Canada, whereas it is strongly securitized in France. In seeking to understand and to explain variation in the intensity of securitized migration, I explore the idea that security is best conceptualized as a continuum rather than as a binary notion.

The next pages are important in setting up the dynamic "story" of the securitization process. In the first two sections of this chapter, I discuss my selection of cases and develop a set of indicators to measure the phenomenon under study. To do so is fundamental for three reasons. First, and contrary to one of the Canadian officials I interviewed who saw "no evidence" that migration is securitized in Canada,[2] I demonstrate that migration *is* securitized in Canada; migration is also securitized in France. Second, I demonstrate that there is a considerable difference in terms of the *levels* of securitization in these two countries. As such, comparing Canada and France is in fact comparing cases that present significant variation in the phenomenon to be explained. Third, I construct a timeline of securitized migration for both countries. The timeline allows me to underscore *when* the securitization process was initiated within the time frame of my study (1989–2005). The timeline also allows me to highlight the pattern of engagement—and its evolution over time—of each securitizing agent with the phenomenon of securitized migration, thereby identifying elements of rupture and continuity throughout the years that my study covers. In Chapters 4 and 5, I will intertwine analysis of the role of several agents in the securitization process with the result obtained here.

The last section of this chapter presents a brief description of the agents and the contextual factors studied as well as a summary of my research strategy for both. This step is of central importance, as the core of my study (Chapters 4, 5, and 6) highlights the securitizing attempts made by agents as well as the relevance of contextual factors in the process of securitizing migration.

Case selection

Immigration is a central question in Canadian history. Indeed, scholarly works published on the question of immigration divide Canadian immigration policy of the past century or so into several phases: each phase has as its heart the theme of nation building. "From confederation in 1867 until today, nation building has been a theme underlying Canadian immigration. Historically, immigration to Canada was sought to expand the population, boost the economy, and develop society. This is still true" (Reitz 2004: 100). Immigration has always been—and continues to be—socially constructed as an integral part of what defines Canada (Adelman 2004; Dauvergne 2006; Dirks 1995; Hawkins 1988; Kelley and Trebilcock 1998). Several factors have sometimes fostered the social construction; others have sometimes constrained it. For instance, the geographic particularities of Canada have long been seen as a crucial factor facilitating the social construction of Canada as a self-defined country of immigration. Other events have put the Canadian welcome mat to the test. On June 23, 1985, a Boeing 747 en route from Canada to India via London exploded as it entered Irish airspace. The plane crashed into the sea killing all 329 people on board, of whom 280 were Canadian citizens (the vast majority of them of Indian origin). The bombing of Air India Flight 182—which led to an investigation and prosecution that took almost 20 years and was the most expensive trial in Canadian history—undoubtedly did set the stage for the process of securitizing migration in the years that my study covers. As well, key judicial landmarks that occurred before 1989 have also been important in setting the stage of the process. Perhaps the most important key landmark is the so-called Singh decision of April 4, 1985. In *Singh* v. *Canada*, the Supreme Court of Canada held that refugee claimants are entitled to claim the protection of Section 7 of the Charter, which provides that everyone should enjoy security of the person. It ruled that the human rights entrenched in the 1982 Canadian Charter of Rights applied to refugee claimants; thereby, the Singh decision extended Charter rights to non-citizens on Canadian soil.

In France, the "story" of immigration policies is characterized by more ambiguity than in Canada. For many years, the "place" of immigration was not highlighted in the history of France. For instance, scholars have suggested that a "collective memory" of immigration has not yet been forged there, and have underlined that, although official rhetoric was eschewing the migratory particularity and history of France, the reality was different. Consequently, scholars have been part of an effort to document the migratory nature of the French nation-state (Feldblum 1999; Noiriel 2006; Wahnich 1997; Weil 2005; Wihtol de Wenden 1987). Just as in Canada, the geographical particularities of France are an important factor in the social mechanisms leading to the securitization process. The "closeness" of north African countries has undoubtedly helped to establish the perception of waves and unstoppable movements of people that have occurred—and that will continue to do so. Other pre-1989 factors have also been important in setting the stage for the process of securitizing migration to unfold. For instance, the larger historical trend of de-colonization (especially in the northern African regions) has certainly influenced the process. Additionally, when in 1984 the extreme-right Front National won municipal elections in Dreux, an industrial town just west of Paris, on a platform calling for a complete halt to immigration as well as the deportation of several hundreds of thousands of African immigrants, a electoral breakthrough was made that would be significant years later as the securitization of migration started to unfold (Geddes 2003; Guiraudon 2000a; Hollifield 2004).

I recognize the general relevance of Canadian and French larger historical contexts, the impact of "geography," the enduring legacy of significant historical events such as the bombing of Air India Flight 182 in 1985, and the importance of key judicial landmarks. However, I have not considered these contextual factors in my study, as some of them fall outside of the years that my study covers (1989–2005) and I had to limit the range of material under investigation.

With respect to the study of the securitization process, Canada and France exhibit similar features, allowing for a high degree of comparative control. Both Canada and France are representative democracies characterized by highly developed, industrial, and capitalist economies. In demographic terms, both societies are under heavy pressure because they both have a relatively low fertility rate[3] (Canada has the lowest rate at 1.6, followed by France at 1.8); as a result, they would have declining populations if it were not for international immigration. A similar inverted diamond shape for the age structure is found in both cases: 18 percent of people fall within the 0–14 years category; 65–69 percent in the 15–64 years category; and 13–16 percent in the 65 years and over category.

Passionate debates about immigration are also taking place in each case, albeit in different forms, thereby signifying the importance of migration issues on the national public agenda. In Canada, the debate currently focuses on the consequences of border control for Canada's sovereignty and its relationship with the United States in a post-9/11 world. In France, the most salient issue is the increasing popularity of the right-wing and anti-immigration Front National led by Jean-Marie Le Pen. Revisions of respective immigration laws have been accompanied by numerous public consultations and public demonstrations, particularly in France.[4]

In immigration terms, both have a positive net migration rate. Whereas Canada is a country founded and populated by immigrants, France has been an immigration country since the mid-nineteenth century. Leaving aside official rhetoric, which eschews regional and migratory particularities, scholarly literature on immigration in France has long recognized and documented the migratory nature of the French nation-state. For instance, Gérard Noiriel, the leading historian of immigration in France, has been engaged in the past decades in an enterprise of debunking the "France unitary myth" (Noiriel 2006).[5] Although the annual intake of immigrants varies significantly between the two countries, as seen in Figure 2.1, the total refugee populations of Canada and France are very similar (132,500 and 139,000 respectively) and were relatively constant between 1995

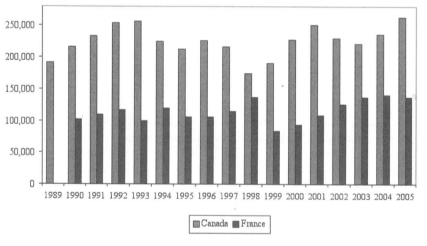

Figure 2.1 Annual intake of immigrants, Canada and France, 1989–2005.

Sources: CIC (2006), Direction de la population et des migrations (DPM) (2005), Comité Interministériel de Contrôle de l'Immigration (CICI) (2006), Coleman (1997), Thierry (2000, 2004).

Note: For both France and Canada data include only "Entrées à caractère permanent"—or "Permanent entry"—thus they exclude "Temporary entry" such as seasonal workers and students. However, in France, for the years 1994–1996, Thierry includes students in his statistics (there is no uniformity on the number of students admitted per year among various French institutions providing statistics; depending on sources, the number of students admitted in these years ranges from 11,000 to 27,000). Whether to include students is a matter of debate between demographers; compare Coleman (1997) and Thierry (2000, 2004).

and 2004. Furthermore, France and Canada rank third and fourth, respectively, among Organisation for Economic Co-operation and Development (OECD) countries regarding the total number of asylum seekers for the period 1980–1999. When the ratio of total asylum seekers to total population is calculated, their rank is also very similar: eighth for Canada and tenth for France.

One of the main challenges of a comparative study is to identify elements of uniqueness intrinsic in each case as well as key differences that could influence our research question. Of course, a key dissimilarity between my two cases is the migration flow. The annual intake is higher in Canada than in France throughout the time period of this study, as Figure 2.1 illustrates. On average, the annual intake of immigrants in Canada between 1989 and 2005 is 224,817, whereas the average annual intake in France between 1990 and 2005 is 114,484. Nonetheless, this dissimilarity has to be qualified. France's official immigration policy since 1974 of "immigration zero"—that is, to stop all immigration and reduce the number of asylum seekers to a minimum—particularly amplified the dissimilarity. Despite this rather draconian goal, France's annual intake has not fallen much below 100,000 since the early 1950s according to Hollifield (2004). For Lynch and Simon (2003), France's annual intake of immigrants is about 130,000 in the 1960s and 1970s, and about 175,000 in the 1980s. Still, and even when these estimates are taken into account, the annual intake of immigrants is far greater in Canada than in France. However, the annual intake merely represents an indication of the success of controlling measures. The annual intake does not explain why France displays a stronger securitization of migration; it only indicates that France's immigration policy is less open than Canada's. In other words, the annual intake of immigrants is a consequence and not a cause of the securitization of migration.

A second and related difference that somewhat complicates the comparison process concerns the immigration system. Although both Canada's and France's immigration policies admit permanent immigrants in three categories—independent, family reunification, and refugees—differences exist in the proportion that each of these classes have of the total annual immigrant intake. Canada's point-based system, introduced in 1967 under the Immigration Act of 1952, gives preference to the highly skilled and independent immigrants, especially since the end of the 1980s. In 2005, the category "independent immigrants" represented about 60 percent of the total immigrant intake while the category "family" represented about 25 percent. In France, for the year 2004, the class "workers" accounted for 5 percent and the "family" class for 73 percent.

Although the difference in terms of immigration system has important socio-political consequences, its impact on national security is less clear. A fragile hypothesis is that, because France admits more immigrants under the family reunification class than Canada, the securitization of migration is stronger in France. In fact, this would be arguing that by definition a "family class" immigrant is more of a security threat than an "economic" immigrant, which is an uncertain foundation on which to theorize.

Also, the dissimilarity, especially when looking at the "refugee class," appears to be overstated. When compared with other OECD countries, the refugee population of Canada and France is very similar and the similarity is relatively constant. The average refugee population between 1995 and 2004 was 139,000 in France and 133,000 in Canada. Again, these numbers are significantly different from those of Germany (1,013,000), the United States (524,000) and the United Kingdom (181,000)—as Table 2.1 summarizes. Furthermore, Table 2.2 shows that France and Canada rank third and fourth, respectively, among OECD countries regarding the total number of asylum seekers for the period 1980–1999. When Canada and France are compared with other OECD countries, the percentage of asylum seekers in the total population is also similar (see Figure 2.2): for the period 1980–1999, the percentage of asylum seekers in the total population was 1.36 in Canada and 0.96 in France.

Another dissimilarity relevant to this study is the criminality of immigrants. As two specialists point out, "there is a fairly common belief in the community

Table 2.1 Stock of refugee population by country of asylum, 1995–2004*

OECD country	1995	1996	1997	1998	1999	2000	2001	2002	2003	2004	*Average*
Germany	1,268	1,266	1,049	949	976	906	903	980	960	877	1,013
United States	623	607	564	534	521	508	516	485	453	421	524
United Kingdom	91	99	108	122	149	186	233	261	277	289	181
Sweden	199	191	187	179	160	157	147	142	112	73	155
France	155	151	147	140	130	133	132	132	131	140	139
Canada	152	138	125	119	123	127	129	130	133	141	133
Denmark	65	66	68	69	69	71	73	74	70	65	69
Australia	62	67	66	70	65	60	58	59	56	64	63
Italy	74	65	67	5	6	7	9	10	13	16	27

Source: United Nations High Commissioner for Refugees (2006).

*In thousands.

Table 2.2 Total number of asylum seekers, OECD countries, 1980–1999

Selected OECD country	Total number of asylum seekers, 1980–1999
Germany	2,584,400
United States	1,296,400
France	581,900
Canada	451,400
United Kingdom	418,800
Sweden	384,600
Switzerland	382,700
Netherlands	376,600
Australia	94,000

Source: OECD (2004, 2010).

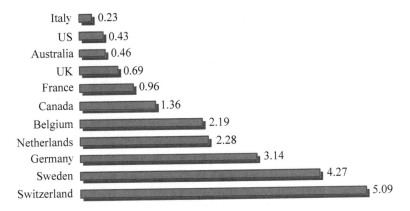

Figure 2.2 Percentage of asylum seekers from 1980 to 1999 in total population as of 2005, selected countries.

Source: OECD (2005).

that the migrant population is more likely than the native population to both engage in criminal activity and persist in such activity over time" (Borowski and Thomas 1994: 633). Furthermore, migration scholars have argued, with caution and reserve, that migration and security were linked for an obvious reason: immigrants are more involved in criminal activities than "local" people (Guiraudon and Joppke 2001). Pursuant to this argument, the "crime" hypothesis contends that a society with a high level of criminal involvement of immigrants would opt for a high level of securitized migration to counter the crime–immigrant linkage. At first sight, the "crime" hypothesis seems conclusive. In the case of France, the criminal involvement rate of immigrants is roughly 2.5 times that of the native-born population. In Canada, numbers shows the opposite: immigrants have a lower rate of criminality than the native-born population (Lynch and Simon 2003). The "crime" hypothesis varies in the same way as securitized migration does across my two cases.

Despite their attractiveness, a careful examination of these statistics is required in the present context for four reasons. First, the concept of criminality fluctuates across my two country cases; thereby, it makes cross-national comparisons of crime involving immigrants difficult. As Lynch and Simon (1999) underscore, differences in the legal definition of criminal acts complicate significantly cross-national comparisons.

Second, statistics on the criminal involvement of immigrants are a function of immigration policies. Restrictive immigration policies coupled with the numerous restrictions on immigrants could induce the detection of criminal activities; thereby, it introduces a negative bias in the statistics. Moreover, a particular policy, despite applying to everybody, induces higher records of criminality for some. For instance, in France everyone is required to carry an identity card at all times, and the police have the right to ask you to officially identify yourself whenever they encounter you. If we add the documented and well-known tendency of French police forces to systematically control the identity of "colored" (read North African) people but seldom the identity of "white" people, it is thus logical that France's statistics are higher in this regard than in Canada where Canadians do not have to carry an identity card with them and the police cannot take repressive measures if a person does not show an identity card when asked.

Third, because only immigrants (and not the total population) are subject to the intense processing for immigration-related offenses, infractions are intrinsically inflated. This is especially the case in France, where the official position since 1974 is that of "zero immigration"—a position obviously disconnected from reality but nonetheless reiterated throughout the time period of this study (Weil 2005).[6]

Fourth, the migration–crime linkage is also, if not principally, a matter of perception and construction rather than an objective reality driving the securitization of migration. When the official rhetoric constantly stresses the negative aspects of migration and points to problems and dangers associated with the movement of people (as in France), the perception of the migration–crime linkage is obviously more predominant than in a society in which immigration is often seen as positive and where difficulties are presented in terms of challenges instead of threats (as in Canada). Indeed, a recent survey indicates that the perception of the criminality associated with migrants is strikingly different in the two countries: a significantly larger proportion of French respondents than Canadian agreed that immigrants increase crime rates (44 percent versus 27 percent respectively) (Jedwab 2006). The important point in the present context is that the migration–crime linkage is largely a question of social construction and, as such, not a social law or reality determining the relationship between movement and order.

In sum, these differences—the migration flow, the immigration system, and the crime rate—between Canada and France can largely be neutralized for the purpose of my study. That is, even though a comparison of Canada and France cannot fully control for all aspects of a country's uniqueness, my comparative project, aiming to suggest factors explaining variation in levels of securitized migration, can hold constant these dissimilarities.

Securitized migration

How to define and measure security is a subject of much contention and intense debate among IR scholars. Some scholars contend that security is an "essentially contested concept"; other scholars argue that security should be defined solely in material/military terms; while still other scholars are in favor of widening and broadening the definition of security.[7] The present study clearly opts for the third line of argument. In the particular context of this study, the fact that I adopt a rather broad definition of security means two things. First, my study needs to establish whether migration is securitized in each country case. Second, my study, based on the assumption that security should not be understood as a binary notion but rather as a continuum involving various degrees of intensity or strength, has to explore whether there is such a variation in the level of securitized migration between Canada and France. Accordingly, I have to rely on indicators allowing me to answer these two questions. Therefore, I have used a combination of indicators offering a nominal measurement (presence or absence of the phenomenon), a degree measurement (providing a rank ordering of my two country cases), and within-case analyses.[8]

Whereas debates surrounding security's definition have proliferated in security studies, the situation is strikingly different in the literature on the migration–security nexus. In fact, very few studies present indicators of *securitized migration* or criteria to evaluate whether migration is securitized or not. Some almost take it for granted; others strive to demonstrate the linkage without aiming to isolate indicators of a securitized migration.[9] In order to better understand the phenomenon of securitized migration, I use two categories of indicators.

The first category is the institutional indicator (indicator *I*). This set of indicators offers both a binary measurement and a degree measurement. First, I have included a legal component in the institutional indicator (indicator *I-1*). I have registered the most important immigration *acts* as well as provisions relating the linkage between migration and security. I have then briefly highlighted their content along the migration–security nexus.

Second, I have explored whether immigration/migration is listed as a security concern in policy statements that relate to security, foreign affairs, and immigration (indicator *I-2*). Furthermore, I have codified the existence (or not) of a particular department or departmental division in charge of border control and national security in which immigration is seen as a key element. I have then placed the results on a timeline in order to pinpoint critical historical junctures in the context of my study, that is, *when* migration entered the list of security concerns in Canada's and France's policy statements.

Third, I have measured the saliency of the link between migration and security within these policy statements (indicator *I-3*). The following questions have oriented a careful reading of how the migration–security nexus was conceptualized in these statements: Is the migration–security nexus at the core (or not) of the document? Is the movement of people discussed under a distinct subheading or is it mentioned only alongside other existential threats? Is migration referred to as one of the most important existential threats?

The second category of indicators of securitized migration concerns the security practices relating to the migration–security nexus (indicator *P*). Two policies/practices are relevant: interdiction (*P-1*) and detention of immigrants (*P-2*). Interdiction offers a binary measurement, whereas detention of immigrants permits an ordinal measurement.

The United Nations (2000) defines interdiction as an activity directed toward preventing the movement of people at the source. Working within the footsteps of the UN's rather broad definition, migration scholars have provided a more comprehensive understanding of interdiction policy, that is, a set of practices that seeks to stop the flow of immigrants by prohibiting, intercepting, and/or deflecting them while they are in movement or before movement is initiated (Davidson 2003; Dench 2001; Dench and Crépeau 2003; Morris 2003; Pratt 2005; Rodier

2006). Interdiction includes the imposition of sanctions on carrier companies that transport illegal or irregular travelers; the requirement that travelers acquire a visa; the placement of immigration officers in foreign airports for detection purposes; the interception of marine vessels in international or territorial waters; and the return of refugee claimants to countries of transit through the use of the concepts "safe third country" or "country of first asylum." As a multifaceted tool, interdiction (P-1) constitutes a powerful instrument to measure the phenomenon of securitized migration.

My second indicator is the magnitude of the detention of immigrants (P-2) as a security practice both in terms of absolute number and in terms of the proportion of detained immigrants versus the immigration intake. Detention of immigrants by completely merging the movement of people with security measures constitutes a central piece of a framework that emphasizes police and repression. Procedures, codes of conduct, and the apparatus of these detention centers strikingly resemble carceral facilities. To be sure, some immigrants are not detained for national security considerations. The breakdown of detention statistics to highlight the security aspect is a difficult, if not hazardous, task. Nevertheless, detention acts as a strong symbol by which immigrants in detention equal dangerous immigrants and, as such, it relates directly to this study.

Canada

The Canadian government has revised its immigration laws several times within the time period that my study covers, as the left-hand column in Figure 2.3 shows. In January 1989, Bills C-55 and C-84 came into effect, introducing many changes to immigration law and the Immigration and Refugee Board (IRB). In 1992, Bill C-86 came into effect, introducing revisions, mostly restrictive, to the refugee determination system. The provision "danger to the public" enters the Immigration Act with Bill C-44 in 1995, by which a person loses the right to appeal the removal order if the Minister of Citizenship and Immigration is of the opinion that a person is a "danger to the public" (Dent 2002; Waldman 2005). In June 2002, Canada passed the *Immigration and Refugee Protection Act,* which has re-enforced security certificates and detention provisions, and expanded the inadmissibility categories to permit refusal of entry on the basis of security.

In terms of whether immigration/migration is listed as a security concern in the priorities of departments in charge of security, foreign affairs, and immigration portfolios (indicator *I*-*2*), one of the most important dates in the case of Canada is 1991. Whereas the previous official document, *Competitiveness and Security: Directions for Canada's International Relations*, published in 1985, was silent on the issue of migration, the document *Foreign Policy Themes and Priorities*, issued in 1991, lists migration as a security concern. To be sure, the initial inclusion of migration in the realm of security was made with caution and mostly in terms of the need for the international community to develop cooperative security. "We need to address transnational security threats such as proliferation, drug trafficking, terrorism, and irregular migration," the document declares (DEA 1991: 91).

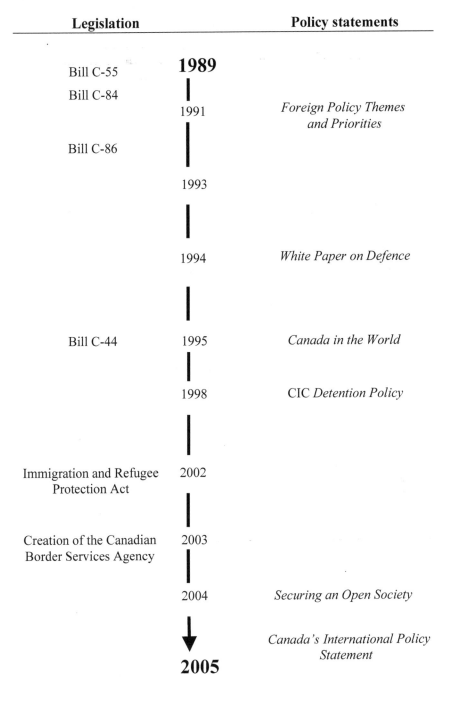

Legislation		Policy statements

1989

Bill C-55
Bill C-84

1991   *Foreign Policy Themes and Priorities*

Bill C-86

1993

1994   *White Paper on Defence*

Bill C-44   1995   *Canada in the World*

1998   CIC *Detention Policy*

Immigration and Refugee Protection Act   2002

Creation of the Canadian Border Services Agency   2003

2004   *Securing an Open Society*

        Canada's International Policy Statement

2005

Figure 2.3 Timeline, institutional indicators, Canada, 1989–2005.

Furthermore, "problems facing the international community that ignore national boundaries [are] growing in length and gravity. Global environmental threats, population and migratory pressures, and proliferation of weaponry can only be addressed on a multilateral basis" (DEA 1991: 90). This position was reiterated in the *White Paper on Defence* (DND 1994) and particularly in *Canada in the World,* published in 1995: "the threats to security now are more complex than before . . . whole range of issues that transcend borders – including mass migration, etc. – have peace and security implication" (DFAIT 1995: ii).

In 1996, Citizenship and Immigration Canada (CIC) issued a new policy statement, *Detention Policy*, which was revised and re-issued in 1998. The new policy sought to instruct immigration officials to use detention as a last resort, justified only in cases in which there was a real possibility that the individual would endanger the Canadian public. The 1998 detention policy adds that immigration officers exercise "sensible risk management practices" (quoted in Pratt 2005: 63) Most sections of the related Citizenship and Immigration Canada immigration manual highlight the importance of the security aspect of immigration officials' work. For instance, the section on inadmissibility instructs immigration officials that the first objective of the Canadian immigration legislation relative to the inadmissibility provisions is "to protect the health and safety of Canadians and to maintain the security of Canadian society" (CIC 2002a: 3). Also, the section on detention informs immigration officers to exercise sound judgment:

> sound judgement not only requires individual assessment of the case, but also an assessment of the impact of release on the safety of Canadian society. Additionally, it requires a risk management approach to make decisions within the context of the following priorities: (1) where safety and security concerns are identified . . .; (2) where identity issues must be resolved before security or safety concerns are eliminated or confirmed; (3) to support removal where removal is imminent and where a flight risk has been identified; (4) where there are significant concerns regarding a person's identity.
>
> (CIC 2002b: 6)

Securing an Open Society: Canada's National Security Policy, issued in 2004, is more precise in declaring the security concern that the movement of people represents for Canada. It applauds the progress made to date "to improve the screening of immigrants, refugee claimants and visitors and to enhance the capacity to detain and remove anyone posing a risk to Canada" (PCO 2004: 41). *Securing an Open Society* also praises Parliament for passing the new "Immigration and Refugee Protection Act, which provides more tools to address security threats" (PCO 2004: 42).

Finally, the Canadian government presented its *Canada's International Policy Statement* in 2005. The statement contains four booklets: "Diplomacy"; "Defence"; "Development"; and "Commerce." While the "Diplomacy" booklet focuses on the smuggling and trafficking of immigrants, the "Defence" booklet argues that "to support more effectively the Government's essential role in providing for the safety and security of Canadians . . . the Canadian Forces will focus their efforts in the following areas . . .: monitoring illegal drugs and immigration activity" (DND 2005: 18–19).

In terms of the existence of a particular departmental division relating to the migration–security nexus, two departmental re-organizations are worth mentioning. First, the new Citizenship and Immigration Canada Intelligence Branch, created after the September 11 attacks, brought together existing intelligence resources in CIC and provided a focal point for sharing information with partners in the intelligence community. Intelligence activities of the CIC concentrate on three main areas: building capacity; improving screening; and managing security within Canada. New funds from the December 2001 budget allowed CIC to place more officers at ports of entry to improve the front-end security screening of refugee claimants and to work with the United States on innovative strategies and policies to address continental migration concerns.

Second, the Canada Border Services Agency (CBSA) was created in December 2003. The CBSA amalgamates several sections (or departmental divisions) in charge of the enforcement of border security, including the Customs program from the Canada Customs and Revenue Agency (CCRA), the Intelligence, Interdiction, and Enforcement program from CIC, and the Import Inspection at Ports of Entry program from the Canadian Food Inspection Agency (CFIA). Building its mandate from the Canada–United States Smart Border Declaration (signed in December 2001), the CBSA is an "integral part of the Public Safety Portfolio, which was created to protect Canadians." Accordingly, the mission of CBSA is "to ensure the security and prosperity of Canada by managing the access of people and goods to and from Canada" (CBSA n.d.). In turn, the Smart Border Declaration is committed to "identify security threats before they arrive in North America through collaborative approaches to reviewing crew and passenger manifests, managing refugees, and visa policy coordination" (DFAIT 2001).

With regards to the level of saliency of the link between migration and security in these policy statements (indicator *I-3*), Canada presents a low level in the context of securitized migration. Despite being listed as a security concern, the movement of people is not at the heart of *Foreign Policy Themes and Priorities*. Likewise, *Canada in the World* acknowledges the new international context in which "threats to security" include mass migration without making the movement of people a conspicuous and prominent issue. In sum, the saliency of the migration–security linkage is relatively low. The same conclusion applies to *Canada's International Policy Statement*. Furthermore, this is a conclusion shared by almost all my Canadian interviewees; that is, they acknowledged, with tangible discomfort for some, that migration is in fact securitized in Canada, only to add hastily that it is a "mild," "low," or "weak" securitization.

As for the first security practices indicator (interdiction, *P-1*), Canada has developed over the years a powerful interdiction apparatus. Indeed, several scholars have aptly demonstrated, for example, that Canada has put in place a strong visa regime and carrier sanctions (Crépeau and Nakache 2006; Davidson 2003; Dench 2001; Dench and Crépeau 2003; Pratt 2005).

Finally, Canada also employs detention for security purposes. There are three reasons why immigration officers may order the detention of an immigrant, namely because the foreign national (including a permanent resident) is (1) deemed a security threat; (2) unlikely to appear for examination; and (3) presenting identification documents do not satisfy the officer. Most Canadian detention centers—and certainly the three principal ones—present carceral features:[10] immigration detainees are held together (co-mingled) with persons held under criminal law; immigration detainees are handcuffed and leg-ironed during transport to and from centers; and detention centers are equipped with solitary confinement rooms for troubled detainees.

Detention of immigrants is fast increasing in Canada. Whereas 6,400 people were detained in 1996, the number of immigrant detainees was over 13,000 in 2003, an increase of approximately 100 percent. Despite this worrying surge in detention, the ratio of immigrants who have been detained to the total number of immigrants accepted in Canada remains relatively low, especially in comparison with France. As Figure 2.4 shows, this ratio is, on average, around 4 percent.

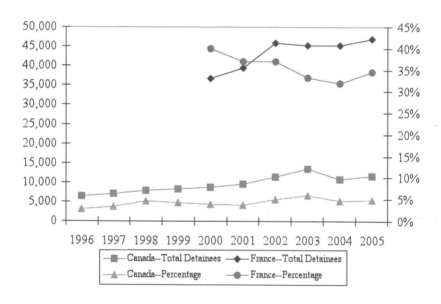

Figure 2.4 Total immigrant detainees and percentage of immigrant detainees vs. total accepted immigrants, Canada and France.

Sources: CIC (2006), Auditor General of Canada (2008), Comité Interministériel de Contrôle de l'Immigration (CICI) (2006), Cimade (2006), Direction de la population et des migrations (DPM) (2005).

Note: To the best of my knowledge, data prior to 2000 for France are not available.

France

In the case of France, the European Union official documents, protocols, and treaties must be taken into account, identified in Figure 2.5 on the left-hand side of the timeline. Of course, the first ones are the Schengen Agreement, signed in 1985, and the subsequent convention implementing its provisions, the Dublin Convention (1990). Both the Agreement and the Convention are well known; thus, suffice it here to mention that they both institutionalize the securitization of migration. The Treaty of Amsterdam (1997) changed the nature of cooperation in the field of justice and home affairs by defnining the area of freedom, security, and justice in more ambitious and more precise terms. Immigration policy became a full community responsibility with the entry into force of the Treaty of Amsterdam. One of the objectives of the treaty is to

> maintain and develop the Union as an area of freedom, security, and justice, in which the free movement of persons is assured in conjunction with appropriate measures with respect to external border controls, asylum, immigration, and the prevention and combating of crime.
>
> (European Union 1997: Article B, p. 5)

Moreover, in December 2003, Javier Solana, the European Union High Representative for the Common Foreign and Security Policy, released *A Secure Europe in a Better World: European Security Strategy,* which sets out the main priorities and identifies the main threats to the security of the EU. The fifth threat identified in the document is organized crime, under which the strategy mentions that illegal migration accounts for a part of the activities of criminal gangs and that it could also have links with terrorism (EU High Representative for the Common Foreign and Security Policy 2003).

France also displays a positive measurement on the legal indicator (indicator *I-1*) of securitized migration. The Pasqua law of 1993 reinforces repressive measures to impede access to French territory, and limits the entry and residence of many categories of migrants. The Debré law (1997) hardens detention provisions and expands police powers. The Sarkozy law (2003) aims at reinforcing measures against illegal migration, and criminal phenomena tied to illegal migration.

In terms of official documents (indicator *I-2*), France's *White Paper on Defence* issued in 1994 discusses the link between migration and security in terms of the threat that the mass movement of people poses to France's security interests.[11] "Disorganized movements of people" are caused by miserable economic conditions, according to the White Paper, and if nothing is done to improve the living conditions of people in developing countries it could provoke mass migratory movements and ultimately crisis and armed conflicts (Ministère de la Défense 1994: 11).

With regard to the internal re-organization of France's security-related department, the Interdepartmental Committee on the Control of Immigration (CICI) is of major importance in the present context. The CICI was created in 2005 and is

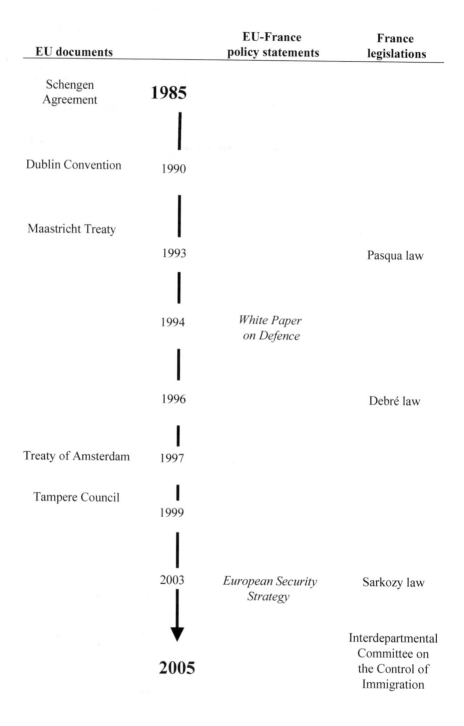

EU documents		EU-France policy statements	France legislations
Schengen Agreement	**1985**		
Dublin Convention	1990		
Maastricht Treaty	1993		Pasqua law
	1994	*White Paper on Defence*	
	1996		Debré law
Treaty of Amsterdam	1997		
Tampere Council	1999		
	2003	*European Security Strategy*	Sarkozy law
	2005		Interdepartmental Committee on the Control of Immigration

Figure 2.5 Timeline, institutional indicators, France, 1985–2005.

presided over by either the Prime Minister or the Minister of the Interior. Its mandates are to reinforce the coherence of the government's action in the context of the fight against illegal immigration and to determine the general orientations of the government regarding the control of migratory flux. Another institution worth mentioning is the Security Division of the Department of Foreign Affairs. Under the direction of strategic, security, and disarmament affairs, the Security Division is in charge of "new threats" including "terrorism, transnational organized crime, drug trafficking, human trafficking and illegal immigration."[12]

In terms of the saliency of the link between migration and security in official documents (indicator *I-3*), France displays a strong level. Although the free movement of persons is inscribed in no more than two articles of the Dublin Convention, the vast majority of the Convention's articles elaborate and develop a strong security system to compensate for the "security lost" by the free movement of persons. Article 5 of the Dublin Convention states that

> for stays not exceeding three months, aliens fulfilling the following conditions may be granted entry into the territories: . . . (e) that the aliens shall not be considered to be a threat to public policy, national security or the IR of any of the contracting parties.
>
> (Dublin Convention 1990)

One should note here that the focus is *not* on immigrants as defined by the United Nations, but rather on the movement of people for whom the stay does not exceed 90 days. The security system involves police cooperation, extradition procedures, a joint information system that assembles all security alerts on persons and disseminates the list among member states, etc. In sum, the Convention, by locking together migration and security throughout the document, scores highly in terms of the saliency of the linkage between migration and security (Bigo 1998b; Bigo and Guild 2003; van Munster 2009).

Regarding security practices indicators, France scores highly. As in Canada, several scholars have documented the use of interdiction (indicator *P-1*) by the French government for security purposes (Bigo and Guild 2003, 2005; Guiraudon 2002; Guiraudon and Lahav 2000; Newman and van Selm 2003; Pratt 2005; Rodier 2006). They all concluded that interdiction is a major component of security practices relating to the movement of people. For instance, Claire Rodier, tracing back to the Dublin Convention of 1990 the use of carrier sanctions for having on-board passengers without proper identity papers, highlights that the rules were "hardened" in the spring of 2001 with the intention of inducing as much control as possible before migrants leave their place of origin. Rodier also underscores the creation of Immigration Liaison Officers (ILO) in 2004, which are national bureaucrats dispatched abroad with the task of "preventing illegal immigration," as evidence of the intensification of interdiction measures (Rodier 2006: 12).

Finally, in terms of detaining immigrants (indicator *P-2*) there are two categories of detention facilities in France. The waiting zones are the first category.

A person is placed in a waiting zone if he has been refused entry to the country because he does not satisfy the conditions set down in the Foreigner Code;[13] if he is a foreigner in transit who has been prohibited from boarding a plane, boat, or train; or if he is an asylum seeker at the border. There are 120 "waiting zones" in airports, ports, and other locations open to the international movement of people.

The administrative holding centers are the second category. A person is detained in an administrative holding center if he is a foreigner subject to a judicial removal measure (removal to the border) or an administrative one (deportation order); if he has been banned by a court from remaining on French territory; or if he is under an enforceable removal measure taken by one of the European Union member countries. There are 22 administrative holding centers in France.

The number of immigrant detainees is considerable in France. More than 47,000 immigrants were detained in 2004. Waiting zones and administrative holding centers have carceral features such as solitary confinement rooms for troubled detainees and handcuffs for detainees during their transport (Welch and Schuster 2005). Also, the sanitary and general conditions of these centers are troubling, provoking a fierce rapport in 2005 from the Council of Europe Commissioner for Human Rights (Commissioner for Human Rights 2006).

Comparing the security practices of detaining immigrants highlights a sharp contrast between Canada and France. In Canada, the average number of immigrant detainees between 1996 and 2003 was about 9,000—a number that represents less than 4 percent of the total number of accepted immigrants. In France, the average number of immigrant detainees between 2000 and 2004 was just under 43,000, representing 28 percent of the total number of accepted immigrants (as previously shown in Figure 2.3). Detention of immigrants is thus significantly higher in France than in Canada.

As Table 2.3 summarizes, the movement of people is securitized today in both Canada and France. I have demonstrated in the previous pages that both Canada and France score on all indicators of securitized migration. Legal instruments and key policy statements listing migration as a security threat have been developed in Canada and France. Furthermore, I have demonstrated that the early 1990s represents a fundamental critical juncture for the study of securitized migration in Canada and France. In Canada, the publication of *Foreign Policy Themes and Priorities* marked the first time that migration was listed as a security concern;

Table 2.3 Indicators, securitized migration, Canada and France, as of 2005

Indicators		Canada	France
Institutional	Legal (*I*-1)	Yes	Yes
	Policy statement (*I*-2)	Yes	Yes
	Saliency (*I*-3)	Low	High
Security practices	Interdiction (*P*-1)	Yes	Yes
	Detention (*P*-2)	Low	High
Securitization outcome		Weak	Strong

in France, the Dublin Convention established how the movement of people was to be viewed for years to come. My third indicator, the saliency of the linkage between migration and security in policy statements, reveals an important difference in levels of securitized migration between Canada and France. I underscored that the saliency is relatively low in Canada and relatively much higher in France. In terms of security practices, I have shown that interdiction policy is used in Canada and France to crack down on migration for security reasons. Finally, the issue of detention of immigrants reveals a considerable difference in the level of securitized migration. Although detention practices are fast increasing in Canada, this country case displays a relatively low level of detention of immigrants. In France, detention of immigrants as a security practice is well established and France has a high level of detention of immigrants.

Clearly then, significant variations exist between the two country cases on the level of the securitization. The outcome for Canada, with low saliency and low detention rates, is a weak level of securitization, whereas the outcome for France, with high saliency and a high level of immigrant detainees, is a strong level of securitization.

Looking ahead

In this chapter I have first presented a rationale as to why comparing Canada and France is feasible in the context of this study, and why that particular comparison is instructive. I have then described the indicators that I used to measure (1) whether migration was securitized in my two country cases and (2) whether there was any variation in the level of securitization between the two cases. Results obtained here are particularly relevant for the following chapters. Although migration is securitized in both Canada and France, there is a meaningful variation in each country's level of securitization. This renders a comparative study of social mechanisms involved in the securitization process particularly relevant. Also, comparing Canada and France in the context of migration is in fact comparing cases that present considerable variation in the phenomenon to be explained.

The next chapter takes a more theoretical turn. In reviewing the existing models proposed to understand the linkage between migration and security, I present the merits of adopting a constructivist perspective in the particular context of this study. The critique of these models (and especially of ST) furnishes the basis for an alternate framework, which is detailed in the last section of this chapter.

3   Constructivism, security, and the movement of people

Since the late 1980s there has been a wave of academic interest in the relationship between the international movement of people and world politics. Unsurprisingly, the nature and mechanisms of the securitization of migration is the subject of considerable debate. In migration studies, a dynamic strand has focused its attention on states' control (or lack thereof) of migration flow with as a starting point the so-called "gap hypothesis"—the gap between the states' intention to adopt restrictionist immigration policy and the actual result of the policy (Brubaker 1992; Cornelius *et al.* 2004; Freeman 1995; Gibney 2004; Guiraudon and Lahav 2000; Joppke 2005; Sassen 1996; Soysal 1994). Other migration scholars have focused their attention on the effects (usually negative) of the securitization of migration on migrants themselves and on the host societies (Caloz-Tschopp *et al.* 2007; Crépeau and Nakache 2006; Freedman 2004; Guild and van Selm 2005). Several scholars have shown that the movement of people has an effect on regional security (as both a potential cause and a consequence) and on the nature of violent conflicts in the international system (Adamson 2006; Kenyon Lischer 2005; Loescher 1992).

In IR, scholars attuned to realist premises of anarchy and material interest argue that Western states should fear the "coming anarchy" associated with mass migration (Huntington 2004; Kaplan 1994). Another stream of theorizing that has its roots in IR is neoliberalism; Christopher Rudolph (2003, 2006) revisits the grand state strategy perspective and contends that the "structural threat environment" is the primary explanatory factor for the securitization of migration. Another model, which takes its cue from critical security studies (largely defined) and political sociology, is the governmentality of unease model. Didier Bigo, one of the most active advocates of this model, argues that the securitization process has to do above all with routinized practices of professionals of security and the transformation of techonologies they use (Bigo 1996, 2002, 2008). Of these models, Securitization Theory (ST) provides the most widely applied and fully developed model of the relationship between migration and security (Buzan *et al.* 1998; Wæver 1995). Yet ST has difficulties finding a place within wider categories of IR theory, as realists and neoliberal institutionalists treat ST with polite neglect and critical theorists find ST not critical enough (Booth 2005; Smith 2005; Wyn Jones 2005).

This study seeks to advance both ST and its engagement with IR theory by linking it to constructivism. Despite ST's architects' open acceptance of some aspects of constructivism, I argue that how ST relates to constructivists premises can be productively explored further. I do not want to suggest that ST should find its "home" in constructivism or to propose that the analytical framework developed in this book should stand in opposition to ST. Rather, my aim is to demonstrate that constructivism offers useful correctives to ST and that these correctives can be integrated within ST without distorting the theory.

In fact, one of the objectives of this study is to take steps in providing an answer to both Alker's (2005) call for further research on whether—and to what extent—identity-specific values are severely threatened enough within particular societies to require securitization responses, and Heisler's (2006) remark that a comprehensive theoretical framework making sense of the securitization process has yet to be produced.

This chapter starts by locating the study within a constructivist approach to world politics. Over the past decades, a community of scholars has been central to the emergence and the establishment of a social constructivist approach in IR. Their achievements have been instrumental in shifting the focus of the analysis of world politics away from merely material factors to include social and ideational factors as well. I then examine current analytical frameworks and attempt to make sense of the phenomenon of securitized migration while paying special attention to ST. The last section of the chapter details my own approach.

Constructivism and power's polymorphous character

The achievement of constructivism in IR is of remarkable significance. In the past two decades, scholars have successfully employed a constructivist approach to describe and explain the vectors of national security, the chemical weapons taboo, the formation of national identity, security communities, new forms of diplomacy, national interest, and the creation of international norms, to name just a few (Adler and Barnett 1998; Finnemore 1996; Finnemore and Sikkink 1998; Hall 1999; Job 2003; Katzenstein 1996; Price 1997).

Despite the upswing of constructivist research—theoretically and empirically—it is difficult to fully encapsulate the basic assumptions and foundations of constructivism. Critics of constructivism were fast in portraying this as a significant weakness. As a friendly critic puts it, "social constructivism is more united on what is being rejected [i.e. mainstream approaches] than on what is being proposed" (Smith 1999: 690). Advocates of constructivism, on the other hand, tend to see such flexibility as one of its main strengths and a noteworthy contribution to the IR discipline.

Unsurprisingly, constructivists differ, in varying degrees, on what the assumptions of constructivism are (see Table 3.1). Emmanuel Adler (2002), following Stefano Guzzini (2000), posits that there are two common grounds shared by the vast majority of constructivists—the social construction of knowledge and the construction of social reality. John Ruggie (1998), focusing heavily on the material/

Table 3.1 Core features of constructivism

Adler (2002), Guzzini (2000)	1. Social construction of knowledge 2. Construction of social reality
Ruggie (1998)	1. International reality is made of material and ideational factors 2. Ideational factors have a normative and an instrumental dimension 3. Ideational factors express both individual and collective intentions 4. Time and place are crucial determinants
Fearon and Wendt (2002)	1. Fundamental concern with the role of ideas 2. Socially constructed agents 3. Methodological holism 4. Central concern with constitutive explanations
Price and Reus-Smit (1998)	1. Importance of ideational as well as material structures 2. Identities constitute interests and actions 3. Agents and structures are mutually constituted

ideational divide, identifies four main features of constructivism: the international reality is made of both material and ideational factors; ideational factors possess a normative and an instrumental dimension; ideational factors express both individual and collective intentions; and time and place are crucial determinants of the meaning and significance of ideational factors. In their article on the rationalism–constructivism debate, James Fearon and Alex Wendt (2002) argue that four characteristics of constructivism can be identified: a fundamental concern with the role of ideas in the construction of social life; socially constructed agents; methodological holism, as opposed to methodological individualism; and a central concern with constitutive explanations rather than uniquely causal explanations.

Acknowledging that the boundaries set by these scholars are not exclusive and that there is actually a lot of crossover among them, the present study adopts Richard Price and Christian Reus-Smit's standpoint. In their seminal article, serving as a bridge between constructivism and critical theory, they state that constructivism emphasizes three core ontological propositions: "the importance of normative or ideational structures as well as material structures; identities constitute interests and actions; agents and structures are mutually constituted" (Price and Reus-Smit 1998: 266). Agents create, reproduce, and transform social structures. Social structures empower and constrain agents, thereby shaping subsequent agents' practices. As Risse (2000: 5) argues, the essential added value of constructivism is not merely the argument that agents and structures are mutually codetermined in a causal way; rather, the fundamental insight is that "social constructivists insist on the mutual constitutiveness of (social) structures and agents."

To be sure, constructivists are not the first ones to insist on the mutual constitution of agent and structure: the assumption has been at the center of other disciplines for a long time. Indeed, Hannah Arendt was already arguing in *The Human Condition* (1958: 9), albeit with different wording, that:

In addition to the conditions under which life is given to man on earth, and partly out of them, men constantly create their own, self-made conditions, which . . . possess the same conditioning power as natural things. . . . [B]ecause human existence is conditioned existence, it would be impossible without things, and things would be a heap of unrelated articles, a non-world, if they were not the conditioners of human existence.

Yet the novelty of social constructivists is to have employed the mutual constitutiveness of agent and structure to demonstrate the socially constructed nature of world politics, as well as the causal role of norms, social values, identities, and cultural practices.

In addition to Price and Reus-Smit's understanding of the constructivist approach, I found the recent work on the concept of power by Michael C. Williams (2003, 2007) and by Michael Barnett and Raymond Duvall (2005) to be extremely useful in a study about the securitization process. Indeed, Williams, inspired by Bourdieu (1990, 1991), has convincingly shown that one of the most powerful forms of power is its cultural and symbolic form.[1] He argues that "particular articulations of the relationship between culture and security [are] crucial forms of power in the production of security practices" (Williams 2007: 2). Similarly, Barnett and Duvall (2005) identify four forms or expressions of power: compulsory, institutional, structural, and productive. For them, such a conceptualization detaches discussions of power from the limitations of IR realism, encourages scholars to see power's polymorphous character, and suggests a framework for integration of power's multiple forms. In the context of my study, these two important standpoints on the concept of power will prove to be extremely useful in better understanding the securitization process for reasons that will be established in the discussions below.

The securitization of migration: the state of the art

Studies of the interconnections of migration and world politics have in recent years become one of the fastest growing areas of research in global politics. The sources, causes, and consequences of international migration have been thoroughly studied using various methodologies and approaches.[2] Two large categories of studies are relevant in the present context: migration studies and IR studies.

Migration studies

Broadly defined, numerous scholarly works tackling the interconnection of migration and world politics have been published in the past two decades. Several studies consist of either an ad hoc list of migration (and diaspora) influences on foreign policy, or observations that migration is a significant factor influencing world politics (Loescher and Monahan 1989; Newman and van Selm 2003; Ong and Nonini 1996; Shain 1995; Shain and Barth 2003; Sheffer 1986).

A dynamic strand of migration studies has focused its attention on the politicization of migration and its associated questions of integration, welfare, multiculturalism, and citizenship (Brubaker 1992; Castles and Davidson 2000; Favell and Hansen 2002; Feldblum 1999; Geddes 2003; Guiraudon 2000a; Ireland 2004; Joppke and Morawska 2003; Weil 2005; Wihtol de Wenden 1987; Zolberg 1992). A nice illustration of this literature is Koopmans *et al.'s* (2005) book. Marrying migration studies and social movement theory, they have applied the political opportunity perspective to understanding the forms and action repertoires of immigrant political activity as well as the mobilization of anti-immigrant sentiment. They have sought to assess whether migrant groups, national conceptions of citizenship, or supranational institutions drive migrants' and anti-migrants' political behavior. They conclude that variable national conceptions of nationhood shape conceptions of belonging and political claims making.

Another large (and equally active) section of migration literature tackles the issue of states' control of migration flows (or lack thereof). The extent to which the nation-state remains capable of regulating and controlling the international movement of people is indeed the subject of considerable scholarly debate (Andreas 2000; Brochmann and Hammar 1999; Brubaker 1995; Gibney 2004; Guiraudon and Lahav 2000; Joppke 2005; Statham and Geddes 2006). Most of the discussions have evolved around the so-called "gap hypothesis"—the gap between the states' intention to adopt restrictionist immigration policy and the actual results of the policy—and its corollary question of whether the state can control unwanted migration (Cornelius *et al.* 1994, 2004). To answer these questions, Gary Freeman (1995, 2002, 2006) has proposed the "client politics model," which argues that lobbying by special interest groups leads governments to adopt more expansionary immigration policies than their official restrictionist rhetoric suggests. Other scholars have put forward the embedded liberalism model, which argues that liberal states accept unwanted migrants because of the influence of embedded liberal ideals and domestic (and, to a lesser degree, international) courts (Guiraudon and Joppke 2001; Hollifield 1992; Joppke 1998). Some have also argued that the diminution of national sovereignty and the growing power of international human rights laws and norms best explain policy gaps (Jacobson 1997; Sassen 1996; Soysal 1994).

Closer to the questions asked in my study, several migration scholars have focused their attention on the effects (usually negative) of the securitization of migration on migrants themselves (Beare 1997; Caloz-Tschopp 2004; Freedman 2004). In a provocative article, Maggie Ibrahim (2005) goes as far as contending that the securitization of migration is the latest and most modern form of racism. Others have highlighted the interconnections of security practices and human rights considerations (Badie and Wihtol de Wenden 1994; Crépeau and Nakache 2006; Devetak 2004; Liotta 2002; Lowry 2002). Similarly, an excellent edited book has sought to investigate the value assessments regarding migrants in Europe, the United States, Canada and Australia—whether immigrants are an asset or a threat—while providing an overview of the impact of international migration on human rights, legal systems, identity, racism, and labor policies (Guild and van

Selm 2005). Migration scholars have also shown that the movement of people has an effect on regional security. Loescher's Adelphi Paper (1992) has attempted to raise the issue of forced migration as both a potential cause and a consequence of insecurity by emphasizing the "high politics" dimensions of the issue. More recently, Adamson (2006) has argued that international migration affects states' interests in three core areas of national security concerns: state sovereignty, the balance of power among states, and the nature of violent conflicts in the international system.

In the context of my analysis, an important limitation of these studies, in spite of the fact that they are significant contributions to the field, is that their aim is not to construct an analytical framework for understanding the securitization process. These studies are simply asking a different set of questions than the ones asked in my study. Indeed, investigating the politicization of migration and its impact on welfare and citizenship, analyzing the rationale as to why liberal states accept unwanted migration, and studying the origins, forms, practicalities, and implications of the gap between official immigration policies and policy practices are different research projects from mine. My aim is not to investigate whether there is a gap (actual or perceived) between states' policies regarding securitized migration and the practices of securitized migration.[3] My focus is not so much on "why" migration was securitized. Similarly, studying the consequences of the securitization of migration on migrants, on host societies, and/or on receiving states is a different set of questions from the ones tackled in my study. Rather, my study is about the social mechanisms of the process of securitizing international migration. The focus is on "how" migration was securitized. Proceeding with a comparative analysis of the cases of Canada and France, the central objective of my study is to gain a better understanding of the securitization process in the context of international migration.

Yet another limit, perhaps even more consequential, of several migration studies is the propensity to treat the state as an autonomous agent. Indeed, influential migration scholars have argued that research on immigration policy "must centre on the state as an international actor" (Zolberg 1992: 316) or that "bringing the state back in" constitutes one of the key contributions of political science to migration studies—that is, to conceptualize the state as a unitary and autonomous actor (Hollifield 2000). Similarly, Rudolph (2003: 606) argues in his study of national security and immigration that the state is "an agent in its own right." In his book, Rudolph devotes a section of its concluding chapter to defending a statist approach to studying migration. One of his arguments is that "whereas domestic interest groups [. . .] tend to be single-issue oriented and define preferences accordingly, the state instead tends to forward a 'national interest' that represents an aggregation of these domestic interests." To be sure, a statist model will have a disadvantage in being able to "account for the nuances involved in the domestic arena," argues Rudolph (2006: 203–4), but scholars should acknowledge that "there is no 'perfect' social science theory."

A constructivist approach highlights that treating the state as a unified agent limits more than it reveals in a study about movement and order. For constructivists, one cannot identify the mechanisms at play in the securitization process without opening the concept of state in order to unravel who the agents are "behind it." For instance, "the" Canadian position on the securitization of migration significantly varies depending on who the Minister of Foreign Affairs is, even when Ministers come from the same political party. In the same vein, "the" French position varies depending on who the Prime Minister is. I argue that, in bracketing the domestic sources of state identity, these studies miss not only the "nuances," as Rudolph simplifies it, but also the sources of change. In fact, sources of change and continuity are treated exogenously. In addition, in conceptualizing the state as an agent rather than as a structure, these studies anthropomorphize collective actors and leave corporate identities un-problematized. These studies also reify the state; they postulate its ever-present and enduring nature. However, the usefulness of reifying the state remains unclear (Cederman 1997; Koslowski 1999; Wight 1999). As Andreas Wimmer and Nina Glick Schiller (2003) underscore, studies that conceptualize the state as an agent fall into the danger of methodological nationalism, that is, "the naturalization of the nation-state by the social sciences." Yet, misrepresenting the state as an agent has an additional cost, as Adler points out in his criticism of Wendt's argument for the value of treating the state as an actor. Wendt "offers a theory and a portrait of agency and the state that [. . .] ultimately gives up on bringing into the theory *the ultimate constructor of worlds,*" argues Adler, "by which I mean the thinking, often reasonable, sometimes surprising, and even at times creative human individual" (Adler 2002: 108, emphasis in original).

International relations/security studies

Most cogent and interesting models for understanding the process by which migration becomes a security issue come from works published mainly in IR literature rather than in migration studies journals. Three traditions in IR scholarship have given rise to five models for understanding and explaining the securitization of migration.

The first two models have their roots in the realist tradition of IR. There is no consensus, however, among advocates of the realist school on the applicability of a realist perspective on the securitization of migration. Indeed, one of the leading advocates of the realist school has circumscribed the focus of security studies to "the phenomenon of war" and, incidentally, defined security as "the study of the threat, use and control of military force." Thereby, he is closing off any possibilities of applying a realist perspective on the securitization of migration (Walt 1991: 212, 2002). Notwithstanding Walt's reticence, scholars have applied the realist model in two ways. First, scholars attuned to notions of structural anarchy and material interest have chosen to present an alarmist picture of the security consequences of the movement of people, that is, the disorder produced by migration. In Robert Kaplan's (1994) famous formulation, Western states should fear the "coming anarchy" associated with mass migration, while, according to Samuel Huntington (2004), the persistent flow of Hispanic immigrants to the

United States constitutes a major potential threat to the country's cultural and political identity. Others view the world as divided into two camps, the rich and the poor, and predict that the poor will either fight the rich or simply overwhelm them (Connelly and Kennedy 1994). Some focus on negative images: "Advanced industrial countries can protect their borders from invading armies but not from hordes of individuals who slip into harbours, crawl under barbed-wire fences, and wade across rivers" (Weiner 1995: 9). Still, albeit in a more gentle way, scholars have argued that *by definition* migration is a security concern: "Migration always is security-sensitive because migration often changes societies and societies often change migrants" (Miller 1998: 25). Second, scholars have explained the security impacts of migration in terms of its potential to induce international crisis and war, arguing that migration should be incorporated into security concerns only when it induces or provokes international conflicts (Weiner 1993).

As numerous critics have pointed out, however, the central explanatory variables of both models are inconclusive (Albert *et al.* 2001; Badie and Wihtol de Wenden 1994; Doty 1998; Guild and van Selm 2005; Newman and van Selm 2003; Tirman 2004; Walters 2002). The structurally deterministic scholarship that underlines the alarmist point of view constitutes an uncertain foundation for theorizing about the migration–security nexus, despite the fact that some politicians have found the alarmist statements attractive. As the next chapters will demonstrate, international migration has been securitized in Canada and France without any clear evidence that it would induce conflicts, let alone conflicts that Canada or France should fear will affect their respective national security interests. Furthermore, perhaps with the exception of a few references in French President Mitterand's speeches, the "story" of the securitization of migration according to the empirical evidences amassed in this study does not support these two lines of argument. That is, neither the concern of structural anarchy nor the concern regarding the inducement of international–regional conflicts arose in Canada's or France's securitization process.

IR neoliberal scholars have also attempted to address the problem of migration–security interaction. Attempting to build a "truly comprehensive theory applicable to more than one state" by revisiting the concept of state grand strategy, Rudolph (2006) argues that the "structural threat environment" is the primary explanatory factor for the securitization of migration. The causal pathway begins with an "external" geopolitical threat, and then leads to state response, and then policy output. Rudolph (2006: 30) aims to "incorporate a constructivist perspective that emphasizes of the role of ideas in shaping outcomes to supplement the IR realist focus on power and interest." Ideas in his model "serve as an intervening variable that shapes particular policy outcomes given a strategic threat environment."

However, constructivism posits a different understanding of ideational factors than the one Rudolph employed. Focusing on the role of norms, knowledge, and culture in world politics, constructivism stresses in particular the role of inter-subjective ideas. A constructivist perspective sees ideational factors as having tremendously more power than being merely intervening variables. For constructivism, ideational factors have constitutive effects on social reality; indeed, for constructivists ideas are at the core of how structural/external threats come to have any meaning. Instead of treating the relationship between structural threats and ideas as, respectively, explanatory and intervening variables, a constructivist study postulates that structural threats cannot exist without the ideational factors that brought them meaning and significance, nor are ideas formulated and created in a structural vacuum. Furthermore, constructivists see a fundamental distinction between brute facts and social facts, the latter being dependent for their exist-ence on socially established convention. Thus, mistaking a social fact such as the "structural threat environment" for a brute fact runs the risk of missing the point that social facts are constructed and open to change. Hence, upon closer exami-nation Rudolph's claim of bringing constructivism into his framework through the inclusion of ideas as intervening variables sits awkwardly with large sections of constructivist scholarships (Adler 1997, 2002; Finnemore 1996; Laffey and Weldes 1997; Price 1997; Price and Reus-Smit 1998; Ruggie 1998).

The fourth model, inspired by Michel Foucault's and Pierre Bourdieu's systems of thought, is the governmentality of unease model.[4] The work of Didier Bigo (1996, 2002, 2008) has been central in developing this approach to security and to the securitization of migration in particular (see also Aradau and van Munster 2007; Ceyhan and Tsoukala 2002; Doucet *et al.* 2010; Huysmans 2006; Walters 2002). Bigo argues that security is not about survival nor is it about urgency and exceptional practices. Rather, security is the result of mundane bureaucratic decisions of everyday politics that create a sense of insecurity, fear, danger, and unease. The securitization process has to do above all with routinized practices of professionals of security, essentially police and bureaucrats. For him, the securitization of migration is "directly related to the [security professionals'] own immediate interests (competition for budgets and missions) and to the transforma-tion of technologies they use" (Bigo 2002: 64). His model identifies a diffuse and overarching system of unease that results in the creation of a transnational field of professionals in the management of unease and contributes to the governmentality of unease.

However, Bigo's exclusive focus on professionals of security as agents involved in the securitization of migration has problematic echoes with constructivist scholarship. Indeed, the usefulness of restricting the category of agents involved in the securitization process to security professionals and to agents specialized in security-related issues remains unclear in light of constructivists' emphasis on the multiplicity of agents of the social world, and on the mutual constitution of agents and structures. In addition, Judith Butler's (1997, 1999) criticism of Bourdieu's account of performative speech acts applies here. In a challenging critique, she argues that Bourdieu tends to assume that the agent who formulates a speech act is positioned on a map of social power in a fixed way and that the success of the speech act depends on whether the agent who performs the speech act is already authorized to make it work by the position of social power he or she occupies. In understanding the relationship between speech acts and agential powers in this way, Bourdieu "fails to take account of the way in which social positions are themselves constructed through a more tacit operation of performativity" (Butler

1999: 122). In that sense, the tacit and performative operation of authorization and entitlement is not always initiated by the agent or by a security professional. Butler (1999: 123) further criticizes Bourdieu for assuming the equivalence between "being authorized to speak" and "speaking with authority," for "it is clearly possible to speak with authority without being authorized to speak." Seen in this lineage, an agent does not have to be a security specialist to present an issue as a security issue—most environmentalists who have successfully stressed that environment degradation is a global security issue are not security professionals, for example. To be sure, a securitizing agent needs to possess social power and social recognition in order to have a significant impact in the securitization process. Yet this social power and recognition does not only come from the realm of security. Furthermore, evidence amassed in my study shows that agents who were not security professionals or particularly specialized in security-related issues have had significant roles in the process of securitizing migration. In addition, my study demonstrates that the rationale for the securitization of migration has often been that migration was a national security issue threatening the survival of the state and/or the society—a situation that requires exceptional measures. Despite these reserves, I shall argue in the concluding chapter that Bigo's set of arguments and the logic behind his model should be seen as a complementary approach to the one developed in this study.

The fifth model is ST (Buzan *et al.* 1998; Wæver 1995). Bringing speech act theory into security studies, ST posits that labeling something as a security issue permeates it with a sense of importance that legitimizes the use of emergency measures outside of the usual political processes to deal with it. For ST,

> the process of securitization is what in language theory is called a speech act. It is not interesting as a sign referring to something more real; it is the utterance itself that is the act. By saying the words, something is done (like betting, giving a promise, naming a ship).
>
> (Buzan *et al.* 1998: 26)

A securitizing speech act attempts to present an issue as an existential security threat to a chosen referent object. In this sense, security is treated as the outcome of a particular social process. As Michael C. Williams (2003: 513) nicely summarizes it, for ST "issues become 'securitized', treated as security issues, through these speech-acts which do not simply describe an existing security situation, but bring it into being as a security situation by successfully representing it as such." For ST, the securitization process involves agents' securitizing moves (i.e. speech acts) and conditions associated with security speech acts.

In recent years, ST has captured the attention of an increasing number of scholars: articles analyzing ST's strengths and weaknesses have been published as leading articles in major IR journals; a peer-reviewed journal has devoted a special issue to ST; and panels on ST have been organized at annual conventions of the International Studies Association.[5] Some scholars have discussed the question of identity and the responsibility of the analyst while others have tackled its normative implications (Eriksson 1999; Huysmans 1993; McSweeney 1996). Other scholars have analyzed the coupling of speech act theory with ST from a gender perspective (Hansen 2000; Kennedy-Pipe 2004). Michael C. Williams (2003) has contended that, by insisting on speech act alone, ST explanatory power is limited because it underestimates other powerful practices such as gesture, the production of image, and the use of symbols. Scholars have also questioned ST's understanding of security (as an existential threat) while advancing an understanding in terms of emancipation (Booth 1991, 2005c). Similarly, scholars have criticized the de-securitization strategy implicitly present in ST. Claudia Aradau's article has indeed spurred an enriching dialog on this question (Alker 2006; Aradau 2004, 2006; Behnke 2006; Floyd 2007; Taureck 2006).

Though stimulated by these contributions, I raise the stakes by identifying limits of ST that have been left relatively untouched by other students of the securitization process. Despite ST's architects' open acceptance of some aspects of constructivism, I argue that how ST relates with constructivists' premises can be productively explored further. In what follows, I identify three limits of ST that are problematic for the study of the securitization process and I offer remedies to these criticisms that can be integrated within the analytical framework laid out by ST. My objective is not to present an alternative framework for the study of the securitization process to the one developed by ST; I do not seek to propose an analysis of the securitization process that would stand in opposition to ST. Rather, my goal is to offer refinements to ST.

First, ST leaves ill-defined contextual factors involved in the securitization process.[6] Instead of talking in terms of contextual factors, ST's architects present two categories of conditions: facilitating conditions and the audience. Facilitating conditions, which are conditions under which the speech act works, are divided into two categories: (1) the internal conditions, that is, a security speech act must follow the security form, the grammar of security; (2) the external conditions, which are subdivided into two types: the social capital of the securitizing actor and the features of the alleged threats. The failure to meet these facilitating conditions, ST argues, leads to a failure of the speech act.

Yet, I argue that working within the umbrella of facilitating conditions—despite being called for by Austin—points the research in the direction of exploring the conditions that *facilitate* the securitization process; it overlooks contextual factors that *limit* or *constrain* a successful securitization. I do not want to highlight that ST has difficulties explaining unsuccessful securitization. Rather, I argue that ST eschews social elements involved in the securitization process that have acted as a limit on a successful securitization—and without which the securitization would have been potentially much stronger. Proceeding within a constructivist approach helps to underscore that linguistic utterances are always produced in particular contexts and that the social properties of these contexts endow speech acts with a differential value system. In other words, an analytical framework for the study of the securitization process should provide theoretical space for research on contextual factors that are inducing the process *as well as* contextual factors that are constraining the process.

Specifying the role of audience is also crucial in working through these issues. In a bold statement, ST asserts that:

> a discourse that takes the form of presenting something as an existential threat to a referent object does not by itself create securitization – this is a securitizing move, but the issue is securitized only if and when the audience accepts it as such. . . . Successful securitization is not decided by the securitizer but by the audience of the security speech-act.
>
> (Buzan *et al.* 1998: 25–31)

I argue that ST's understanding of the role of audience is misleading for several reasons. To start with, ST treats the sequence of the securitization process in a unidirectional fashion in which audience stands only at the very end. According to the theory, securitizing agents initiate the securitizing process and audiences terminate the process by either approving or disapproving agents' securitizing attempts. By positing that the audience merely participates in the final phase of the process, ST eludes notions of feedback and multidirectionality between securitizing agents and audiences that are, I contend, at the core of the securitization process. Moreover, one must ask who precisely comprises the audience. Instead of breaking down the audience into categories, ST's response of adding adjectives to the word "audience" succeeds merely in confusing things. In *Security: A New Framework for Analysis* (Buzan *et al.* 1998), ST's architects refer to a "significant" audience (p. 27), a "sufficient" audience (p. 204), and "those the securitizing act attempts to convince" (p. 41). Elsewhere, Wæver talks about the "relevant" audience (2000: 251, 2009: 21). Yet what is a "sufficient" audience? How do we measure a "significant" audience? What is the "relevant" audience in the case of migration? If migration is a societal security concern, then should "those the securitizing act attempts to convince" be the society supposedly under threat? In a liberal democracy, can the ultimate audience be something other than the general population?

Two scholars have recently discussed the issue of audience. Mark Salter (2008) further disaggregates the audience into four types (elite, technocratic, scientific, popular). Yet Salter does not seek to analyze what kind of powers contextual factors such as the audience possess in the securitization process. Thierry Balzacq (2005) raises the stakes and argues that the units of analysis of ST "negates the audience." He proposes instead that an effective securitization should be "audience-centered" and that "a securitizing actor is sensitive to two kinds of support, moral and formal" (p. 184). However, Balzacq's claim that ST "negates the audience" does not sit well with ST's aforementioned claim that "successful securitization is . . . decided . . . by the audience of the security speech-act" (Buzan *et al.* 1998: 25). To be sure, ST leaves the "audience" unspecified as we have seen, but the theory clearly does not negate its existence or its role. In addition, Balzacq's argument is cast in terms of what kinds of *support* a securitizing actor must seek. It is not understood in terms of what kind of powers contextual factors such as the audience possess in the securitization process—whether they have facilitating or constraining powers. Hence, I argue that a departure from the conceptual devices of "conditions" to a constructivist approach stressing socio-historical, ideational, and contextual factors is necessary.

Second, I argue that ST cannot explain variation in levels of securitized migration. ST treats security as a binary notion: either an issue is securitized or it is not. The only variation that ST recognizes is along the spectrum of non-politicization, politicization, securitization, and de-securitization. As Mark Salter (2008) points out, ST appears to represent securitization as a threshold: either a threat is represented and then accepted as a security issue, or it remains contested within the realm of normal, deliberative politics. Salter highlights correctly that this does not match the complexity of contemporary social dynamics of security. I would add that, in conceptualizing the securitization in this way, ST is not capable of distinguishing the issue of intensity of securitization. Once an issue reaches the securitization phase, ST does not distinguish whether the issue is strongly securitized or weakly securitized. The question of levels of securitized migration could be asked in two ways. This is problematic because scholars self-consciously following in the footsteps of ST, as currently organized, cannot empirically problematize whether intensity in securitized migration exists or not. The literature certainly reflects that situation. Most of the studies have been case studies of one phenomenon in one country. In the narrower field of securitized migration, the vast majority of studies are single case studies as well. To my knowledge, Melissa Curley and Wong Sui-lun's (2008) edited book is the only study looking at the securitization of migration across country cases while employing ST. This has two implications. The intensity of securitized migration could vary *over time* in the same country case. At first sight, international migration certainly seems more securitized in several OECD countries today than in the 1970s. Or the intensity of securitized migration could fluctuate *across cases*. One can observe a disconnection between ST and empirical evidence; as my previous chapter has demonstrated a considerable difference exists in the level of securitized migration between Canada and France. Yet there is no theoretical space in ST to tackle the question of levels of securitized migration and, consequently, to provide adequate guidance for the suggestion of hypotheses accounting for variations either within cases across time or across cases.

The third limit of ST is that it presents a thin understanding of the concept of power. To be sure, power is discussed in relation to securitizing actors. For ST, a securitizing actor must be in a position of authority and have the power to define security, even though power is never absolute and that authority should not be defined as official authority. In addition, one could distillate a conception of power in the discussion of the agent–audience relationship. ST sees the power of agents in terms of their *ability to convince* the audience while it understands the power of the audience in terms of its *capacity to approve* agents' securitizing moves. However, there is a sense of incompleteness in how ST treats power. In the past few years, scholars working within the constructivist family, broadly defined, have put forward ideas and arguments about the notion of power that ST could integrate into its framework. In particular, I think of the Bourdieu-inspired work by Williams (2003, 2007) on the symbolic forms of power and of Barnett and Duvall's (2005) sophisticated understanding of power.

In the following pages, I look to offer remedies to these criticisms. Indeed, I argue that constructivism offers sound theoretical foundations to propose refinements to ST. Against ST's focus on facilitating conditions and on audiences' mere "approval" capability, I put forward a constructivist approach that acknowledges the polymorphous character of power by positing the enabling and/or constraining powers of contextual factors such as the audience. Against ST's lack of distinction between different levels or intensities of securitized migration, I suggest an analytical framework that possesses theoretical and empirical spaces to understand and explain variation in levels of securitized migration. Yet I contend that these elements can be integrated within the analytical framework initially laid out by ST.

The argument

Undoubtedly there are methodological, theoretical, empirical, and normative issues about the securitization process on which there is substantial disagreement among scholars that this chapter cannot fully engage with. The process of securitizing migration is a wide-ranging and complex process that the next few pages cannot do justice to; the framework briefly presented here is by no means intended to be comprehensive. Rather, I propose to focus on the fundamental social components of the process of securitizing international migration, bringing out the original contributions of my set of arguments and laying out foundations on which ST could be improved.

In a study about the securitization process it is important to distinguish between the politicization of migration and the securitization of migration. As previously mentioned, securitization refers to the process of integrating migration discursively and institutionally into security frameworks that emphasize policing and defense. In contrast, the politicization of migration refers to the process of taking migration out of restricted networks and/or bureaucracies and bringing it into the public arena (Guiraudon 1998; Huysmans 2006). Politicization can have both positive and negative overtones concerning the movement of people. When an agent is underscoring the positive contribution of immigrants to a country's history or culture, she or he is making a positive politicization. When an agent is criticizing the efficiency of the refugee recognition process, she or he is making a negative politicization. This is not to say that there is no "politics" in the securitization process or that the two processes are not related—the politicization of migration could lead to the securitization of migration and vice versa. Yet I contend that a politicization of migration does not necessarily equate with a securitization of migration; an agent can politicize an issue without securitizing it. It is one thing to question the overconcentration of migrants in large urban agglomerations, refugee adjudication, the adequacy of settlement services, and the failure to recognize overseas professional credentials. It is an altogether different one to declare that migration is a security threat.

Working within the footsteps of ST, I argue that agents' security speech acts are an essential social constituent of the securitization process.[7] Speech acts intend to present international migration as an existential security threat—that is, agents' securitizing moves. Following prevailing treatment in securitization research, a securitizing agent needs to possess social power and social recognition. In my reading, ST's conceptualization of the securitizing agents' social power contains sufficient flexibility to recognize the importance of the social conditions for the possibility of speech acts [this would alleviate Bourdieu's (1982) criticism of Austin's theory]. Yet an element perhaps left under-theorized by ST is that social recognition could be institutionalized (e.g. a politician in power), but it could also be an emergent recognition. That is, while a social agent (e.g. an environmental activist) may have little social power and recognition at the beginning of the process, the agent's social recognition and thus social power could increase precisely because of the questions she or he is raising and the way she or he is doing so. It is indeed important to recognize and incorporate the issue of *emergence* of social power and social recognition in the analytical framework. This would help reduce the tension identified by Butler (1997, 1999) that speech act theory neglects the extent to which performative speech acts are themselves contributing to agents' social positioning, power, and authority.[8]

Securitizing moves both percolate from the environment in which they are made and are constrained by the same environment. As such, agents' securitizing moves have to be analyzed within the context in which they have been made. An investigation of the process of securitizing migration must address whether securitizing attempts were made at a particular point in time, whether they were made before or after a major international event, whether they found an echo in the collective identity schema of a particular society, and whether the audiences reacted to these securitizing attempts with enthusiasm or with reluctance.

This brings to the forefront the issue of the relationship between securitizing agents and contextual factors. Building upon constructivists' premises and Bourdieu's ideas, I propose to understand the relationship as mutually constituted, durable but not static, generative, and structured. Indeed, one of the central premises of constructivism is the mutual constitution of agency and structure. That is, constructivists contend that agents do not exist independently of the constraining and enabling power of structures whilst structures "do not exist independently of the knowledgeable practices of social agents" (Price and Reus-Smit 1998: 266–7). Agents create, reproduce, and transform social structures. Social structures empower and constrain agents, thereby shaping subsequent agents' practices. Such an understanding is in line with Bourdieu's system of thoughts. As Williams (2007: 24) underlines, "in his own words, the position Bourdieu adopts is that of a 'constructivist structuralism or of a structuralist constructivism' that attempt to link agency and structure in a comprehensive conception of practice." In other words, the idea that human action is linked to the subjective constitution of social reality needs to be supplemented by a similar focus on structural elements that comprise that constitutive process.

Seen in this light, agents do not work in a vacuum. How the agent anticipates the likely reception of his/her securitizing move operates as an incentive or a constraint on the very process of elaborating the speech act and the actual practice of making the speech act. Securitizing agents cannot exclude themselves from environments in which they formulate their securitizing attempts; they do not navigate freely toward a successful securitization. To be sure, agents do have some autonomy; socio-historically and culturally produced knowledge enables individuals to construct and give meaning to contextual factors. Yet they are not free agents and their capacity to change, reproduce, and remodel the security realm is not unbounded. A security speech act does not constitute a securitization; it only represents an attempt to present an issue as a security threat.

In the same way, the meaning and construction of contextual structures is dependent on ideas and agents' interpretations. Contextual factors (e.g. the terrorist attacks of 9/11) do not objectively exist out there waiting to exercise influence. Multifaceted contexts in which agents operate cannot "impose" a securitization without agential powers; they do not simply drive securitization in some objective way. Contextual factors do not speak for themselves. Rather, they have to be interpreted as having security implications for them to have security impacts.

Conceptualizing the relationship between agents and contextual factors as mutually constituted not only allows for the inclusion of feedback and multidirectionality in the analytical framework but also permits a fruitful understanding of the issue of power in the securitization process. To capture the process, power needs to be understood as symbolic power—that is, "the ability to use symbolic structures or representation and the occupation of social positions from which they can be effectively enacted, and social and material power thereby mobilized" (Williams 2007: 65). Social structures/contexts possess the power to legitimize and authorize, to include and exclude, and, as such, they exercise considerable power on agents—most notably by accrediting and conferring authority to a particular agent. Following Barnett and Duvall (2005), I contend that structural positions do not generate equal social positions, or social privileges. Structures allocate differential capacities to different actors in different social positions. Social capacities of actors are not only socially produced but social structures also shape actors' self-understanding and subjective interests. Furthermore, structural/contextual factors also produce subjectivity in systems of meaning and signification. This form of power entails generalized and diffuse social processes and focuses on systems of signification and on networks of social forces perpetually shaping one another.

Seen in this light, agents' powers comprise not only the ability to try to convince an audience that international migration is a security threat but also—if not somewhat more profoundly—the ability to reproduce, transform, and remodel the security architecture of a referent object (society, state, etc.). Furthermore, it is because the relationship between agents and contexts is so interwoven that an agent can employ symbols that carry security meanings in one context but not in another. To paraphrase Bourdieu, the symbolic power of securitizing moves is defined in and through a given relation between those who exercise power and those who submit to it, that is, in the very structure of the field in which belief is produced and reproduced.

In this study, I explore the role of two agents in the process of securitizing migration: political agents and media agents. This selection of agents is not a theoretical statement on who constitutes a securitizing agent; in designing the study, I had to limit the range of agents under investigation. Nonetheless, I argue that assessing the value of these two agential hypotheses is fundamental in the context of the securitization of migration. To be sure, the relationship between political agents and media agents is a complex and multifaceted one that the present study only slightly explores. However, for the purpose of my study, I contend that the relationship is one of continuous interaction. Rather than automatically seeing political agents as the initiators of the securitization process, I contend that political agents can, in some cases, be the initiators of a particular security policy and, in other cases, be transmitting players (e.g. by giving institutional support to media's and/or audiences' security demands). Similarly, media agents can in some cases be initiators of the securitizing process (e.g. by making securitizing moves before political agents formulate one, thereby pressing both the government and the audiences to adopt a particular security policy). In other cases, media agents can be transmitting players (e.g. by supporting political agents' securitizing moves or by voicing and articulating audiences' security demands).

In turn, I contend (contra ST) that the audiences' powers (and by extension contextual factors' powers) do not function in a binary and direct way as merely the capacity to approve or disapprove securitizing agents' moves. Rather, I argue that the power of structural/contextual factors operates in a diffuse yet tangible way, through social processes embedded in the historically contingent and multifaceted cultural settings. Seen in this light, the power of contextual factors is best understood as a continuum ranging from the power to *enable* to the power to *constrain* securitizing agents. Socio-historical and structural contexts not only enable (or constrain) particular agents to make security speech acts but also enable (or constrain) agents to make particular security speech acts at a particular point in time. For instance, the power of the audience resides precisely in its social capacity to either enable an agent to make securitizing attempts or constrain a securitizing agent who attempts to securitize migration—although the same audience could be an enabling force at a particular point in time and a limiting force at another point in time.

In the following chapters, I examine the role of two exogenous shocks, the so-called "refugee crisis" of the early 1990s and the terrorist attacks of September 11, 2001, and the role of domestic audiences in the process of securitizing migration in Canada and France.

As previously mentioned, several scholars who have worked on the concept of audience in securitization research disaggregate audience into categories. Salter (2008) proposes a fourfold distinction and Balzacq (2005) talks about the "target" audience. This emphasis on the role of audiences in the securitization process is worthy and essential. For instance, Salter's argument to distinguish between elite, technocratic, scientific, and popular audiences represents a key contribution to this research agenda. Yet pushing Salter's argument a step further in understanding the role of these four audiences in terms of their enabling and/or constraining powers is fruitful in the present context. For example, elite audiences could induce the securitization process by enabling agents to make securitizing moves (e.g. the elite audience of a political party known to have far-right inclinations will enable agents in making securitizing attempts). Or an elite audience could impede the securitization process by constraining the scope, the nature, and the strength of an agent's anticipated securitizing attempts (e.g. given the tradition, history, and political orientations of an organization, association, or political party). Similarly, a mass or popular audience could induce the securitization process by enabling agents to make security speech acts (e.g. by demanding the implementation of security practices after the arrival of a boatload of refugees on its shores). A mass audience could also limit the securitization process by constraining the scope, the nature, and the strength of agents' securitizing attempts (e.g. by showing a constant reluctance to see international migrants as a security threat).

In turn, such an understanding of power offers insights into the issue of variation in intensity or levels of securitized migration. Rather than seeing security as a binary notion, integrating the polymorphous character of power into the analytical framework allows us to understand security as a continuum. It also offers guiding principles to make sense of the distinction between a strong securitization and a weak securitization. Conceptualizing the power of contextual factors as enabling and/or constraining capability suggests that, when particular and important contextual factors act as constraining or limiting factors on agents' securitizing attempts, the outcome will be a weaker securitization. In contrast, when contextual factors act as enabling or inducing factors on agents' securitizing moves, the framework suggests that the outcome will be a stronger securitization.

Looking ahead

In the past few years, several IR scholars from various traditions have proposed models to study the securitization process. In my mind, ST undoubtedly offers the most creative and productive analytical framework. One of ST's greatest strengths is that it shifts the focus of analysis away from merely material factors to include socio-cultural ones as well. Acknowledging the intersubjective dimension of security and of securitization, ST postulates the social construction of threats and referent objects.

Despite representing a landmark work, ST is not immune from criticism. There is room for refinement. As I have sought briefly to show, both ST and its engagement with IR theory would gain by linking ST to constructivism to a greater degree than it currently is. Seeking to offer remedies to these criticisms, I have further argued that my correctives could be integrated within ST without distorting the original framework.

At a time when international migration is increasingly perceived as a security concern, this chapter has sought to offer refinement to the current benchmark in securitization research in the hope of taking a few steps toward answering both Alker's and Heisler's call for further research on an analytical framework for the study of the securitization process. Whereas this chapter had a clear theoretical outlook, the following chapters will focus on empirical findings. In order to facilitate comparison across my two country cases, I have structured the next two chapters according to the two securitizing agents explored in the study. Chapter 4 examines the role of political agents; Chapter 5 analyzes the role of media agents. I explore the role of exogenous shocks and audiences in Chapter 6.

Part II

The securitization of migration in Canada and France

4   Political agents and their security speech acts

Closing the door is not the answer.

(Lucienne Robillard 1998)

A strong immigration is an investment in our future. Immigration, in short, is a successful economic, social, and cultural strategy.

(Elinor Caplan 1999)

We are strengthening inadmissibility criteria so that criminals, security risks, and violators of human rights will not be given access to Canada.

(Elinor Caplan 2000)

Uncontrolled migratory movement would be a threat against our fundamental national interests.

(Philippe Marchand 1991)

France does not want to be an immigration country anymore. The objective is now "immigration zero."

(Charles Pasqua 1993)

You take a father with three or four wives and 20 children who gets 50,000 francs in welfare payments – naturally without working. Add the noise and the smell; the French worker on the same corridor goes crazy.

(Jacques Chirac 1991)

Whereas questions of identity, social construction, and discourse were barely touched on by international scholars or theorists twenty years ago, these issues are now at the forefront of the discipline. Since the mid-1980s, scholars have started to widen the concept of security and to offer new perspectives on issues such as national security, taboos, norms, collective identity, and ideational factors. In the particular context of the present study, this opening had fundamental consequences. As we have seen in Chapter 3, a pertinent theoretical framework in understanding and explaining the phenomenon of securitized migration is Securitization Theory, a theory that gives a prominent place to discourse.

In exploring the role (or lack thereof) of these political agents in the process of securitizing migration, my aim is twofold. First, I want to conduct a temporal analysis, that is, contrasting *when* the securitization of migration was initiated with *when* political agents of each country case made their securitizing moves. As I have demonstrated in Chapter 2, the early 1990s represents a fundamental critical juncture in my study of securitized migration in Canada and France, with the publication of *Foreign Policy Themes and Priorities* (DEA 1991) in Canada and the signing of the Dublin Convention (1990) in the case of France. Thus, I will highlight the pattern of engagement of each political agent with these respective critical junctures. Second, I want to underscore each political agent's securitizing moves (or lack thereof) in regards to migration between 1989 and 2005, that is, investigating how each agent relates with the phenomenon of securitized migration. Overall, I seek to gain a better understanding of the social mechanisms involved in the securitization process within and across cases.

For the purpose of this study, political agents are elected politicians and members of the government—those who are in power. I have focused my analysis on the leaders of the governing political party as well as on the ministers in charge of the foreign affairs and immigration portfolios; therefore, I have not included leaders of the opposition in my study. Of course, several other agents could be said to be political and contribute to the securitization of migration. For purposes of feasibility, I am confining my exhaustive analysis to a particular set of securitizing agents that are undeniably powerful without discounting that others play roles as well. As such, this selection of agents is not meant to be a theoretical statement on who constitutes a securitizing agent. In Canada, my selected political agents are Prime Ministers, Ministers of Foreign Affairs,[1] and Ministers of Citizenship and Immigration.[2] In France, I chose Presidents, Prime Ministers, Ministers of Foreign Affairs, and Ministers of Interior. To allow for within- and across-case comparisons, I have systematically retrieved, collected, and analyzed the complete set of speeches made by each agent between 1989 and 2005, a total of about 3,500 speeches.[3]

Collecting and analyzing the complete set of speeches, although putting important pressures on research effort, reduces considerably several biases rightfully associated with discourse analysis (Milliken 1999). First, this study largely avoids the media-interpretation bias by which a scholar, instead of retrieving the original speech, uses portions of the speech reported in a newspaper article. Analyzing sections of a speech that have been quoted in a newspaper article gives, by definition, a sense of incompleteness to the analysis. The present study has taken great care in steering away from such a bias. And, second, this study also avoids the partial-research bias by which a scholar, instead of retrieving the complete set of primary sources, focuses only on a partial set of primary sources or on speeches surrounding an isolated crisis in time. Inevitably, the scholar enters a fragile zone in which he or she must justify the selection procedures allowing him or her to collect one speech and not another. Such a research strategy leaves some room for uncertainty. Because I aim to conduct a systematic investigation, reducing as much uncertainty associated with the research material as possible is imperative.

I have conducted a content analysis of every speech by a given agent to understand how this particular agent perceives the issue of international migration (and its derivatives such as refugees, illegal migrants, etc.). What is he/she talking about when he/she talks about the movement of people: is it to highlight the benefits of multiculturalism, to underscore the difficulties of immigrants to integrate the job market, to celebrate the diversity and the richness that immigrants bring to the host society, to question to efficiency of the refugee determination process, and so on. In the next step, I have isolated the securitizing moves, that is, when a political agent argued that international migration is a security concern for the state and/or the society. I have then worked to intertwine the security speech act with the rationale justifying the securitizing move. It is important to note that although I use statistical analysis to provide a graphic overview of the pattern of engagement of each securitizing agent with the phenomenon of securitized migration, a traditional content analysis constitutes the primary method of investigation.

This chapter contains two main sections. The first section examines the case of Canada; the second focuses on France. A concluding section summarizes the key findings and introduces the next chapter.

Canada

Prime Ministers

In Canada, each new parliamentary session is marked by the Governor General's Speech from the Throne in the Chamber of the Senate outlining the government's legislative agenda. It is widely acknowledged that the Prime Minister is, in fact, the principal architect of the text; thus, the text constitutes a reliable source to indicate the general orientation and position of the government as well as the Prime Minister's political agenda.[4]

What is fascinating is that the first such securitizing move in the period under investigation was made in October 1999—specifically, the Speech from the Throne opening the second session of the thirty-sixth Parliament of Canada. As we have seen in Chapter 2, one of the key dates in the case of Canada is 1991, with the publication of the policy document *Foreign Policy Themes and Priorities*. Therefore, there is a temporal gap of eight years between the securitization of migration and the first securitizing attempt made by the Prime Minister through the Speech from the Throne.

Two notes are important here. First, there were only two Speeches from the Throne in the early 1990s—on May 31, 1991 with Brian Mulroney as Prime Minister, and on January 17, 1994 with Jean Chrétien as Prime Minister. One explanation for the gap of eight years mentioned above might be that during Prime Minister Kim Campbell's government (in office from June 13, 1993 to October 25, 1993) there was not a Speech from the Throne—for reasons that will be become clearer in my discussion of Prime Ministers' speeches. Had she and her political party won the federal elections of November 1993, we might have seen securitizing moves in a Speech from the Throne. Second, one should note the increasing number of securitizing moves in the past six years (from 1999 to 2005). When these securitizing moves are juxtaposed with the use of "migration" in the Speeches from the Throne, an increasing interest in issues of migration as well as its security implications in Canada is indicated.

An investigation of Prime Ministers' speeches (527 speeches) is more revealing. Kim Campbell made the very first securitizing moves in the summer of 1993, as shown in Figure 4.1. Her swearing-in speech of June 1993 is noteworthy for two reasons. First, it was the first time a Prime Minister officially linked migration and security. Prime Minister Campbell told her audience that the new Public Security portfolio "consolidates the responsibilities for policing, border protection, customs, processing of immigrants' applications and the enforcement of immigration laws" in order to ensure that Canadian society was not at risk (Campbell 1993). Second, the speech came nearly two years after the publication of the official Canadian document initiating the securitization of migration (1991). As in our study of the Speeches from the Throne, a time gap exists between the initiation of the securitization process and the first securitizing move made by the Prime

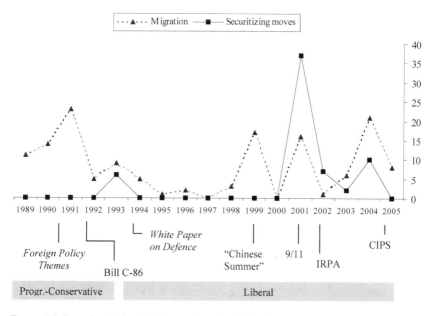

Figure 4.1 Speeches, Prime Ministers, Canada, 1989–2005.

Note: The dashed line represents the use of "migration" (and its derivatives such as immigration, refugee, illegal migrant) in a speech; the solid line represents securitizing moves – i.e. when migration was said to be a security concern for Canada; "Chinese Summer" refers to the arrival of four boats of Chinese would-be immigrants to British Columbia's shores; the grey horizontal line indicates which political party was in power. Although I present some of the results with the help of a figure, it is important to underscore that the primary research method that I employ is a traditional content analysis of each speech. CIPS, Canada International Policy Statement; IRPA, Immigration and Refugee Protection Act.

Minister. However, the time gap (two years) is considerably smaller than the one with the Speeches from the Throne (eight years).

Second, Campbell's securitizing moves were idiosyncratic attempts. They were all made within a very short period of time and they were made in a particular historical context in Canada. Replacing Brian Mulroney, who left after two mandates in power as the leader of the Progressive-Conservative Party, Campbell's Progressive-Conservative Party suffered its biggest defeat in history in the 1993 federal election, going from a majority government (169 seats) to losing its status as a recognized political party by Elections Canada (only two seats).

Between Campbell's securitizing move made in 1993 and the terrorist attacks of September 2001, the Prime Minister of Canada did not make a single speech act securitizing migration. However, it is not as though the opportunity did not exist. The arrival of 599 would-be Chinese immigrants near Vancouver during the summer of 1999—the so-called "Chinese Summer of 1999"—resulted in a groundswell of emotion across Canada, and could have easily resulted in a bold statement to the effect that the movement of people was disturbing Canada's security. Nevertheless, the Prime Minister made no declaration to that effect.

Of course, Jean Chrétien repeatedly mentioned the movement of people in 1999, as Figure 4.1 illustrates; yet, it is important to note that it was a politicization with positive overtones. As well, the "Chinese Summer of 1999" did not simply drive securitization in some objective way—although I will discuss this issue in detail in Chapter 6. Indeed, the Prime Minister had to interpret the exogenous shock in one way or another along the migration–security nexus; he also had to put forward his understanding of that event's implications for Canada. Contextual factors—such as the "Chinese Summer of 1999"—constitute resources upon which securitizing agents can make security speech acts or not.

Obviously, the attacks of 9/11 did have a huge impact on the linkage between migration and security. In his address during a special House of Commons debate in response to the terrorist attacks in the United States, Prime Minister Chrétien did not hesitate to establish the linkage. However, and perhaps an indication of the long-term Canadian position, Chrétien also noted that Canada would not give in to the temptation of creating a security curtain, and declared that his government would not be "stampeded in the hope—vain and ultimately self-defeating—that we can make Canada a fortress against the world" (Chrétien 2001). Furthermore, one should also notice the sharp decrease, as early as 2002, in the linkage between migration and security in the Prime Minister's speeches.

Overall, one finding stands out clearly from the analysis of Prime Ministers' speeches from 1989 to 2005 in the particular context of this study: the Prime Minister of Canada has not been the key securitizing actor in the process of securitizing migration. Indeed, an investigation of Speeches from the Throne as well as an analysis of Prime Ministers' speeches reveals that the Prime Minister has not historically been a key actor in the initiation of the securitization process. Semi-structured interviews conducted in the fall of 2005 corroborate this conclusion. Every senior analyst/bureaucrat interviewed (from four departments: the Privy Council Office, Foreign Affairs, Citizenship and Immigration, and Transport) has indicated that the Prime Minister was not a key player in the process of securitizing migration.

This is not to say that the Prime Minister is not involved in the general process. As one of my interviewees explained:

> Every cabinet document that has something to do with immigration would go through the [respective] Secretary of PCO and there would be analysts within that [section] who would be specialists in immigration. If a major document was going through . . . they would be looking at whether there was some money to be spent, whether all government's departments that were involved were on side, and so on. But I do not think it would be right to see PCO as the driver in most circumstances [that touch on migration issues].
>
> (Interviewee #7, Privy Council Office, October 31, 2005)

Furthermore, the relationship between migration and security in the Prime Ministers' speeches displays no systematic and consistent direction. Simple correlation coefficients calculated for each year indicate that the two variables are uncorrelated.

Ministers of Foreign Affairs

A thorough examination of the speeches of Canada's Ministers of Foreign Affairs (384 speeches) reveals that the Ministers appear to have been the key players in the process, as Figure 4.2 shows. Indeed, a temporal connection emerges between a security speech act and the initiation of the securitizing process.

Barbara McDougall, in the second Progressive-Conservative majority government, was the first Foreign Affairs Minister[5] in the period under investigation to declare that migration was a national security concern for Canada. In a speech she gave on December 10, 1991 to the conference commemorating the sixtieth anniversary of the Statute of Westminster, she declared that "in adopting [a] wider concept of security, Canada will be more aggressive and active in tackling transnational threats to security such as weapons proliferation, drug trafficking, terrorism, and irregular migration" (McDougall 1991). In an address given in January 1992 to the Council of Ministers of the Conference on Security and Cooperation in Europe, she identified cooperative security as a fundamental factor "apt to reduce the threat of mass migrations" (McDougall 1992a). A few months later, in another international address [to the Association of Southeast Asian Nations (ASEAN) post-ministerial conference], McDougall reinforced the idea that a security dialog between countries to deal with the movement of people was needed. The securitization of migration was later reaffirmed in a domestic address. At the official opening of the Canadian Foreign Service Institute in Ottawa, the Minister told the audience that "the challenges of our foreign services are increasingly complex and diverse. Mass movements of populations . . . have changed forever the way our immigration officers work. The work they do is crucial to the well-being and long-term security of all Canadians" (McDougall 1992a,b).

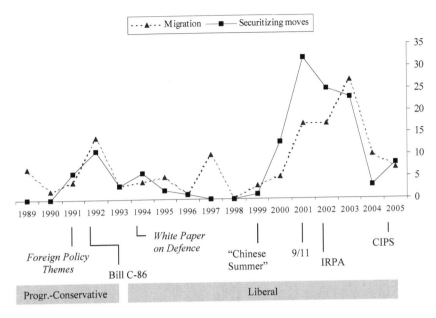

Figure 4.2 Speeches, Ministers of Foreign Affairs, Canada, 1989–2005. See notes to Figure 4.1 for explanation.

We observed a relative continuity in the way that migration is seen with the change of government (from a Progressive-Conservative majority to a Liberal majority) in 1993. André Ouellet, the new Liberal Minister, told the audience at the International Institute for Strategic Studies, London, in September 1994, that if Canadians were asked what development outside of Canadian borders is threatening Canadian security the answers would likely be global in nature. "Unchecked movements of peoples across frontiers" is found alongside international crime, drugs, disease, and nuclear proliferation in Ouellet's answer to this hypothetical question (Ouellet 1994).

The rationale behind the securitization of migration in these years is rather simple for some. One of my interviewees, who was directly involved in the writing of the 1995 Canada foreign policy statement, *Canada in the World*, told me quite candidly that Canada had linked together migration and security partly because "every other government was doing it, so we made the link."[6]

The arrival of Lloyd Axworthy in the Lester B. Pearson building marks a sharp decrease in the securitization of migration. Axworthy, despite being a heavy consumer of words such as "security" and "threat," rarely spoke of the movement of people in terms of a security issue *for* Canada. During one of the longest terms as Minister of Foreign Affairs in Canadian history (from January 25, 1996 to October 16, 2000), Axworthy securitized migration on only two occasions.

In fact, the angle of analysis preferred by Axworthy was brought onto the scene in the summer of 1999 with the arrival of four boats of Chinese would-be-immigrants to British Columbia's shores. Instead of mounting a charge to the effect that immigration was bringing all sorts of security problems to Canada, Axworthy cast the whole incident under the human security agenda. That is, the arrival of the boats "brought home to Canadians the ugly reality of another human security threat of global proportions—the smuggling and trafficking of human beings" (Axworthy 1999). Or, as this passage illustrates nicely,

> millions of vulnerable people have been forced from their homes; been driven to borders which are open one minute and closed the next; forced into hiding; separated from their families; made to act as human shields; stripped of their identities; sexually abused; and callously killed. The need to combat these threats has become the basis of the Canadian approach to foreign policy.
>
> (Axworthy 2000)

Undoubtedly, the linkage between migration and security is established under Axworthy; however, the link is constructed with a rather different angle from the one previously made. Securitized migration in this context is about the security of the migrants; migration is not conceived as a "threat" to Canada. Rather, the linkage is made in terms of security *for the migrants*; an unsurprising finding given Axworthy's record of accomplishment as one of the most well-known public figures to have put human security in the international arena.

Axworthy's successor, John Manley, had a different understanding of how the movement of people should be interpreted. In his very first speech as Minister of Foreign Affairs, and in front of a Canadian audience, Manley made it clear that under his leadership the department would see migration as a salient security issue. "We are facing new and complex security threats: including illegal migration, crime, terrorism, disease, illegal drug trafficking, and computer-based crime," he argued at a forum on Canada's foreign policy agenda and priorities in October 2000 (Manley 2000).

As expected, the linkage between migration and security became especially acute after 9/11. Immigration, security, terrorism, border controls, and security screening are fused into the same conceptual category both in domestic speeches, such as the Standing Committee on Foreign Affairs and International Trade, and in international speeches such as at the 56th Session of the UN General Assembly. Furthermore, the idea of the Smart Border Declaration, a key document signed by the United States and Canada in the aftermath of the 9/11 attacks, is built around securitized migration. The first pillar of the Declaration's action plan, entitled "The Secure Flow of People," undoubtedly links migration and security in a formal and perhaps enduring way:

- We will implement systems to collaborate in identifying security risks while expediting the flow of low risk travelers.

- We will identify security threats before they arrive in North America through collaborative approaches to reviewing crew and passenger manifests, managing refugees, and visa policy coordination.
- We will establish a secure system to allow low risk frequent travelers between our countries to move efficiently across the border.

(DFAIT 2001)

A major change is brought, albeit in a subtle manner, to the general way that the movement across borders is perceived. Indeed, the spectrum of security has significantly shrunk: someone is either a security "risk" or a "low risk" migrant. Tellingly, the category "not a risk" is totally absent from the document—as is any conceptualization of the movement of people that is not from a "risk" or a "threat" perspective. From the very beginning, the migrant (and even the frequent traveler) is a security concern. In addition, it is important here to point out that, since its signature in 2001, all Ministers of Foreign Affairs have praised the success, the coherence, and the structure of the Smart Border Declaration.

Hence, in the particular context of the securitization of migration, a content analysis of speeches made by Ministers of Foreign Affairs is tremendously informative. First, securitizing moves made by Minister Barbara McDougall are temporally connected in a systematic way with the initiation of the securitizing process, thereby conferring to McDougall a particularly important role in the context of migration. Second, several Ministers of Foreign Affairs have played a crucial role in the process throughout the years that this study covers. In recent years, John Manley (both pre- and post-9/11) and Bill Graham pushed hard to securitize migration. Third, the analysis underscores the necessity of distinguishing the different individuals who have held the position of Minister of Foreign Affairs. For example, Lloyd Axworthy has been more a de-securitizing force than a securitizing force.

Ministers of Citizenship and Immigration

My analysis of speeches made by Ministers of Citizenship and Immigration between 1989 and 2005 underscores the important role of this particular agent in the process of securitizing migration. It also highlights two critical junctures: the arrival of four boats of Chinese would-be-immigrants to British Columbia's shores and the terrorist attacks of September 11, 2001.

The role of the Minister of Citizenship and Immigration in initiating the securitization process is harder to evaluate as the majority of speeches by Minister Bernard Valcourt (Minister from April 1991 to November 1993) is closed to the public. Notwithstanding, I was able to collect seven speeches from 1992 and two speeches from 1993 with the help of several archivists of Library and Archives Canada and a request under the Canadian Access to Information Act. Valcourt made no securitizing attempts in either 1992 or 1993 except to mention once the need to protect Canadian society from abusers of the immigration program. This gives us the following picture: Ministers of Citizenship and Immigration made almost no securitizing moves between 1989 and 1998.

Although there was no systematic securitizing move in the early years that the study covers, there have been increasing securitizing moves of late by the Ministers, as Figure 4.3 illustrates. To understand this rupture, it is important to trace back the evolution of Ministers' speeches. Indeed, one of the most telling examples of the increasing securitization of migration is the way that those who abuse the immigration system were discursively presented throughout the years that this study covers. To be sure, the "abusers" of the immigration system have always been a key concern for Ministers of Citizenship and Immigration; however, a change occurred in 1999. In the early 1990s, the rationale was a matter of control: it was important to focus on those who tried to abuse the Canadian system in order to justify the argument that a large intake of immigrants to Canadian society would not jeopardize Canada's social cohesion. "The Canadian public," argued Bernard Valcourt in 1992, "will support open and generous immigration and refugee programs as long as they feel those programs are under control" (Valcourt 1992). A few years later, the same logic was restated. Lucienne Robillard, who is often described as one the best Ministers of Citizenship and Immigration of the

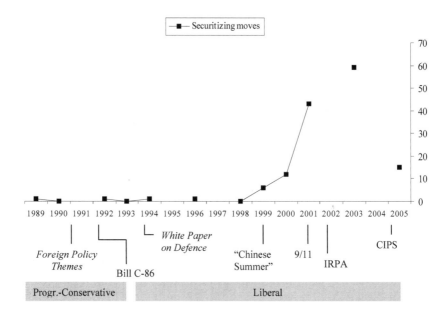

Figure 4.3 Speeches, Ministers of Citizenship and Immigration, Canada, 1989–2005. See notes to Figure 4.1 for explanation.

Note: Even though it is breaking with the overall structure of how graphs of speeches are presented, I did not include "migration" in this particular graph because the Minister uses the word so often that it would "hide" the results for securitizing moves.

recent past, told the Standing Committee on Citizenship and Immigration that "to protect the integrity of our program, we cannot turn a blind eye to the minority that do not honour their commitments . . . we are targeting the problem area: we are focusing on the small number of people who default" (Robillard 1998).

Up to this point, the focus on the "abusers" had no particular security lens attached to it. Indeed, Ministers of Citizenship and Immigration had made almost no securitizing moves up until the summer of 1999. The cabinet shuffle of the summer of 1999 (naming Elinor Caplan as the new Minister) and two particular international events changed the dynamic.

Although the Prime Minister and the Minster of Foreign Affairs made no securitizing moves on or shortly after the "Chinese Summer of 1999"—as we saw in the previous section—Minister Caplan decided to interpret differently this exogenous shock. In one of her first speeches following the event, Caplan kept the focus of Citizenship and Immigration Canada on the "abusers" while adding something new: a security component through the issue of detention.

> We know that if an accelerated process is part of the solution, so is an enhanced detention policy. . . . We have already announced proposals to increase deten-tion if a person is undocumented and uncooperative. . . . We will take every action necessary to deal with the abuse of immigration and refugee processes.
> (Caplan 1999a)

This official position was restated on several occasions in the following months (Caplan 1999b,c, 2000a,b, 2001a,b). Sometimes, the targeted group was clear: "Foreign nationals convicted of serious crimes. War criminals, terrorists, those posing risks to national security. I want them out of here. They are strictly inadmissible, and unwelcome." Sometimes, the target was more diffuse: "How do we maintain a proper balance between our humanitarian objectives regarding newcomers and the need to maintain security in the face of global migration" (Caplan 2000c,d).

As well, a twist to the general argument was sometimes brought up. The Minister occasionally argued that the experience of the summer of 1999 led her to consider detention as a human security—that is, in cases where the persons may themselves be at risk from the smugglers and the organized crime behind their journey (Caplan 1999a, 2000b).

While the arrivals of four boats in the summer of 1999 did initiate the link-age between migration and security, the terrorist attacks of September 11, 2001 undoubtedly hardened both the linkage and the discourse associated with that connection. In one of the first speeches following the terrorist attacks, Caplan opts to send a strong message by powerfully linking migration and security:

> Canadians are looking to us for reassurance that we can protect their health and safety, and the security of our society. . . . These begin with the welcome we offer to immigrants and the haven we provide for refugees from around the world. I am proud to say that this is very tough legislation for those who

pose a threat to public security, and for those who do not respect our laws. . . .
We will crack down on criminals and security threats, and those who would
abuse our laws.

(Caplan 2001c)

Throughout the months following 9/11, the Minister kept pushing for the
securitization of migration. "In my own portfolio—immigration—we have acted
quickly and firmly to deal with threats against the safety and security of Canada
and its neighbours," Caplan declared in November 2001. The Minister also
applauds the introduction of a new permanent resident card, the enhancement
of Canada's security screening of refugee claimants, and the increased capacity to detain and deport "those who pose a risk," as well as the passing of the
Immigration and Refugee Protection Act (IRPA). These measures "will allow
us to protect our values and pursue the Canadian way together, in security and
freedom from fear," according to the Minister (Caplan 2001d).

The tone of securitizing moves considerably hardened with the arrival of
Denis Coderre as the new Minister. Coderre told his audience in March 2003
that as the Minister responsible for one aspect of Canada's security he would
make sure his department would take a number of measures to enhance security.
Pointing out that "CIC have been operating within an intensified security framework since 9/11," he adds that the "Canadian government is vigilantly assessing
threats to national security. . . . Canadians can be sure that we will do our
utmost to ensure the nation's security" (Coderre 2003a). Applauding measures
such as the introduction of immediate and in-depth security checks for refugee
claimants, the denial of access to the Canadian refugee determination process to
those who would abuse it, and the systematic fingerprinting and photographing
of all refugee claimants, Coderre pushes securitizing moves in two perceptible
directions.

The first is to situate citizenship and immigration within a bigger, nearly
global process. "Canada today is entering a new world order," points out Coderre,
adding that this "new world order" demands that all levels of government adopt
new approaches to enhancing the safety and security of all Canadians at home
and abroad (Coderre 2003b). As such, Coderre insists that Citizenship and
Immigration Canada "continues to find new ways to work cooperatively with
other federal agencies, provincial and municipal governments and police forces.
. . . We are fully committed to protecting the safety and security of Canadians"
(Coderre 2003c).

Second, Coderre places a strong emphasis on surveillance and monitoring
through the use of biometrics and particularly the potentiality of an ID card. For
Coderre, the introduction of a Canadian identity card is not a matter of "reacting
to the US, but rather an issue of international security." He argued further, "Yes,
it will prevent terrorism" (Coderre 2003d). For Coderre, biometrics will enhance
border security and keep out security risks. In October 2003, he further contended
that

document integrity is a fundamental way to help improve our personal and national security in an uncertain world. I know that improved document integrity is just one important component of our security strategies. It fits with our commitment to border protection, intelligence services, and screening by immigration officers at ports of entry into Canada and internationally.

(Coderre 2003e)

In conclusion, a content analysis of speeches made by Ministers of Citizenship and Immigration highlights that several Ministers have made numerous securitizing moves. Elinor Caplan and Denis Coderre have played a particularly important role in the securitization of migration. While the arrival of four boats in the summer of 1999 triggered these securitizing moves, the terrorist attacks of 9/11 undoubtedly hardened the discourse. However, one should note that the increasing frequency of securitizing moves—both in number and intensity—happen before the terrorist attacks of September 11, 2001. In fact, 70 percent of the securitizing moves made by the Minister of Citizenship and Immigration in 2001 were made before 9/11. Notwithstanding, the terrorist attacks dramatically altered the position of all Ministers of Citizenship and Immigration, from Elinor Caplan onwards.

France

Presidents

In the particular context of this study, one of the first securitizing moves made by the President of the Republic was in a discourse from June 18, 1994 on French foreign aid of the last thirty years, as illustrated in Figure 4.4. Francois Mitterand, toward the very end of his second mandate, advised Western countries' leaders not to ignore tumultuous events unfolding in Africa because, with such a policy, we could observe "the proliferation of several types of disorder against which the atomic bomb would be useless: drugs, epidemic, erratic migratory movements, environmental problems" (Mitterand 1994a).[7] We must convince ourselves, he adds, that "these dangers will not be limited to their countries of origin." Nearly three months after the end of the Rwanda genocide, as well as the terrorist attacks in Paris in the summer of 1994, Mitterand reiterates his position in a speech on Africa's democratization. "What a risk it is," he told his audience, "to observe, with extreme poverty as background, the birth of plagues against which even the most hermetic border will never protect us: drugs, epidemics, erratic migratory movements, terrorism, and environment problems" (Mitterand 1994b).

Jacques Chirac, newly elected president in May 1995, formulated a similar policy in the first year of his first mandate, largely on the theme of French insecurity and the need to remedy the situation. In a speech before the U.S. Congress in January 1996, he warned his audience that massive immigration from poor countries was a risk for future generations. Neither accumulating arms nor creating useless barriers would ensure successful protection. Rather, "the best security

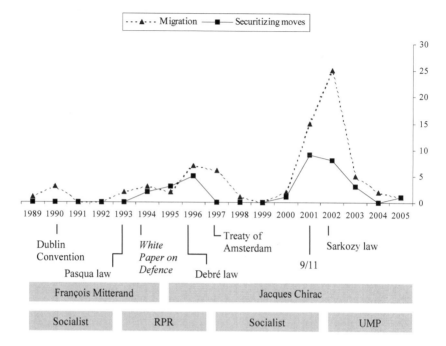

Figure 4.4 Speeches, Presidents, France, 1989–2005.

Note: The dashed line represents the use of migration (and its derivatives such as immigration, refugee, illegal migrant) in a speech; the solid line represents the securitizing moves – i.e. when migration was said to be a security concern for France; the first grey horizontal line indicates who was President at a particular point in time; the second grey horizontal line indicates which political party was controlling the government. Although I present some of the results with the help of a figure, it is important to underscore that the primary research method that I employ is a traditional content analysis of each speech. RPR, Rally for the Republic; UMP, Union for Popular Movement.

today is solidarity" (Chirac 1996). Later the same year, Chirac argued that France had to understand the consequences of a new era in world politics. France's Department of Defence, he contends, was leading the path out of the woods by identifying novel, more diffused, and unpredictable threats to France—of which migration was listed alongside the renewal of ethnic hatred and fanaticism.

Contrary to widespread perception, more than 85 percent of the discursive linkages between migration and security made in 2001 were actually made *before* the 9/11 attacks. Indeed, two months after 9/11, Chirac was stressing the elements of continuity in the assessment of France's national security. Although the fight against terrorism certainly called for an adaptation of France's security system, declared Chirac, it did not provoke a profound revision of that system. "The main threats to the security of France remain the same. They did not change" (Chirac 2001a).

Furthermore, in an exchange with a journalist about the relationship between Europe's and France's security interests, Chirac insisted that France was fully aware of the existence of a number of dangers (expressed in terms of instability, migrations, and conflicts) at its borders. "Our interest is to neutralize these dangers that can carry many difficulties for France. In other words, Europe, in enlarging, is actually reinforcing its zone of security" (Chirac 2001b).

We observe a decrease in the link between migration and security immediately after the presidential election of April 2002, which Chirac won by a landslide against the controversial right-wing, anti-immigrant Jean-Marie Le Pen. However, Chirac re-affirmed his strong stance on the issue toward the end of his second mandate. Speaking to the French-German Chamber of Commerce in April 2005, he declared: "There are some domains in which Europe needs to give member states the opportunity to join forces." Some of these areas are "security, to fight illegal immigration networks, international terrorism, and organized crime" (Chirac 2005).

In sum, this analysis of Presidents' speeches since 1989 (449 speeches) invites two conclusions. First, the President appears to have had a relatively low influence on the process of securitizing migration; and, second, the terrorist attacks on the United States were not a trigger effect in the particular context of this study. This finding suggests that the exogenous shock of 9/11 did not operate as an objective factor; rather, the President had to interpret the exogenous shock in one way or another along the migration–security nexus. He had to talk into existence his particular understanding of the implications of 9/11; the securitization of migration appears not to have been one of them.

Prime Ministers

Michel Rocard, Prime Minister from May 1988 to May 1991, holds a significant place in the story of securitizing migration attempts in France. Indeed, an analysis of the Prime Minister's speeches (801 speeches) reveals that the linkage between migration and security was first established in 1989, as Figure 4.5 shows. "Internal security of our country has its European dimension," Rocard declared in Strasbourg on June 15, 1989, regarding the Schengen Agreement. The transfer of some aspect of France's internal security to the European level is a trade-off with the free movement of people within the country, members of the audience were told. The objective is to provide a "guarantee for both security and human rights" in this regard. "What would be the point of being rigorous in our foreign policy if European frontiers were open all the way down and if the free movement of people would be merged with the free movement of terrorists?" (Rocard 1989).

However, it is probably for his strong politicizing moves that Rocard is best remembered. In a speech in which migratory pressures, especially labor migration, were presented as a fundamental problem requiring urgent measures, Rocard declared, "France is no longer an immigration country. I have said it and I am reaffirming here: We cannot welcome all the misery of the world" (Rocard 1990).

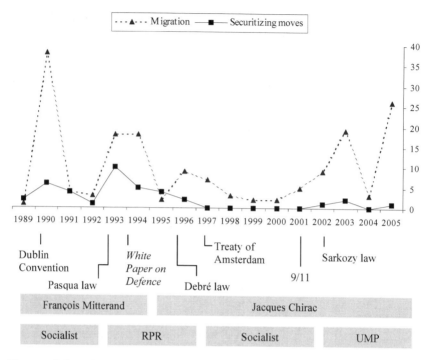

Figure 4.5 Speeches, Prime Ministers, France, 1989–2005. See notes to Figure 4.4 for explanation.

This particularly strong standpoint was reiterated a few months later, albeit with slightly different wording.

Rocard's successor as Socialist Prime Minister, Édith Cresson, made it clear that she intended to pursue a policy of continuity. In her first speech as Prime Minister, she argued that the central mission of the state is to guarantee the security of its citizens. She further contended:

> It is true that a feeling of insecurity, individual and collective, is strong. These security expectations logically indicated the objectives [of the government]: the defense of our national interests, the fight against drugs, the full control of migratory flux, a neighborhood-oriented police service.
>
> (Cresson 1991)

In September 1991, she proposed—to the surprise of many Socialists—the organization of charter flights to ensure (and speed up) the deportation of unwanted immigrants.

The Rally for the Republic (RPR) won the legislative election of early 1993, producing what has been called the "cohabitation" (i.e. a Socialist President, François Mitterrand, working with a center-right parliament, headed by Édouard

Balladur). This represents a fundamental turning point for the study of the securitization of migration in France. The declaration of the general policy of Balladur's government was indeed unequivocal.

> A coherent immigration policy firstly requires that irregular situations must be ended and that decisions of expulsion must be carried out with strength. . . . However, applying the law is not enough; the law must be changed when it is no longer in line with the needs. Condition of entry of foreigners in France must be defined more strictly. France is an old nation which intends to remain itself.
>
> (Balladur 1993a)

Such a strong stance on this issue was reiterated in different settings, which indicated the depth and strength of the position. For example, at the inauguration of the new headquarters of Paris' police forces, Balladur stated that the new headquarters constituted a symbol of the political willingness to ensure the security of the French in a world filled with difficulties. Indeed, the new headquarters reflect the image of the security policy pursued by his government—that is, a sharp increase in identity control and in the control of immigration. In fact, Balladur's government was involved in a broader enterprise of recovery, of which a tougher stance on migration was a central aspect.[8] The linkage between migration and security was in fact cast in an emergency, worst-case scenario type of reasoning. "We should be very careful. If we do not implement the necessary measures to fight clandestine immigration, then what is happening elsewhere would happen in France: the reactions of opinion would put principles to which we are profoundly attached in serious peril." Furthermore, according to the then Prime Minister, the period was a matter of such grave concern, in fact "the most difficult period since the war," that the left and right divisions should be bridged (Balladur 1993b).

The return of a Socialist government, under a new leadership, in the National Assembly in June 1997 did change the political-security agenda in the particular context of this study. In contrast with the harsh rhetoric of the previous center-right government as well as the left-wing government of the early 1990s, Lionel Jospin, in the first Declaration of general policy, made it clear that his government was seeing migration from a rather different point of view. In fact, Jospin made no securitizing moves in his entire mandate as Prime Minister (five years), as Figure 4.5 shows.

One could argue that Jospin did not have to make a securitizing move since the previous government had already securitized migration. However, three elements indicate that such a conclusion appears to be erroneous. First, Jospin's government did indeed try to create a rupture in migration policy. "We will abrogate the Pasqua and Debré laws,"[9] mentions the Socialist Party electoral platform (quoted in Weil 2005: 297). An intense debate about the reformulation of an immigration law was engaged, of which the Chevènement law, adopted on May 11, 1998, was the legislative outcome. The Chevènement law did not reject all the repressive dispositions included in the Pasqua and Debré laws, but certainly did bring some significant changes. According to Weil, the anti-immigrant discourses became so costly politically at that time that even the leader of the right and Jospin's predecessor as Prime Minister, Alain Juppé, was starting to hope that a consensus on immigration was in the making. "I must admit that the [Jospin's government] has somewhat defused the immigration issue," said Juppé (quoted in Weil 2005: 302).

Second, and more importantly in the context of this study, one observes a refusal to frame migration in a security setting. The new thinking is not just about legislative reformulations (and "old wine in new bottles"); rather, it is about a profound change in the way that migration issues are dealt with. Indeed, for Jospin, "those who preach the intolerance and the hatred of the Other exploit realities, such as misery, unemployment, personal and social insecurity, and manipulate representations such as the foreigner" (Jospin 1998). Accordingly, they must be combated. Furthermore, at the very beginning of his mandate, Jospin asked Patrick Weil, one of the most important specialists on migration issues in France, to lead a team of thinkers and intellectuals to report on the current situation and to "propose simple, realistic, and human rules for the entry and the sojourn of foreigners" (Weil 2005: 297). The report came out in July 1997 with 140 propositions touching on the right of asylum, family reunification, student migration, and so on (Weil 1997).

Third, despite one of the most powerful opportunities to formulate securitization, that is, the terrorist attack of 9/11, Lionel Jospin made no speeches to that effect. In his speech that followed the attacks, Jospin does not mention once the word "migration" or its derivatives.

In fact, we have to wait until July 2003 (and the return of a center-right government) to note a strong securitizing move. Jean-Pierre Raffarin, appointed Prime Minister by Chirac after the May 2002 legislative election, made a clear link between migration and security on the basis of criminality. In his speech in the National Assembly, Raffarin told the parliamentarians that,, since their first day in power, his government undertook to regain French confidence in the Republic by "insisting on what constitutes the core of the Republic: security for all. Security . . . is the first liberty" (Raffarin 2003a). Praising his government for its tough stance on criminality, he then announced that his government would continue to work on this path when discussing two important texts: one on immigration and the other on the right of asylum. Two months later, Raffarin made an even clearer linkage. "[Others'] insecurities bring different difficulties. I am thinking of course here of important topics such as the European enlargement. We are asking ourselves: 'How will we manage the migratory flux?' " (Raffarin 2003b).

Overall, the Prime Minister has played a strong role at the beginning of the securitization of migration, but a subtler role from the Jospin mandate onward. An analysis of Prime Minister Dominic de Villepin's speeches during the civil unrest in the fall of 2005 is telling in this regard. In these very intense four weeks—when three people lost their lives, thousands of vehicles were burned, a state of emergency was declared, more than 200 cities were affected, and the monetary damage was estimated at 200 million euros—de Villepin was extremely careful, unlike the Minister of the Interior, Nicolas Sarkozy, not to merge and fuse together ethnicity, integration, poverty, youth, migration and security. No securitizing speech act was pronounced; most, if not all, of his declarations were on themes such as calmness and complexity (and the danger of reducing the crisis to one factor).

Ministers of Foreign Affairs

As my discourse analysis of Ministers of Foreign Affairs' speeches (738 speeches) reveals, migration has not been of particular interest for successive Ministers since 1989. With the exception of the year 2003, Ministers of Foreign Affairs have barely touched on the issue of migration, as Figure 4.6 illustrates. For the first ten years that this detailed analysis covers, migration has been mentioned on average only a little more than once a year. Unsurprisingly, given this clear lack of interest, securitizing moves have not been numerous. From 1989 to 2003, securitizing moves have been made only in 1995 and 1997; furthermore, the moves uttered in these two years have been relatively weak.

The strongest and clearest linkage between migration and security was made in June 2003 by then Minister of Foreign Affairs, Dominique de Villepin. Revisiting a few dispositions of the Chevènement law regarding asylum and refugee issues, de Villepin argued for the necessity of giving the French Office for the Protection of Refugees and Stateless Persons the entire responsibility of verifying that

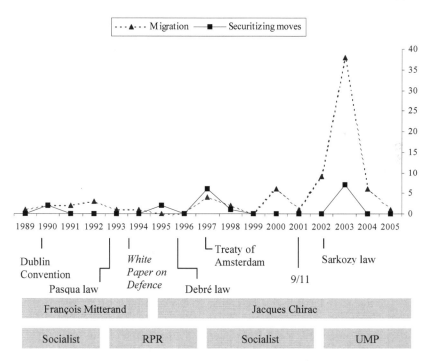

Figure 4.6 Speeches, Ministers of Foreign Affairs, France, 1989–2005. See notes to Figure 4.4 for explanation.

"asylum seekers did not constitute a threat to public order, public security or state security."[10] He further argued that "it would not be responsible to ignore the security of our citizens when dealing with the issue of asylum. We all know that international displacements could bring risks in terms of traffic and violence" (de Villepin 2003).

More recently, Philippe Douste-Blazy, in a speech on France's foreign policy priorities and diplomatic action, has used terrorist attacks in Madrid and London to link migration and security, albeit indirectly. "And now security," he declared, "our citizens need to know that Europe is capable of protecting them from the threat that is assailing us. More than ever we have to focus our efforts to reinforce our control at the frontiers, through biometric visas" (Douste-Blazy 2005).

A relative lack of securitizing moves does not forbid rather bleak rhetoric on the question, however. For instance, in an intervention in the French National Assembly, Hervé de Charette, Minister of Foreign Affairs from May 1995 to May 1997, argued that it was up to France to undertake the particular dispositions and practices to make the Schengen Agreement "work." "The Schengen Agreement should not be held responsible when [the French] services do not conduct appropriate controls. In other words, it is up to us to start sweeping in front of our doors" (de Charette 1995).

In light of this detailed discourse analysis from 1989 to 2005, we can conclude that France's Minister of Foreign Affairs has not been a central securitizing actor in the context of migration. As one of our interviewees confirms: "The Department of Foreign Affairs, despite being involved at some point, has been and remains a minor player in the process."[11] Indeed, every senior analyst/bureaucrat interviewed (from three departments: Interior, Foreign Affairs, and Defence) has indicated that the Quai d'Orsay has played almost no role in the process of securitizing migration.

Ministers of the Interior

The Department of the Interior and Regional Development has five central missions, one of which is to "protect the population against risks and calamities of all kinds and against the consequences of an eventual conflict" (Ministère de l'Intérieur et du Développement Régional 2009). It is therefore not surprising to find several powerful securitizing speech acts in relation to migration made by numerous Ministers, as Figure 4.7 shows.

Three points stand out from an analysis of the speeches of the Ministers of the Interior. First, security speech acts made by Ministers of the Interior are temporally connected with the beginning of the securitization process, thereby rendering the Minister a particularly influential securitizing agent in the context of this study. Whereas the Presidents and the Ministers of Foreign Affairs made no securitizing moves in the early 1990s, the Ministers of the Interior made several, thus establishing a clear and important temporal connection between securitizing moves and the initiation of the securitization of migration in France.

As early as 1991, Minister of the Interior Philippe Marchand made an important securitizing move. One of the four priorities of the national police, according to

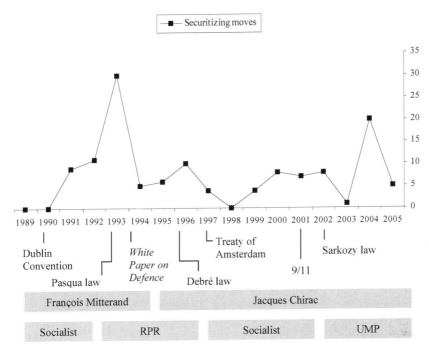

Figure 4.7 Speeches, Ministers of the Interior, France, 1989–2005. See notes to Figure 4.4 for explanation.

Note: Even though it is breaking with the overall structure of how graphs of speeches are presented, I did not include "migration" in this particular graph because the Minister uses the word so often that it would "hide" the results for securitizing moves.

Marchand, was the control of migratory flux. "If immigration is not controlled," he declared on November 20, 1991, "it will become a destabilizing factor for our security. . . . Uncontrolled migratory movement would be a threat against our fundamental national interests" (Marchand 1991). Marchand's successor, Paul Quilès, further established the linkage between migration and security, as Figure 4.7 shows. Among members of the center-left governments in power between 1989 and 2005, Quilès represents one of the securitizing agents who made the most powerful and repeated securitizing moves in the context of migration. Furthermore, Charles Pasqua, the Minister of the Interior under the newly elected center-right government of Édouard Balladur in 1993, solidified the role of the Minister of the Interior as the initiator of the securitizing migration process by making the themes of migration and security a central concern of its mandate.

The second important element that stands out from an analysis of speeches of the Ministers of the Interior is the rationale behind securitizing moves: the initial and basic justification for making a securitizing move is the danger to France's social cohesion that an uncontrolled movement of people represents. Indeed, from 1989 to 2002, the fundamental rationale behind the numerous securitizing moves was the notion of social cohesion. That is, the movement of people, if not controlled, would certainly lead to the explosion of France's national cohesion.

While Philippe Marchand first elaborated this standpoint, Paul Quilès, Minister of the Interior from January 1992 to March 1993, established on firmer ground the rationale behind the securitization. "The strength of a country is also its social and territorial cohesion which are provided by its security" (Quilès 1992). Given this, the Schengen Agreement must be applied, according to Quilès, in order to compensate the loss of security caused by the free movement of people.

Many Ministers did reiterate this standpoint between 1991 and early 2002, incidentally, making social cohesion the fundamental reason invoked by various Ministers to try to legitimize the securitization of the movement of people. For instance, Charles Pasqua undoubtedly hardened the tone and the message; however, the rationale for the securitization was still cast in terms of social cohesion. In his first speech as Minister, Pasqua declared, "Clandestine immigration is a new phenomenon that we urgently need to combat if we do not want to see our national cohesion explode" (Pasqua 1994). Pasqua reiterated his position in several subsequent speeches—sometimes speaking in terms of the loss of France's identity, sometimes highlighting the necessity of protecting the "national community" from threatening "perils," and still sometimes arguing that France "suffers" from migratory movement that could lead it to "explosion." Pasqua further contended in introducing his immigration law that the law constitutes the "last chance to save France's integration model," a law that had at its core the linkage between migration and security (Pasqua 1993a,b).

Pasqua's successor, Jean-Louis Debré, also worked to securitize migration using the same logic. "We cannot give up in front of the numerous clandestine immigrants in France," he warned his audience on March 6, 1996. "To give up would be too great a risk for our social cohesion . . . and for public order. It is also too big of a risk for our nation, as irregular immigrants induce racism, xenophobia, and anti-Semitism" (Debré 1996). The logic of social cohesion as justifying the securitization of migration crosses political formation. For instance, Daniel Vaillant, Minister of the Interior in the Jospin government, reiterated themes now well known. "As Minister of the Interior, I ought to underscore the extremely pernicious consequences of clandestine immigration both for the security of our country and for the immigrants. Clandestine immigration is by definition a factor of instability and potential problems. It nourishes exclusion" (Vaillant 2001).

Finally, the third crucial point that this study highlights is that elements of a profound shift from social cohesion to the theme of criminality in the securitization's rationale were introduced as early as 1993, gaining increasing power ever since, especially from the period of 2002 onwards. One of the strongest advocates of the linkage between criminality and migration as a justification for the securitization of migration was undoubtedly Charles Pasqua. In his speech in front of senior police officers (France's *commissaires*) on May 10, 1993, Pasqua told them, "your priority will be to fight against two phenomena increasingly interconnected: drugs and clandestine immigration . . . Clandestine immigration is a natural pond for delinquency" (Pasqua 1993c).

This strong and powerful linkage between criminality and migration found an echo almost a decade later, with the nomination of Nicolas Sarkozy to the position of Minister of the Interior. "The time of taboos is over," Sarkozy told his audience on September 2, 2002, "delinquency has taken new forms that we cannot ignore. . . . Aggressive mendacity and clandestine immigration ought to be dealt with by giving the police a strong capability to act. . . . We cannot fight against these plagues, which are the gangrene of everyday life of the French, by closing our eyes to their international dimension" (Sarkozy 2002a). In another speech he made on the same day, Sarkozy made an even more powerful securitizing move in declaring that the success of a internal security policy was conditioned by the fight against clandestine immigration, organized crime, and terrorism. Sarkozy's successor, Dominique de Villepin, has pursued a similar set of arguments, albeit in a less provocative way. "To reduce insecurity in a enduring way, we must tackle the core of the problem. That is the direction that I choose in fighting against drug trafficking, cyber criminality, and irregular immigration" (de Villepin 2004).

In fact, from 2002 onwards (specifically beginning with the so-called Sangatte crisis and the Saint-Denis's church crisis in which immigrant families and *sans-papiers* had taken refuge in the church), clandestine or irregular immigration, delinquency, criminality, and drug trafficking are fused into the same conceptual category—as fundamental vectors of insecurity that need to be vigorously fought. By discursively linking these themes in such a consistent way, Sarkozy and de Villepin have undoubtedly made powerful securitizing moves in the context of migration.

Conclusion

Summing up the evidence amassed in the previous pages allows me to explore how each political agent relates with the phenomenon of securitized migration described in Chapter 2. Drawing together the pattern of engagement of political agents under study with the phenomenon of securitized migration is important because it provides a better understanding of the social mechanisms involved in the securitization of migration. It also permits a temporal analysis, that is, contrasting *when* the securitization of migration was initiated in the period under investigation with the result obtained for each political agent.

In Canada, the pattern is clear. Among the actors I examined, the role of the Minister of Foreign Affairs is paramount in initiating the securitization process. Whereas Joe Clark (Minister of Foreign Affairs from September 1984 to April 1991) made no securitizing moves in the last two and a half years of his mandate that this study covers, his successor Barbara McDougall (April 1991 to June 1993) made numerous and repeated securitizing moves in the crucial year of 1991, as well as in 1992 and 1993. McDougall was very influential in initiating the process of securitizing migration in Canada.

Although the securitization of migration could hardly have occurred without the Prime Minister's engagement or tacit accord (given Canada's political system), my findings suggest that the Prime Minister has not been the key securitizing agent initiating the securitization process. Brian Mulroney made no securitizing attempt throughout the last four years of his mandate that this study covers. The first securitizing attempts were made by Prime Minister Kim Campbell during the Fall 1993 federal election.

The role of the Minister of Citizenship and Immigration in initiating the securitization process is harder to evaluate, as the majority of speeches by Minister Bernard Valcourt (Minister from April 1991 to November 1993) is closed to the public. Yet, results based on collected material indicate that Ministers of Citizenship and Immigration made almost no securitizing moves between 1989 and 1998.

The temporal pattern is less clear in the case of France. Both the Prime Minister and the Minister of the Interior were significant players in the early stage of the securitization process. In 1989, Prime Minister Michel Rocard was already making securitizing moves; in doing so he was setting the securitization process in motion. Of all the years that this study covers, the year 1990 contains the second most numerous securitizing attempts made by the Prime Minister; only 1993 saw more securitizing moves. Rocard's successor, Édith Cresson (Prime Minister from May 1991 to April 1992), pursued a policy of continuity in this regard, thereby re-enforcing the role of the Prime Minister in initiating the securitization process.

Even though Minister of the Interior Pierre Joxe (May 1988 to January 1991) made no securitizing moves in 1990, Socialist Ministers of the Interior Philippe Marchand (January 1991 to April 1992) and Paul Quilès (April 1992 to March 1993) became strong and influential proponents early in the process. In terms of total securitizing moves made on a yearly basis, 1991 and 1992 are both within the top five of all the years that this study covers.

Whereas Rocard, Marchand, and Quilès had important roles early in the securitization process, Minister of Foreign Affairs Roland Dumas and President François Mitterand were not key agents in initiating the process. Dumas made no securitizing moves throughout his mandate that this study covers (1989–1995); Mitterand made his first securitizing attempt only in 1994.

Drawing together the pattern of engagement of political agents also allows a comprehensive understanding of the role of each political agent throughout the years of this study (1989–2005). Here, the pattern in Canada is less clear than in France.

In Canada, neither Jean Chrétien nor Paul Martin (who together were in power for thirteen of the seventeen years that this study covers) made repeated and systematic securitizing moves in the context of migration. Figure 4.8 presents the evolution of securitizing moves across political agents between 1989 and 2005. To be sure, we observe a rise in the number of securitizing moves shortly after the terrorist attacks of September 11, 2001: more than 80 percent of all securitizing moves made in 2001 were actually made after 9/11. However, these securitizing attempts were not made on a systematic and repeated-over-time basis. As early as 2002, the number of securitizing attempts by the Prime Minister drops significantly. It has remained relatively low since then.

Several Ministers of Foreign Affairs have had an important role in the securitizing process. Ministers Barbara McDougall, John Manley (October 2000 to

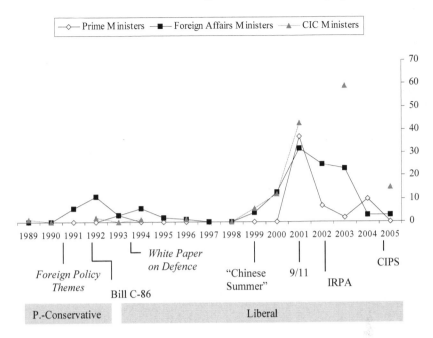

Figure 4.8 Securitizing moves across agents, Canada, 1989–2005. See notes to Figure 4.1
for explanation.

February 2002) and Bill Graham (February 2002 to July 2004) repeatedly and
with fervour made securitizing moves in the context of migration. It is important
to note that there was a significant rise in the number of securitizing attempts by
the Minister of Foreign Affairs before the terrorist attacks of September 11, 2001.

However, the Department of Foreign Affairs has not spoken in a unified voice
during the time period of this study. Whereas Ministers McDougall, Manley,
and Graham were all influential proponents of the securitization of migration,
Lloyd Axworthy, during one of the longest terms as Minister of Foreign Affairs
in Canada's history (from January 1996 to October 2000), did not support the
securitization of migration. In fact, Axworthy was more a *de-securitizing* agent
in the context of migration, although a full narrative of his efforts to de-securitize
migration were not the purpose of this study.

Finally, Ministers of Citizenship and Immigration Elinor Caplan and Denis
Coderre were also key securitizing agents. The first Minister of Citizenship
and Immigration to introduce a security component into how the movement of
people should be seen in Canada was Elinor Caplan (Minister from August 1999
to January 2002). From Caplan's initial securitizing move onward, Ministers of
Citizenship and Immigration have all been important agents in the securitization process. Denis Coderre (Minister from January 2002 to December 2003)
undoubtedly hardened the tone and the message; thus, he is one of the Ministers
most involved in the securitization process.

Furthermore, "migration" and "security" are, perhaps unsurprisingly, the discursive turf of Ministers of Citizenship and Immigration and Ministers of Foreign Affairs respectively. Indeed, Ministers of Citizenship and Immigration have talked about migration far more than the two other political agents (85 percent of the total results); similarly, Ministers of Foreign Affairs have discussed issues of security considerably more often than Ministers of Citizenship and Immigration and Prime Ministers (70 percent of the total results). In addition, a distribution of all securitizing moves across political agents indicates a near equal distribution between Ministers of Foreign Affairs and Ministers of Citizenship and Immigration. The former have made 40 percent of all securitizing moves; the latter, 41 percent.

In France, the pattern of engagement of each political agent with the phenomenon of securitized migration is clearer than in Canada. Ministers of the Interior are without a doubt central players in the securitization of migration, as Figure 4.9 illustrates nicely. Ministers of the Interior have made 60 percent of all securitizing moves in the context of migration. Ministers Philippe Marchand (January 1991 to March 1992), Charles Pasqua (March 1993 to May 1995), Jean-Louis Debré (May 1995 to June 1997), and Nicolas Sarkozy (May 2002 to March 2004) were the most influential Ministers in the securitization process. The theme of security is a central concern for Ministers of the Interior.

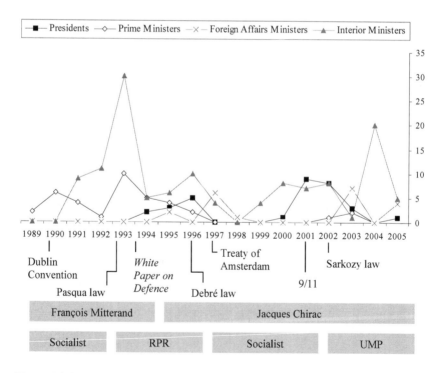

Figure 4.9 Securitizing moves across agents, France, 1989–2005. See notes to Figure 4.4 for explanation.

Prime Minister Édouard Balladur (March 1993 to May 1995) was also an important securitizing agent in the context of migration. Balladur noticeably pushed for the securitization of migration in 1993; in fact, in the twenty-six months that he was Prime Minister, Balladur made 41 percent of all securitizing moves made by Prime Ministers between 1989 and 2005. However, the Prime Minister's office has not spoken in a unified voice throughout the years that this study covers. Indeed, Socialist Prime Minister Lionel Jospin (June 1997 to May 2002) made it clear in his first Declaration of general policy (1997) that his government was seeing migration from a rather different point of view. Not only did Jospin make no securitizing attempt throughout his government's mandate, he also pushed for the *de-securitization* of migration in many regards.

Presidents François Mitterand (1981–1995) and Jacques Chirac (1995–2007) both made several securitizing attempts in the context of migration. Mitterand made his securitizing moves at the very end of his second presidential mandate, whereas Chirac made numerous securitizing attempts in the first two years of his first presidential mandate and shortly after the terrorist attacks of September 11, 2001. However, their direct role in the securitization of migration appears to be relatively low.

Finally, no Minister of Foreign Affairs has been an important agent in the securitization of migration. In fact, the total number of securitizing moves made by all Ministers of Foreign Affairs represents only 8 percent of all securitizing moves made by all political agents—a small figure when compared with those made by Ministers of the Interior (60 percent).

Overall, the pattern of engagement of agents' securitizing moves with the phenomenon of securitized migration has been relatively different in my two country cases. In Canada, political agents from both Departments of Foreign Affairs and Citizenship and Immigration Canada have been at the heart of the securitizing process. In France, influential political agents have all been Ministers of the Interior, with the exception of one Prime Minister.

Security is neither a fact of nature nor merely a question of material factors. In this chapter, I have underscored that several securitizing agents have pushed for the securitization of migration. In addition, I have described which political agents have attempted to present migration as a national security concern. I have also traced when and how political agents have made their securitizing moves. This is not to say that security speech acts can alone successfully securitize migration. They are securitizing moves. The next two chapters will further explore social constituents of the securitization process by analyzing the role of another agent (editorialists) and the role of contextual factors.

5 Media, migration, and security
An obvious link?

> Media are highly significant vectors of the link between migration and security.
> (Interviewee #14, Department of Foreign Affairs, France, 2006)

> Media are significant agents of the securitization of migration.
> (Interviewee #1, Privy Council Office, Canada, 2005)

This chapter examines a set of arguments often invoked but rarely unpacked—that is, that popular written media are influential actors in the securitization of migration. Several interviewees in both Canada and France indeed ranked the media as a highly significant actor in the process of securitizing migration, as the aforementioned quotes illustrate. Some scholars also impute at least partially the securitization of migration to media (Cholewinski 2000; Ibrahim 2005; Vukov 2003). Sean Hier and Joshua Greenberg (2002: 493), in their discussion of how Canadian media reported on the arrival of four boats carrying 600 would-be immigrants from China to the shores of British Columbia in 1999, argue that "newspaper media very quickly and uncritically used" the arrival of the boats to present migrants as signifying "a sense of collective uncertainty pertaining to matters related to Canadian immigration and refugee policy, as well as the more generalized notions of national security and identity." Others argue that, despite the fact that there is no direct causal link between the media coverage of immigration and the numerous aggressions against migrants in Italy and Greece in the 1990s, one should not forget that the "media plays a crucial role in the process of construction of the migratory threat" (Tsoukala 2005: 180).

The set of arguments presented by these scholars comes at a great cost: most of the studies arguing that media constitute important securitizing actors are treating media as a unitary actor. Yet there are many types of media (newspapers, radio, TV, Internet), and even within the newspaper category there are several ramifications of the type of newspaper (tabloid, broadsheet, national/regional circulation) as well as its content (front pages, columns, photos, editorials). To lump all these differences under the umbrella concept of "media" limits more than it reveals in the context of this study. Scholars working on the assumption that "media" is a unitary actor would indeed have missed the fact that some editorialists have chosen to interpret the movement of people as having security implications (for the state and/or society), that some have been reluctant to do so, and that others have argued against doing so.

In addition, I demonstrate in this chapter that there is a disconnection between the set of arguments according to which "media" are important securitizing actors and the empirical evidence amassed in my study. Indeed, my analysis of editorials of four national newspapers in Canada and France between 1989 and 2005 shows that the pattern of engagement of these editorialists in the social construction of securitized migration varies considerably within and across cases.

I have limited my analysis to the editorials, that is, the articles expressing the opinion of a newspaper's editors or publishers. Whereas speeches constitute the loci of political claims by securitizing political agents, editorials are newspapers' own explicit voice in public debates. Because newspapers' editorials possess a detailed argumentative structure, an investigation of editorials permits an analysis of interpretive frames behind the newspapers' official positions, proposals, and demands regarding the migration–security nexus.

In total, I have systematically retrieved, collected, and analyzed nearly 900 editorials. Collecting the complete set of editorials that discuss migration issues largely avoids potential bias. The most important bias that this study avoids is the "rebound" one. As editorialists usually write their editorials just a few hours after an event takes place, focusing solely on editorials published shortly after a crisis (e.g. Chinese refugee crisis in Canada in the summer of 1999 or the 2001 East Sea crisis in France) could significantly bias the analysis in one way or another.[1] Providing an analysis of the evolution of a newspaper's official position that is not biased by events isolated in time is crucial to fully understand the role played by editorialists in the process of securitization over the relatively long time period that this study covers (1989–2005). This is a research effort that will prove to be important in the particular context of this study, especially in the case of *The Globe and Mail*'s and *La Presse*'s reactions to the terrorist attacks of September 11, 2001, as we shall see.

Similar to the objectives of the previous chapter on political agents, my aim in this chapter is twofold. First, I want to carry out a temporal analysis, that is, to contrast *when* the securitization of migration was initiated in each respective country case in the period under investigation with *when* media agents of each country case started their securitizing. As I have demonstrated in Chapter 2, the early 1990s represent a fundamental critical juncture in my study of securitized migration in Canada and France, with the publication of *Foreign Policy Themes and Priorities* (DEA 1991) in Canada and the signing of the Dublin Convention (1990) in the case of France. Thus, I will highlight the pattern of engagement of each media agent with these respective critical junctures. Second, I want to underline each media agent's attempt (or lack thereof) to securitize migration between 1989 and 2005, that is, to investigate how each editorial relates to the phenomenon of securitized migration.

The chapter contains two sections. The first part focuses on the case of Canada, in which I analyze editorials of *The Globe and Mail* and *La Presse*. *The Globe and Mail* is a broadsheet English-language nationally distributed daily newspaper. With a weekly circulation of 2 million copies, it is Canada's largest-circulation national newspaper (it calls itself "Canada's National Newspaper"). The readership of *The Globe and Mail* includes intellectuals, policy makers, bureaucrats, politicians, and the general public. The newspaper has been generally supportive of the Liberal Party of Canada in the 1990s and early 2000s. *The Globe and Mail* is considered the winner of what has been called the "national newspaper war"—a war that started with the launch of another English-language national newspaper in 1998, the *National Post*. As the *National Post* does not cover the entire time span of the present study, I have not included it in the study. *La Presse* is a broadsheet French-language daily newspaper published in Montreal. Although *La Presse* is mostly distributed within the province of Quebec, the newspaper is distributed across Canada. *La Presse* is the largest-circulation newspaper in Quebec with a weekly circulation of 1.5 million copies. The aimed readership of *La Presse* is the general public, policy makers, bureaucrats, and politicians. I opt for *La Presse* over *Le Devoir*, which aims for a more intellectual readership, because the weekly circulation of *Le Devoir* is significantly smaller (180,000 copies) as well as *Le Devoir* being minimally distributed across Canada.

The second section concentrates on the case of France where I examine editorials of *Le Monde* and *Le Figaro*. *Le Monde* is one of France's leading broadsheet daily newspapers with a weekly circulation of 2.4 million copies. *Le Monde* is distributed throughout France, with a readership that includes intellectuals, policy makers, politicians, and the general public. *Le Monde* is often described as a center-left newspaper and has generally been supportive of the Socialist Party. *Le Figaro* is also a broadsheet French-language daily newspaper. With a weekly circulation of 2 million copies, *Le Figaro* is one of the largest newspapers in France. *Le Figaro* is considered a conservative newspaper and has generally been supportive of Jacques Chirac's and Nicolas Sarkozy's political parties.

I have conducted a content analysis of every editorial in which migration was the main topic[2] to understand how editorialists perceive the issue of international migration (and its derivatives such as refugees, illegal migrants, etc.). What is the editorialist talking about when he/she talks about the movement of people: is it to highlight the benefits of multiculturalism, to underscore the difficulties of immigrants in integrating the job market, to celebrate the diversity and the richness that immigrants bring to the host society, to criticize the efficiency of the refugee determination process, and so on. In the next step, I have isolated the securitizing moves, that is, when an editorialist argued that international migration is a security concern for the state and/or the society. I have then worked to intertwine the security speech act with the rationale justifying the securitizing move. It is important to note that although I use statistical analysis to provide a graphic overview of the pattern of engagement of each securitizing agent with the phenomenon of securitized migration, a content analysis constitutes the primary method of investigation.

Canada

The Globe and Mail

> If there is anxiety to be suffered on account of the cultural changes immigration produces, it is the first-generation immigrants who have the greatest claim to it rather than Canadian society.
>
> (Editorial, *The Globe and Mail* 1997)

In February 1989, Radio-Canada (Francophone national public television) aired a documentary called *Disparaître: The Inevitable Fate of North America's French-Speaking Nation.*[3] The documentary argued that an increasing number of immigrants who do not speak either French or English would bring racial disharmony and, more importantly, would threaten the province of Quebec's fundamental character. "Quebecers," the host of the show Lise Payette said, were "living dangerously."

The Globe and Mail's editorial, entitled "The Panic Button," published in the following days was noticeably critical of the documentary (*The Globe and Mail* 1989). The editorial first contended that the documentary was not an isolated gesture; rather, it was part of a general trend in Quebec (as an element of proof, the editorial brings in a quote from then Premier Robert Bourassa, saying that a "deep feeling of insecurity" exists among francophones). The editorial then rejects both moves: "The danger with such tracts as Disparaître and the apocalyptic musings of politicians is that they promote a bunker mentality, marketing the unwarranted belief that the language and culture of French-speaking Quebecers is seriously threatened." "Insecurity on that scale," the editorials persists, would create a scare that "is not justified by the facts" (*The Globe and Mail* 1989).

Furthermore, while editorialists of *The Globe and Mail* made no systematic and repeated securitizing moves in the early 1990s, they also stayed away from perceiving immigration as a threat to Canada's cultural identity. "If there is anxiety to be suffered on account of the cultural changes immigration produces, it is the first-generation immigrants who have the greatest claim to it rather than Canadian society." "It is their children," the editorial continues, "who will be palpably different from them" (*The Globe and Mail* 1997).

Along the same lines, an editorial of 1998 notes that

> the news that Toronto will in a few short months become a majority non-white city has been anticipated all decade long. . . . The fear was that such a radical shift would spell social dislocation, ethnic tension and crime. Nothing of the sort happened. . . . The big news story is how little of a news story this revolution is.
>
> (*The Globe and Mail* 1998)

This pro-immigration stance was reiterated more recently. "This country is being transformed by waves of immigrants from the Far East, Africa and other distant points. Yet, there is scant evidence of the fear or anxiety that often accompanies rapid change. Canadians like what is happening to their country" (*The Globe and Mail* 2004).

The recurrent praise of the Canadian immigration system also illustrates the continual refusal to conceptualize migrants as existential threats to Canadian society. "Canada's immigration and refugee policy is among the world's most liberal," contends a 1993 editorial (*The Globe and Mail* 1993). Several editorials mention the generosity of Canada's immigration system—"one of the most generous in the world"—as well as the idea that immigration enriches Canada, thereby making Canada a much more vibrant nation as a result.[4]

In 2000, the editorial board of *The Globe and Mail* even went a step further in rejecting a securitization of migration. The editorial of January 31, 2000 is worth quoting at some length.

> Fear of drugs, migrants and terrorists slipping into the U.S. from Canada has many Americans so twitchy that they are pressuring the Clinton administration to impose security measures on their neighbour to the north akin to those used along the border with Mexico. . . . The prospect is daunting. . . . Since that degree of security [the high degree of security of the U.S.-Mexico border] has not stopped the flow of illegal migrants from Mexico into the U.S., it seems only reasonable to ask whether it is even possible to secure the Canadian border. . . . Even if it were possible, is it worth it? . . . [F]utile attempts to inspect and track everybody and everything that crosses the border creates a problem instead of a solution.
>
> (*The Globe and Mail* 2000)

In sum, editorialists of *The Globe and Mail* made almost no securitizing moves in the context of migration between 1989 and 2001. However, it is not as though the opportunity to make securitizing moves did not exist. Following the considerable windows that constitute the so-called "1999 Chinese Summer crisis," editorials did promote repressive measures against migrants, but not under a security agenda. Following the arrival of the 599 would-be Chinese immigrants an editorial of *The Globe and Mail* (1999) "applaud[s] holding the migrants in detention until their cases can be decided." However, it did not applaud the detention because Chinese would-be immigrants represented a serious national security threat; rather, the detention of immigrants was welcomed on the basis that "releasing the first group of them has been disastrous from a public-relations perspective" as it is widely assumed that they went underground in the United States to work off their debts to snakeheads in sweatshops or prostitution rings. Clearly, polishing the Canada–U.S. relationship was a greater concern than the logic of securitization.

In fact, *The Globe and Mail*'s editorial position regarding the "Chinese Summer of 1999" nicely illustrates that this exogenous event did not drive securitization in an objective way. In order to become a security concern, the "Chinese Summer" incident had to be read and interpreted as such. Evidence amassed in my analysis of *The Globe and Mail*'s editorials shows that editorialists have not interpreted this particular event as having national security implications.

Moreover, a refusal to securitize migration (at least in the pre-9/11 period) does not mean a refusal to politicize the issue—that is, the process of taking an issue *out* of restricted networks and/or bureaucracies and bringing the issue *into* the public arena (Guiraudon 1998; Huysmans 2006). Migration is indeed a recurrent theme in *The Globe and Mail*'s editorials from 1989 to 2005, as Figure 5.1 shows. Migration constitutes the main topic of eleven editorials per year on average. Among the recurrent themes that *The Globe and Mail*'s editorials politicize, but do not securitize, are the categories of immigrants, the discretionary power of the Minister, the refugee determination system, the economic contribution of immigrants, and so on. In many instances, the politicization has positive overtones. This does not mean that no harsh words were written or that no inconsiderate positions were taken. For instance, one of the editorials urges, on economic grounds, that the Minister exclude prospective immigrants carrying the AIDS virus.[5]

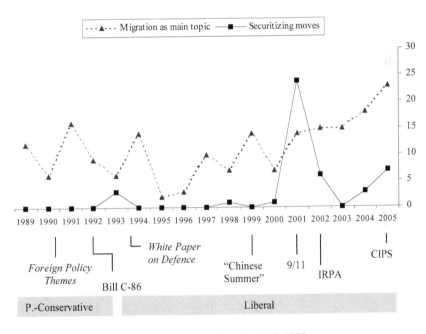

Figure 5.1 Editorials, *The Globe and Mail*, Canada, 1989–2005.

Note: The dashed line represents the use of migration (and its derivatives such as immigration, refugee, illegal migrant) in an editorial; the solid line represents the securitizing moves – i.e. when migration was said to be a security concern for Canada; the vertical filled column refers to one of the key years in the securitization process; "Chinese Summer" refers to the arrival of four boats of Chinese would-be immigrants to British Columbia's shores; the grey horizontal line indicates which political party was in power. Although I present some of the results with the help of a figure, it is important to underscore that the primary research method that I employ is a traditional content analysis of each editorial. CIPS, Canada International Policy Statement; IRPA, Immigration and Refugee Protection Act.

Overall, pre-9/11 editorials not only unequivocally reject the securitization of migration, but also they constantly highlight the overwhelming contributions of migration to Canada. This is not to say that no *The Globe and Mail* editorials argued for the securitization of migration between 1989 and 2005. The gist is that these securitizing moves were made after the terrorist attacks of September 11, 2001.

Indeed, we have to wait until the terrorist attacks of 9/11 to see a clear rupture in *The Globe and Mail*'s editorials. In fact, we have to wait until the week after the terrorist attacks because the anti-securitization stance is even stronger than before in one of the editorials written shortly after the attacks. The editorial of September 19, 2001 argues that rewriting Canada's immigration laws to keep any possible terrorist or agent far from Canadian shores is an unnecessary, unworkable, and undesirable reaction to 9/11. Changing immigration laws in order to try to block every possible terrorist agent is undesirable, according to the editorial, not only because such policies would be a fundamental redefinition of Canada's values, but also because "any attempts to build a foolproof immigration system would only lead to a false sense of security." In sum, it would be a "panicked reaction" to change hastily "an essential characteristic of Canadian society" (*The Globe and Mail* 2001b).

A first element of rupture appears three days later, on September 22, 2001. The editorial, while applauding the Canadian government's effort to tighten border security and "clamp down on loopholes in our immigration policy so that we don't play an unwitting role in a future disaster," criticizes Canadian authorities for not going far enough (*The Globe and Mail* 2001c). The editorial of September 29, 2001 pushes the demand higher: "Canada faces the greatest threat to its security since the Second World War." Accordingly,

> bringing our defences up to scratch will require more than the sort of tinkering – locked cockpit doors, new security passes for some airport workers – that we have seen from Ottawa so far. What is needed is wholesale rethinking of our security policy, from defence to law enforcement to immigration. It must be sweeping and it must be fast.
>
> (*The Globe and Mail* 2001d)

Further and more considerable elements of rupture came into sight in December 2001 and January 2002. The editorial of December 4, 2001 contends that few Canadians would disagree with the announcement made in early December 2001 that Canada and the United States will cooperate to improve border and immigration security (the Smart Border Declaration). "It is logical, even reassuring," the editorial argues, that both governments will expand the use of police, customs and immigration enforcement teams. "Increased security will benefit Canada as much as the United States. Not only will it detect suspected terrorists, but it should find more criminals of every sort." For the editorialist, the only troubling aspect to the security plan "is the unilateral deployment of military personnel to patrol the border" (*The Globe and Mail* 2001e). The editorial of January 12, 2002 discusses a possible federal cabinet shuffle. Elinor Caplan, then Minister of Citizenship and Immigration, has earned, according to the editorial, a one-way ticket to the backbenches because "she is an 'open door' kind of liberal who appeared philosophically uncomfortable with the law-and-order toughness Canadians were seeking after Sept. 11. She resisted amending Canada's immigration legislation for too long this fall" (*The Globe and Mail* 2002).

All of this represents a profound turnaround—if not a complete contradiction—of *The Globe and Mail*'s editorials regarding the migration–security nexus. Whereas securitizing the border was previously seen as unreasonable, unworthy, and creating a problem instead of offering a solution, the securitization of immigration was now "logical" and "reassuring." Whereas rewriting Canada's immigration laws were deemed an undesirable reaction to 9/11, a "sweeping" and a "wholesale rethinking" was now needed—and the Minister of Citizenship and Immigration should lose her cabinet membership because she resisted rewriting Canada's immigration laws. Whereas the prospect of security measures at the U.S.–Canada border was previously "daunting," it was now beneficial for both countries to increase security at the border. Whereas attempts to track everybody crossing the border were previously seen as "futile," it was now assumed that the same attempts would be successful in detecting suspected terrorists and criminals. Whereas policies that intended to block every possible terrorist agent were previously characterized as a "panicked reaction" that would alter a fundamental aspect of Canadian society, it was now thought that being philosophically uncomfortable with the law-and-order toughness approach to immigration made you an "open door" minister.

In sum, an analysis of *The Globe and Mail* editorialists establishes that before 9/11 they did not understand and perceive international migration to be a threat to Canada's national security and collective identity. It is not as if editorialists had no interest in migration issues or no opportunity inducing them to formulate securitizing moves, as we have seen. Nevertheless, the editorialists decided not to see the movement of people as a security issue and, accordingly, have formulated no securitizing moves and have argued against the securitization of migration. My investigation also demonstrates that the terrorist attacks of 9/11 constitute the source of a profound rupture—if not a complete contradiction—in the way editorialists saw the movement of people. Evidence also suggests that 9/11 did increase the number of editorials in which migration was the main topic. Yet editorialists of *The Globe and Mail* have formulated a relatively low number of securitizing moves in the years following the terrorist attacks—casting perhaps some doubts on the lasting effects of 9/11.

La Presse

In one of his last editorials before retiring from the editorial board of *La Presse*, Pierre Vennat wrote the only editorial associating immigrants with a loss of Quebec's cultural identity, in the years that the study covers. "Those [immigrants] who will refuse to accept that in Quebec 'it is in French that things are done' will have to be redirected somewhere else," the editorialist contends in October 1989. The editorial entitled "Immigration and the survival of a francophone Quebec" argues that francophones' anxiety toward immigration is fully legitimate because "it is provoked by the real threat that immigration, in the actual period, poses to the survival of a francophone Quebec" (Vennat 1989). Undoubtedly, this constitutes a strong securitizing move in the context of my study.

However, instead of representing *La Presse*'s editorial line over time, this securitizing move turned out to be an idiosyncratic editorial, as Figure 5.2 illustrates. In fact, several editorials of *La Presse* written between 1989 and 2005 have rebutted, in a systematic way, the logic behind Vennat's securitizing move. For instance, the editorial of August 19, 1993 contends that Kim Campbell's cabinet reshuffle and the transfer of many immigration responsibilities to a newly created department—the short-lived Department of Public Security—runs the risk to "exacerbate xenophobia and intolerance" (Gruda 1993a). Since the sole purpose of the Department of Public Security is to track criminals of all sorts, Campbell's move to associate migrants with criminals gives a false sentiment of control and order when the real target is a very thin portion of all migrants. "There are many people who swindle social security programs, others who defraud employment insurance: this is not a reason to place all welfare recipients or all workers under the responsibilities of the public security department. Why would we do that in the case of immigrants?" (Gruda 1993a).

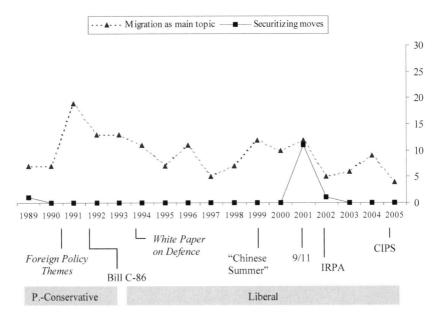

Figure 5.2 Editorials, *La Presse*, Canada, 1989–2005. See notes to Figure 5.1 for explanation.

In December 1993, editorialist Agnès Gruda also argued, based on a study produced by the *Conseil Supérieur de la Langue Française*, that the new reality of Quebec negates the immigrant stereotype as a "cultural stealer." "The study," the editorialist notes approvingly, "actively refuses to comply with those who think that the best way to fight for the survival of French is to cultivate the fear of the Other" (Gruda 1993b). Between 1996 and early 2001 (i.e. before 9/11), several editorials narrate case studies of the government's decision to treat immigrants as dangerous criminals or case studies of refugees who, after deportation, were (or could be) tortured, and of situations where human rights considerations were not applied. These editorials argue that the government was clearly "paranoiac" with its security concerns, that it "cultivates a cult of hostility," and that attempting to create a security fortress is pointless from the beginning (Gruda 1996, 1999). Furthermore, in two editorials written a few months before the terrorist attacks of September 11, 2001, Agnès Gruda contends that Canada holds a dual responsibility concerning refugees. Canadian authorities, by making it harder and harder for a refugee to be recognized as such, have created a system that invites internal abuses. Still, Canadian authorities, by closing its doors to refugees, are also partially responsible for the terrible travel conditions that many would-be immigrants are willing to accept. The more a rich country tries to build a fortress against the movement of people, the more it will induce organizations to go "illegal" and to organize less and less safe travel "arrangements" (Gruda 2001).

Yet, arguments opposing Vennat's point of view have become the established position on the issue; an editorial published ten years after Vennat's is one of the best illustrations of this. In October 1999, the Parti Québécois held its National Congress. The radical wing of the Party put forward propositions to the effect that immigration was largely responsible for the "decline" of the francophone, who would become a minority in Montreal within fifteen years, thereby making immigrants a threat to "Québécois de souche." To add to the controversy, the Party's leader and Premier, Lucien Bouchard, somewhat concurred with the radicals' position. Such a position brought a vitriolic reaction from *La Presse*'s editorialist, Alain Dubuc. To play the "Québécois de souche" against the others is "odious because it recreates ethnic cleavages. It is also stupid because the thirty percent of allophones do not constitute a homogenous group but a mosaic that includes several cultures and languages." The editorialist went on to attack the minister in charge, accusing her of managing the linguistic file with fundamentalist inclinations "that do not correspond to the values of Francophones from Quebec." Indeed, on this issue the minister is, "to use a French analogy, much closer to the Front National [of Jean Marie Le Pen] than to the Socialist Party." In sum, the initiative of the Parti Québécois is "despicable" and "constitutes a twenty-five year step backward" (Dubuc 1999). Therefore, while an idiosyncratic editorial published in 1989[6] argued that francophones' anxiety was legitimate because immigrants were a "real threat" to the survival of a francophone Quebec, several subsequent editorials have precisely attacked such sets of arguments by describing them as "odious" and "despicable."

Similar to that of editorialists at *The Globe and Mail*, editorialists of *La Presse*'s refusal to securitize migration does not equate with the non-politicization of the issue. Migration is a recurrent theme in *La Presse*'s editorials from 1989 to 2005. As shown in Figure 5.2, migration is the main topic of more than nine editorials per year on average. The politicization of migration reaches a peak in 1991, that is, when the Quebec–Canada Accord on immigration was signed and at a time when the Mohammed Al-Mashat affair was making the headlines.[7]

Unlike *The Globe and Mail*, however, several editorialists of *La Presse*, between 1992 and 1994, have directly questioned the contributions of immigrants (Dubuc 1993, 1994). *La Presse*'s editorialists politicize several topics, such as the category of immigrants, the Quebec–Canada relationships concerning migration issues, and immigrants' economic impact.

Among these politicized topics, the question of the refugee determination system is particularly revealing of politicization that did not lead to securitization. In a vitriolic and controversial editorial published in March 1992, *La Presse*'s editor-in-chief, Alain Dubuc, contends that refugee advocacy groups are responsible for portraying Canada as a closed and unjust country (Dubuc 1992a). Perhaps out of guilt, media have become "accomplices of that propaganda" by never denouncing the untrue and biased messages portrayed by these pressure groups. The focus of attention is more on idiosyncratic cases of rejection and arbitrary expulsion, which "by definition will [make people] cry," than on giving due recognition to Canadians and Quebecers who are making efforts to open their doors to refugees by paying taxes and by adapting themselves to the cultural shock. For Dubuc, Canada "is too generous." The only winners of Canada's strategy of "opening its arms and closing its eyes" are the swindlers. Hence, rethinking Canada's position is crucial. To do so, a good starting point would be, according to the editorialist, to ask the following questions:

> Is it normal that the principle of "non-refoulement" is applied even when the applicant's narrative makes no sense? Is it normal that refugees waiting for their application to be processed have the right to obtain legal counselling, which constitutes an invitation to delay due process and to multiply claims? Is it normal that social security be automatically granted to refugees and that a refugee with a dubious claim can rent an apartment and work? Is it normal that an accepted refugee become automatically an immigrant when the right of asylum is temporary and should stop when the situation in the home country goes back to normal?
>
> (Dubuc 1992a)

Obviously the editorial provoked strong reactions, especially from targeted advocacy groups. In his rejoinder to the "letters to the editor" that he received, the editorialist even goes a step further by insisting: "It is impossible to propose critical thinking on important issues such as refugees without provoking mafias' thunderous reaction, who seize the monopoly of truth." Society needs to be able to count on an objective point of view regarding important topics, argues the editorialist. However, non-governmental organizations such as refugee advocacy groups are not objective because they are militant organizations and "the exigencies of [their] struggles has priority over the search for the truth." Media are the only providers of objectivity. However, in this particular case the media have not been able to play their noble role, according to the editorialist, partly because of the strength of the pressure from these non-governmental organizations. Hence, refugee advocacy groups "are largely responsible for the imperfections of the system" (Dubuc 1992b).

This is politicization at its highest level, yet no securitizing moves were made. *La Presse*'s editorialist, in his editorial as well as in its rejoinder, never casts the discussion in terms of security concerns for Canada or Quebec. The editorialist never forwarded the argument that migration constitutes an existential threat necessitating and justifying emergency measures, nor did he argue that migrants were vectors of fundamental loss to Canada's identity. Rather, in the midst of the controversy are matters of principle and perceptions of reality. Certainly, one can easily debate the editorialist's standpoint, notably his understanding of humanitarian concerns and the media's objectivity. The point remains, however, that *La Presse*'s editorialist made no securitizing moves.

The terrorist attacks of September 11, 2001 fractured the continuous rejection of the securitization of the movement of people. Indeed, 9/11 has hardened *La Presse*'s editorial point of view on the migration–security nexus. The terrorist attacks have made the balance between security and migration harder to assess, thus bringing its fair share of contradictions among editorials.

In one of the first editorials written after 9/11, the editorialist contends that it would be too easy, but wrong, to hold the Canadian refugee system partially accountable for the tragedy. However, the editorialist, while acknowledging that none of the terrorists who carried out the attacks were refugees, also applauds the adoption of hardened refugee admission measures (i.e. security checks imposed on all refugee claimants). In the face of the new reality provoked by 9/11, Katia Gagnon (2001) argues that these repressive measures against refugees answer "the legitimized demand of security by North-Americans" by establishing a "dense security net," as if to say that refugees had conducted the attacks.

One of the best illustrations of the blurring effect of 9/11 on the point of view of *La Presse*'s editorials is how editorialists have come to see the role of bureaucrats in managing the migration–security nexus. In April 2003, an editorial strongly criticized Canadian bureaucrats in charge of immigration and refugee issues for showing "a strong tendency to forget the poignant human tragedies behind their books of norms." Bureaucrats ought not to focus solely on their role as security providers; they "should also let themselves be moved by the tragedies they are managing" (Gagnon 2003a). Four months later, the same editorialist took the opposite position. In the summer of 2003, six families who refused to go back to their countries of origin, arguing that they would be persecuted and/or tortured if sent back, were in sanctuary in Canadian churches in a last-resort move to stay in Canada. The ensuing editorial, published on August 9, 2003, was unequivocally hard. "To give the benefit of the doubt to every refugee who sought sanctuary in a church and who pretended to be victim of an injustice is unbearable," the editorialist contends. "Canada has given itself rules to evaluate the veracity of each of 50,000 refugee claimants who knock on our door every year. These rules are clear and they are generous" (Gagnon 2003b). Bureaucrats should then simply apply the "clear and generous" rules that compose their book of norms.

In conclusion, my investigation of *La Presse*'s editorials reveals that editorialists have overall rejected the securitization of migration between 1989 and 2005. In addition, although 9/11 has shaken the position of *La Presse*'s editorialists, the terrorist attacks have not been as influential on editorialists' point of view as many would have presumed.

France

Le Monde

> The way France treats the stranger from within, the immigrant, has a direct impact on how France is perceived internationally.
>
> (Éditorial, *Le Monde* 1997)

My analysis of the complete set of editorials of the French newspaper *Le Monde* reveals a clear pattern of engagement of this particular media agent in the social construction of securitized migration. Except for a rather ambiguous editorial published in 2002, *Le Monde*'s editorialists made no securitizing moves throughout the years that the study covers.

It is not, however, as though the opportunity did not exist. For example, the arrival on February 17, 2001 of the freighter *East Sea*, which deliberately ran aground on a French Mediterranean beach carrying 900 Kurdish refugees, resulted in a groundswell of emotion across France and could have easily induced a bold editorial to the effect that "uncontrolled" migration was jeopardizing France's security. Equally, the entry into force of the Pasqua law of 1993, the Debré law of 1996, or the Sarkozy law of 2003 have all created a good deal of political attention, as Figure 5.3 illustrates. Nevertheless, editorialists of *Le Monde* made no securitizing moves. As such, one should note here that the *East Sea* crisis of 2001, for example, did not simply drive securitization in some objective, deterministic way. *Le Monde*'s editorialists had to interpret the crisis along the migration–security nexus; they opted not to understand this event in terms of a security concern for France.

Furthermore, the direct and immediate effects of one of the most important exogenous shocks of the past two decades—the terrorist attacks of 9/11—are hard to identify in *Le Monde*'s editorials. While debates surrounding the Pasqua law and the Debré law constitute the main explanation for the rise in editorials that have migration as their main topic, the attacks of 9/11 are not the central event with which migration is anchored in 2001 or 2002. Indeed, *Le Monde*'s editorialists rarely discuss the terrorist attacks in conjunction with migration in the weeks/months following the attacks. The presidential election and the European Summit

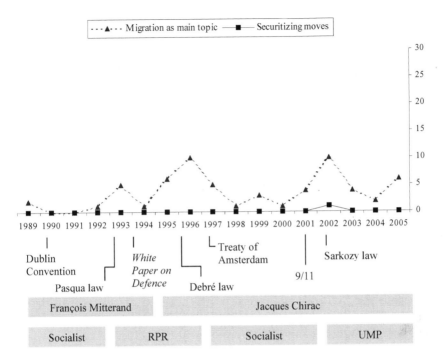

Figure 5.3 Editorials, *Le Monde*, France, 1989–2005.

Note: The dashed line represents the use of migration (and its derivatives such as immigration, refugee, illegal migrant, etc.) in an editorial; the solid line represents the securitizing moves – i.e. when migration was said to be a security concern for France; the first grey horizontal line indicates who was President at a particular point in time; the second grey horizontal line indicates which political party was controlling the government. Although I present some of the results with the help of a figure, it is important to underscore that the primary research method that I employ is a traditional content analysis of each editorial. RPR, Rally for the Republic; UMP, Union for Popular Movement.

held in Seville, Spain in June 2002 are the two key issues associated with the rise in the number of editorials that have migration as the main topic. Thus, the trigger effect of 9/11 appears to be considerably less significant for *Le Monde*'s editorialists than for editorialists of *The Globe and Mail,* as we have seen. The terrorist attacks induced no significant change in *Le Monde*'s editorials.

My investigation of *Le Monde*'s editorials underscores that editorialists have repeatedly and specifically argued against the securitization of migration. For instance, the editorial of November 8, 2003 argues that, instead of perceiving the movement of people and the arrival of immigrants as a existential threat to its cultural identity, France should see migration as a "chance for plurality" (*Le Monde* 2003). An editorial published during the 1995 presidential election campaign opposing Jacques Chirac and Lionel Jospin wishes that both candidates "would not succumb to the temptation of opportunistic political discourse on clandestine immigration and security" (*Le Monde* 1995). Moreover, the general debate surrounding the Debré law of 1996 confirms, according to the editorial of December 21, 1996, that "the obsession of the migratory risk nourishes a repressive spiral that has devastating effects for the nation-state" (*Le Monde* 1996). In the year that saw the unexpected appearance of Jean-Marie Le Pen in the runoff election against the incumbent Chirac, several editorials vigorously denounce the apparently winning combination of Islam–immigration–insecurity. Equally, editorialists decry the "discourse of order" on the basis that it is producing a "social stigmatization" and that "police responses are short-sighted" (*Le Monde* 2001a, 2002).

Furthermore, editorialists repeatedly aim at reorienting the way in which the movement of people is seen in France. For instance, argues *Le Monde*, instead of accepting the "simple answers" provided by the culture of insecurity, one should understand and acknowledge the complexity of migration. Instead of limiting its response merely to the repressive aspect, the government should systematically give preference to building a more balanced "social model." Instead of seeing migration through an "accountant lens" in which only "useful" migrants are noticed, France should widen its perspectives (*Le Monde* 1993, 1996, 2001a, 2004, 2005). "The heart has its arguments that reason must listen to," the editorial of February 22, 2001 reminds its readership (*Le Monde* 2001b).

In sum, my investigation of *Le Monde*'s editorials demonstrates that *Le Monde*'s editorialists have made no securitizing moves throughout the years that this study covers and, as such, have not been important securitizing agents. Furthermore, my analysis suggests that the terrorist attacks of September 11, 2001 have had a very limited impact on the editorial line of *Le Monde*.

Le Figaro

> In some areas, the number of immigrants is one-third more than citizens who really come from here; the integration in these areas could work in reverse. Our good Republic cannot resign itself to such permanent drifting.
>
> (Suffert 1997)

My analysis of *Le Figaro*'s editorials from 1989 to 2005 reveals a completely different pattern of engagement. *Le Figaro*'s editorialists made several securitizing moves throughout the years that this study covers, as Figure 5.4 illustrates. These repeated securitizing moves were not just made in a given year or after a particularly important exogenous shock (as in Canada after 9/11). Rather, evidence demonstrates that editorialists made several securitizing attempts in the context of migration in almost every single year between 1989 and 2005.

Editorialists of *Le Figaro* formulated strong securitizing moves as early as 1990. It was argued that "we must suspend immigration otherwise everything is possible: the country is one the verge of burning fiercely" (Giesbert 1990a), that "the phenomenon of immigration is currently de-structuralizing French society" (Giesbert 1990b) and that in France "11 percent of the population were strangers. How can we be surprised that cities are sometimes burning?" (Giesbert 1991a).

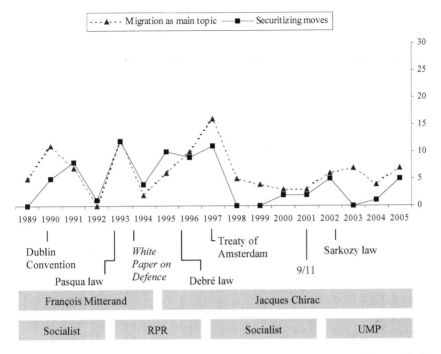

Figure 5.4 Editorials, *Le Figaro*, France, 1989–2005. See notes to Figure 5.3 for explanation.

In 1992 an editorialist contended that, in the face of immigration pressure, French people were wondering about their identity and whether they had a future as *a nation* (Lambroschini 1992). In May 1993, Xavier Marchetti argued that "France's national identity is at risk . . . The government must start to tackle [immigration]; the mood of the nation is at stake" (Marchetti 1993)

As such, one of the most important findings of my investigation of *Le Figaro*'s editorials from 1989 to 2005 is that *Le Figaro*'s editorialists have been key securitizing agents in initiating the process of securitizing migration. A temporal connection is present between editorialists' securitizing moves and the beginning of the securitization process. As Figure 5.4 illustrates, *Le Figaro*'s editorialists made several securitizing moves in the early 1990s, which as we have seen in Chapter 2 constitutes a critical juncture in the study of securitized migration in France.

Editorialists put forward two rationales for the securitization of migration. The first and most important argument is the fear of social explosion, which we found throughout the years covered by this study. Several editorialists argued that the unity of society was seriously at risk of social explosion (Giesbert 1991a; Lambroschini 1992). Some urged the government to see the "problem" as "a new form of war" (Marchetti 1995), others praised the 1996 Pasqua law as "un-attackable in its principles" (Rebois 1996). "We must urgently control the migration flow – both legal and clandestine," wrote an editorialist in 2005, "otherwise in fifteen years from now it is the children of the newly arrived immigrants who will light the suburbs on fire" (Brézet 2005). If the migratory pressure is not controlled, it will become a "source of tension threatening France's social cohesion" argued another editorialist in January 2005 (Thréard 2005).

Another vector of the securitization of the movement of people for *Le Figaro*'s editorialists is the issue of numbers. The idea that France is facing a tremendously high level of migratory pressure has indeed been at the centre of many editorials. On several occasions, editorials raise the issue of mass movements of people, which they often deem as unstoppable and bound to grow significantly in the near future, as a security concern for France. France is confronted with massive immigration in such a way that firmness will not be enough to control it: "the wave will never stop growing" (Rioufol 1996). In May 1990 the editorialist Franz-Olivier Giesbert, while recognizing that the proportion of foreign population in France at the beginning of the 1990s was the same as in 1926, argued, "it is still too much, especially when we know that new waves of immigration are under way" (Giesbert 1990b). Oddly, a year later, Giesbert (1992b) was considering the same statistic dubious: "official statistics are telling us that the number of foreigners in France has been constant since 1982 and that the number is very similar to 1931's number. Bizarre. We should look into that more closely", warned the editorialist, as if these numbers were a manipulation. Similarly, not only should Western governments realize that the "demographic explosion of the Third World" is currently posing a threat to developed countries (Rebois 1991), but also this threat requires "out of the ordinary measures" (Rebois 1993).

Sometimes the issue of numbers is not taken in absolute terms but rather in relative terms: "In some areas," Georges Suffert wrote in 1997, "the number of immigrants is one-third more than the number of citizens who really come from here; the integration in these areas could work in reverse. Our good Republic cannot resign itself to such permanent drifting" (Suffert 1997). This echoed a theme from 1990. "In areas where the immigrants are becoming a majority, it is the French people who are feeling excluded" (Marchetti 1990). This is an unacceptable state of affairs requiring drastic measures (most notably stopping definitely some aspects of immigration), according to the editorialist.

A related finding concerns the sequential connection. As I hypothesized in Chapter 3, two roles are particularly important for media agents in the securitization of migration. Media agents can be initiators of the securitizing process (e.g. by making securitizing moves before political agents, thereby pressing elite audiences to adopt a particular security policy and/or to prepare the ground for policy reforms), or they can be transmitting players in the securitization process (e.g. by cueing in on political agents' securitizing moves after the fact).

In the context of this study, evidence seems to suggest that *Le Figaro*'s editorialists have been active initiators in the securitization process. To be sure, editorialists often aim at influencing the mass public. Notwithstanding, several editorials were prescribing to an elite audience what they ought to do in the context of the movement of people, as well as which position they should adopt. In fact, the particular role of *Le Figaro*'s editorialists is best illustrated when their securitizing moves are juxtaposed with Ministers of the Interior's securitizing moves at two critical points in the securitization of migration: the Pasqua law of 1993 and the Debré law of 1997.

In both cases, editorialists formulated their securitizing moves shortly before Ministers of the Interior did. Although the Pasqua law was introduced in August 1993 in the National Assembly, *Le Figaro*'s editorialists were making securitizing moves as early as April 1993—a few days after Pasqua (and the new Balladur government) were sworn into power in March 1993. In May 1993, Marchetti was arguing that "France's national identity is at risk . . . The government must start to tackle [immigration]; the mood of the nation is at stake" (Marchetti 1993). Editorialists formulated almost all of their securitizing moves before the Minister of the Interior started to make strong securitizing moves. The 1997 episode saw the unfolding of the same sequential connection. In August 1996 editorialists' securitizing moves were made before the Debré law was introduced in the National Assembly and before Debré made his securitizing moves. As such, evidence suggests that editorialists' securitizing moves were setting the tone for Pasqua's and Debré's securitizing moves in the following months.

Le Figaro's securitizing moves also come with a high level of politicization of migration, referring here to the process of taking an issue *out* of restricted networks and/or bureaucracies and bringing the issue *into* the public arena. Surely, the number of editorials with migration as the main topic is particularly important in the case of *Le Figaro*, as Figure 5.4 has shown. Editorialists of *Le Figaro* have devoted on average more than six editorials per year to migration—almost twice as many editorialists of *Le Monde*.

However, what is the most surprising in this intense "interest" in migration from editorialists of *Le Figaro* is the near total absence of positive dispositions toward the issue of immigration. I have encountered only a few editorials in which immigration or immigrants were discussed in positive terms. When the topic managed to reach the top of an editorialist's agenda it was for its negative, dangerous, and threatening aspects. A clear sense of bitterness and aggressiveness toward the phenomenon of the movement of people is hard to miss. Negative stereotypes are often presented as pure facts. In two editorials published on July 14—France's national holiday celebrating the storming of the Bastille in 1789 during the French Revolution—the editorialist Gérard Nirascou was particularly harsh. The two editorials, one published in 1997 and the other in 2000, used almost the same formulation. Immigrants should realize that "to be French, it is not only receiving family allowances or unemployment indemnities, it is perhaps, one day, fulfilling one's duty to give one's life [for France]" and that "to be French, it is not only to benefit from social programs, but also to participate in the history of a great nation" (Nirascou 1997, 2000). It is important to re-affirm this, according to Nirascou, because the immigration "problem" is, at the dawn of the twenty-first century, of a particular acuity rarely seen in the history of France.

Furthermore, the word "problem" precedes immigration in most, if not all, editorials. For example, Suffert in an editorial published in December 1997 argued that "immigration is a problem that touches every single French citizen" (Suffert

1997). In 1990 Marchetti was telling his readers that "we have to acknowledge that the problem of immigration, which is felt deeply in people's souls and which is a carrier of risks of all kinds, has been tossed away for too long" (Marchetti 1990). The reiteration of the "problem of immigration" in *Le Figaro*'s editorials reached an apogee in November 2001 to explain the lack of national identity in youth immigrants. "Experts in falsification and apostles of repentance have not stopped in the last fifteen years to qualify France as a racist nation and to present colonization as an abject enterprise," argued editorialist Alexis Brézet. "How, then, could youth living in suburbs," he continued "wish to claim French identity if France is shameful of her own identity? Why would they love a nation that does not love herself?" (Brézet 2001).

Counterintuitively, given the numerous securitizing moves made by *Le Figaro*'s editorialists prior to 9/11, the terrorist attacks of September 11, 2001 have had almost no effect on *Le Figaro*'s editorialists. None of the securitizing moves made in 2001 and 2002 have had the terrorist attacks as its rationale. Some of these editorials discuss a disruptive event in a sports competition in which immigrants have booed *La Marseillaise* (France's national anthem); others discuss the European asylum policies or the results of Jean-Marie Le Pen in the first round of the 2002 presidential election. In sum, none of the securitizing moves by *Le Figaro*'s editorialists has a clear link with 9/11.

Conclusion

"The media play a key role in the organization of the society; they are powerful actors in the political and social structure," argues a major figure in the field of communication studies (Siegel 1996: 18). In the context of this study, several bureaucrats as well as scholars indeed assume that media are influential actors in the securitization of migration. Yet my comparative analysis casts serious doubt on the argument that media are important securitizing agents in the process of securitizing migration. It is not necessarily wrong to argue that media are securitizing agents, only that this argument does not tell us much about the process of securitizing migration.

Evidence amassed in this chapter suggests that the role of the editorialists of two major newspapers in each country case varies considerably within and across cases. Canada's biggest national newspaper, *The Globe and Mail*, made securitization moves only following the terrorist attacks of September 11, 2001. Canada's biggest francophone newspaper, *La Presse*, made almost no securitizing moves throughout the years that this study covers. Similarly, editorialists of France's newspaper *Le Monde* have not argued for the securitization of migration for the entire period that this study covers. Finally, editorialists of *Le Figaro* are the only ones who have made several securitizing moves in a forceful and repeated way.

There is also a clear temporal disconnection between the initiation of the securitization process and editorialists' securitizing moves in three of the four newspaper sets of editorials studied. None of the editorials published by *The Globe and Mail*, *La Presse*, and *Le Monde* is temporally connected with the initiation of the securitizing process, that is, the early 1990s. Only the editorialists of *Le Figaro* made securitizing moves during a crucial time period.

This chapter has also shown that the effects of 9/11 have been more important on *The Globe and Mail*'s editorialists than on the editorialists of the other three newspapers. The terrorist attacks of September 11, 2001 have created a profound rupture—if not a contradiction—in the editorial line of *The Globe and Mail*. Although 9/11 has shaken the position of *La Presse*'s editorialists, the terrorist attacks have not been as influential on the point of view of editorialists as many would have presumed. In the case of France, the terrorist attacks have had almost no impact on the securitization of migration, either on *Le Monde*'s or *Le Figaro*'s editorial line.

This chapter completes my investigation of social agents involved in the securitization of migration. In the next chapter, I will turn my attention to contextual factors.

6   The powers of contextual factors

It is hard to reduce the entire cosmos to a grand narrative, the physics of subatomic particles to a text, subway systems to rhetorical devices, all social structures to discourse.

(Latour 1993: 64)

The previous two chapters have argued that it is essential to analyze agents' security speech acts (or lack thereof) in a study about the securitization process. This chapter rests on the premise that it is equally essential to study how agents' securitizing moves relate to the cultural and socio-historical contexts in which they are made.

Agents do not work in a vacuum. Securitizing agents cannot exclude themselves from environments in which they formulate their securitizing attempts; they do not navigate freely toward a successful securitization. To be sure, agents do have some autonomy; socio-historically and culturally produced knowledge enables individuals to construct and give meaning to contextual factors. However, they are not free agents and their capacity to change, reproduce, and remodel the security realm is not unbounded. A security speech act does not constitute a securitization; it represents only an attempt to present an issue as a security threat. In the same way, the meaning and construction of contextual structures is dependent on ideas and agents' interpretation. Contextual factors do not objectively exist out there waiting to exercise influence. Multifaceted contexts in which agents operate cannot "impose" a securitization without agential powers; they do not simply drive securitization in some objective way. Contextual factors do not speak for themselves. Rather, they have to be interpreted as having security implications for them to have security impacts.

Seen in this constructivist lineage, a study about the structural/contextual factors involved in the securitization process calls for an analysis of an range of factors: whether securitizing attempts were made at a particular point in time; whether they were made before or after a major international event; whether they found an echo in the collective identity schema of a particular society; and whether domestic audiences relate to these securitizing attempts with enthusiasm or with reluctance.

Guided by a constructivist perspective, I have argued in Chapter 3 that the power of structural/contextual factors operates, in a diffuse yet tangible way, through social processes embedded in the historically contingent and multifaceted cultural settings. The power of contextual factors is best understood as the power to *enable and/or constrain* securitizing agents. The power of contextual factors resides precisely in their social capacity to either enable an agent to make securitizing attempts or constrain a securitizing agent attempting to securitize migration—of course, the same factor could be an enabling force at a particular point in time and a limiting force at another point in time. Indeed, socio-historical and structural contexts not only enable (or constrain) particular agents to make security speech acts but also enable (or constrain) agents to make particular security speech acts at a particular point in time.[1]

Such an understanding of the power of contextual factors offers guiding principles to account for the variation in levels of securitized migration. Linking a polymorphous understanding of power with the question of intensity allows me to suggest that, when the contextual factors represent a relatively constant constraining force on agents' securitizing moves, the outcome is a weak securitization. In contrast, when the contextual factors are a relatively constant inducing force on agents' securitizing attempts, the outcome is a strong securitization.

In a study about securitized migration, contextual factors can include several elements: large historical contexts of a country; the "geographic" location of a country; key judicial landmarks; the enduring legacy of significant historical events; and so on. Although these factors are important factors in understanding securitized migration, the securitization of migration cannot be understood without an appreciation of the necessary role played by two particular contextual factors: exogenous shocks and domestic audiences. Exogenous shocks refer to an event or groups of events that induce points of departure from established sociological, cultural, and political patterns. Exogenous shocks often offer a "window of action" to agents for the transformation of social structures. None of these events objectively produces a significant change in world politics. Rather, they constitute resources that are interpreted by and potentially acted upon (or not) by agents. I explore two exogenous shocks that are particularly relevant in the context of this study: the refugee "crisis" of the early 1990s and the terrorist attacks of 9/11.

Regarding domestic audiences, several scholars have tried to further disaggregate the concept of audience in securitization research (Balzacq 2005; Buzan *et al.* 1998). Salter's (2008) argument to distinguish between elite, technocratic, scientific, and popular audiences represents a key contribution to this research agenda. The following pages will build on Salter's categorization by underscoring the role of elite audiences and of popular/mass audiences in Canada and France.

Even when the audience is subdivided into more circumscribed elements, there are still significant obstacles to operationalize a disaggregated audience. I draw on three principal sources to discern how elite and mass audiences have shaped the securitization process. With regard to elite audiences, I have collected, coded, and analyzed the manifestos from the main federal political parties in Canada, as well as most important presidential candidates in France, along the migration–security nexus. Political parties' manifestos are a valuable source of information on elite audiences' involvement mainly because an elite audience will allow the point of view of an individual to be presented as the official position of the political party, and because parties' manifestos set out their strategic direction as well as outlines of prospective legislation should they win the election. Furthermore, I have examined manifestos over a relatively long time span (from 1945 to 2005 in Canada; from 1974 to 2005 in France), rendering possible an analysis in terms of rupture and continuity.

A second option to determine an elite audience's role in the securitization process is to ascertain the extent to which the legislative branch of government has allowed or constrained securitizing actors' moves. I have analyzed whether the most important immigration laws sailed through Parliament, whether they were narrowly passed, or whether they were defeated. Legislative outcomes are a particularly good measure of elite audiences' roles in the securitization process because they constitute a final decision in which the dominant view is expressed; furthermore, they are a package of administrative powers and procedures setting the framework for practices related to national security.

To analyze the role of popular/mass audiences in the securitization process, I have examined public opinion on questions related to the migration–security relationship. I have collected results of public opinion polls for all the years that my study covers. Ideally, public opinion on immigration should be put in some historical context to counter the volatility of an analysis based on idiosyncratic measurement. Without situating public opinion in time, we have no reference through which to determine if profound change happens or if continuity is what drives the thinking about a given issue. Moreover, it is crucial to look at this issue *over time* because the nature of a mass audience's involvement is not static. A mass audience could have been a constraining force in the past whereas it constitutes a facilitating force in a more recent period, or vice versa. To evaluate whether there has been rupture or continuity in a mass audience's involvement, the analysis needs to be carried out over a relatively long period of time. For that reason, when possible, I have situated all measurements of public opinion in historical context, and I have also relied directly on primary data from pollsters instead of distilling the information from media sources. Doing so renders possible an analysis of the evolution of public opinion between 1989 and 2005 as well as an analysis of how public opinion relates to the specific pattern of securitized migration in Canada and France (detailed in Chapter 2).

To be sure, none of these proxies—electoral platforms, Parliament's decisions, and public opinion—can alone assess and measure the role of audiences. Nevertheless, I argue that when they are grouped together to form an aggregate these proxies constitute powerful tools for understanding how audiences shape the securitization process.

The "refugee crisis" of the early 1990s

A first exogenous shock that had a significant impact on the securitization of migration was the so-called "refugee crisis" of the early 1990s. In the late 1980s and early 1990s, regional and civil wars resurfaced around the globe, inducing important migratory movements. The refugee streams resulted from the conflicts in the Horn of Africa and Afghanistan, as well as from the first Gulf War, ethnic strife in Rwanda, and the disintegration of the former Yugoslavia. In addition, the fall of the Berlin Wall induced mass movements of people within Europe. While the number of refugees worldwide was 9 million in 1984, it reached a peak in 1992 with more than 18 million—an increase of 100 percent in less than a decade (Figure 6.1). It thus gave rise to all sorts of projections, scenarios, and arguments, such as the image of a wave of refugees, an uncontrollable and unstoppable movement of people.

In the literature on the linkage between migration and security, rising numbers of refugees gave strength to Kaplan's (1994) notion of "coming anarchy," but also, and more importantly, to studies seeking to raise the profile of international migration in the eyes of security studies. Two of the most important works were Myron Weiner's edited volume *International Migration and Security* (1993) and Gil Loescher's Adelphi Paper *Refugee Movements and International Security* (1992).[2] The primary objective of both studies was to raise the issue of international migration as both a potential cause and a consequence of insecurity. The gist of their arguments was that mass migrations and refugee movements could create domestic instability and threaten regional and international security; hence, security studies should pay close attention to the phenomenon.

Although the surge in the total number of refugees worldwide reveals an important pattern, breaking down receiving states in categories is more enlightening in the present study. Indeed, it was not merely the increase in the absolute number of refugees per se that prompted governments to regard the movement of people with suspicion, but also the rising proportion of refugees attempting to enter developed countries at that particular point in time.

The estimated proportion of refugees in developed countries versus worldwide refugees has significantly increased in recent years, from about 15 percent in the late 1980s to 30 percent in 1996 (Figure 6.2). Furthermore, although the total number of refugees has declined since the peak of 1992, the proportion of

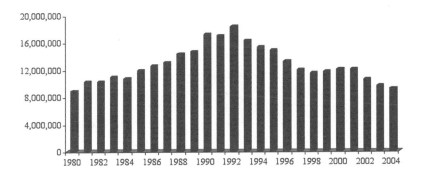

Figure 6.1 Number of refugees worldwide, 1980–2004.

Source: United Nations High Commissioner for Refugees (2006).

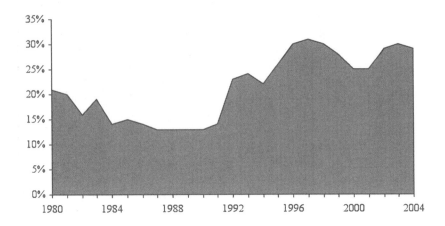

Figure 6.2 Proportion of refugees in developed countries versus worldwide refugees, 1980–2004.

Source: United Nations High Commissioner for Refugees (2006).

refugees accepted by the more developed countries has continued to increase; since 1995, it has never gone below 25 percent of worldwide refugees.

These trends in the movement of people had important implications for the securitization of migration. The rise in numbers of refugees worldwide as well as the increasing refugee pressure on industrialized countries came to be interpreted as a national security issue. That is, mass migrations not only became a regional security concern in war-torn areas, but also, to varying degrees, became socially constructed as a national security concern for Western states.

Advocates of securitized migration were keen on using the symbolic power of the metaphor of invasion, presenting images of tidal waves of refugee movements, alarmist perceptions that Western countries were being flooded with migrants, and views of looming large-scale immigration as imminent threats to national security. As Reg Whitaker (1998: 414–15, emphasis in original) points out, in the early 1990s the refugee had been "reconstructed in the dominant state discourses as an object of fear . . . . At worst, the refugee is criminalized or politicized as a threat to order . . . . Images are invoked of *tidal waves* of refugee movements threatening to engulf and overwhelm the host country, if not checked." The most important rationales advanced to justify the securitization of migration were, according to Whitaker, the image of the apocalyptic threat of a desperate, hungry human tidal wave washing relentlessly westward. While Whitaker was writing mainly about the Canadian context, Christina Boswell (2006) finds similar conclusions in the European context. She notes that rising numbers of asylum seekers have fed alarmist tendencies, reinforcing the notion that Europe is being flooded with migrants from poorer regions. Similarly, Joanne van Selm (2000, 2003) argues that fear of massive movements of people fuelled fears of yet more massive displacements, which in turn have set in motion concerns about insecurity. It is precisely the "refugee crisis" that has enabled certain securitizing agents to make securitizing moves at this particular point in time. As Mark Miller (1997) and Charles Keely and Sharon Russell (1994) all argue, the perception of large movements of refugees was provoking major security concerns for European governments in the late 1980s and early 1990s. Because refugees were perceived as a threat to national security, underscores Vaughan Robinson (1998), the implementation and/or the reinforcement of security practices such as the repatriation of refugees were undoubtedly seen as one of the main solutions to the refugee crisis of the early 1990s.

My analysis of agents' speeches points in the same direction. In Canada, mass movements of people have indeed been a key concern for political agents under study. Barbara McDougall, then Minister of Foreign Affairs, spoke of the threat of "mass migration" on a number of occasions. In an address given in January 1992 to the Council of Ministers of the Conference on Security and Cooperation in Europe, she identified cooperative security as a fundamental factor "apt to reduce the threat of mass migrations" (McDougall 1992a). A few months later, McDougall reinforced that a security dialog between countries was needed to deal with the movement of people. The securitization of migration was later reaffirmed in a domestic address. At the official opening of the Canadian Foreign Service Institute in Ottawa, the Minister told the audience, "the challenges of our foreign services are increasingly complex and diverse. Mass movements of populations . . . have changed forever the way our immigration officers work. The work they do is crucial to the well-being and long-term security of all Canadians" (McDougall 1992b). Prime Minister Kim Campbell also spoke about the "inescapable" connections between "population flows" and "fundamental sources of insecurity" (Campbell 1993).

In France, the effects were, if anything, more intense and more direct on agents' speeches. Indeed, key political agents jumped on this issue to push their agenda. In June 1991, Jacques Chirac, then Mayor of Paris, complained about the smell and the noise of immigrants, as the epigraph of Chapter 4 illustrates. A few weeks later, Prime Minister Édith Cresson publicly introduced the idea of organizing charter flights to ensure (and speed up) the deportation of unwanted immigrants—an idea that did not sit well with her fellow Socialists. In September 1991, former President Valéry Giscard d'Estaing warned the French of the "invasion" of immigrants. As Alec Hargreaves (2001: 29) puts it in a piece written before the 2002 presidential election, "shortly after this series of highly publicized statements, support for Le Pen's ideas hit an all-time high, despite the fact that the FN leader has been largely out of the limelight during the preceding months."

Additionally, we saw in Chapter 4 that controlling the migration flux was the focus of numerous securitizing moves made by Interior Ministers. "If immigration is not controlled," Socialist Interior Minister Philippe Marchand declared in 1991, "it will become a destabilizing factor for our security. . . . Uncontrolled migratory movement would be a threat against our fundamental national interests" (Marchand 1991). Marchand also stated that a more considerable migration flux might come, which would pose even greater security challenges and, as such, the flux had to be controlled.

The impact was perhaps best illustrated by *Le Figaro*'s editorialists. The idea that France was facing a tremendously high level of migratory pressure had indeed been at the center of many editorials. On several occasions in the early 1990s, editorialists raised the issue of mass movements of people as a security concern for France; migratory flux was often deemed "unstoppable" and bound to grow significantly in the near future. "The migration pressure won't stop overnight," concluded an editorialist. In May 1990, an editorialist, although recognizing that the number of foreign people in France at the beginning of the 1990s was the same as in 1926, argued, "it is still too much, especially when we know that new waves of immigration are under way." Evidently, the perception of waves and unstoppable movements of people was strongly established (Giesbert 1990, 1991; Rebois 1991, 1993).

In sum, mass movements of people and the increasing "refugee pressure" on industrialized countries have been socially constructed as having security implications for Western states in general, and particularly for Canada and France in the context of my study. This is not to say that numbers of refugee movements are not accurate. Rather, the point is that numbers are only numbers; they do not operate in an objective way on the securitization of migration. Refugee movements have to be read and interpreted as having national security implications for them to have some. In this light, the refugee crisis constitutes a powerful "window of action" in which some agents decided to push for the securitization of the movement of people—transforming at the same time the security architecture of a society/state. An exogenous shock acquires security meaning only if it is interpreted to have security implications. Evidence amassed here suggests that the "refugee crisis" of the early 1990s was constructed as having security implications; as such, this exogenous shock appears to be a component of the social mechanisms involved in the securitization process.

Regarding the issue of variation in levels of securitized migration, the hypothesis that rising numbers of asylum seekers explains much of the variation seems convincing at first. Indeed, when the numbers of asylum seekers are compared on an annual basis, the "refugee pressure" is substantially stronger in France than in Canada, as Figure 6.3 illustrates. Between 1989 and 1991, France received nearly twice as many asylum applications as Canada. It would then be logical to observe a stronger securitization of migration in the country where the "refugee pressure" is higher. This would indeed provide a simple and convincing explanation to the question of variation in levels of securitized migration.

However, the reality is more complex. First, the inflow of asylum seekers was, in some years, higher in Canada than in France—for example Canada received more asylum applications than France in 1992 as well as between 1995 and 1998. Second, when the ratio of the total number of asylum seekers to the total population of each country is calculated, the results point in the opposite direction. Figure 6.4 shows that the percentage of asylum seekers in the total population is significantly higher in the case of Canada than in France. For all the years

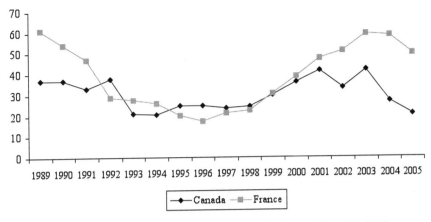

Figure 6.3 Asylum applications in Canada and France (in thousands), 1989–2005.
Sources: INSEE (2005), CIC (2006).

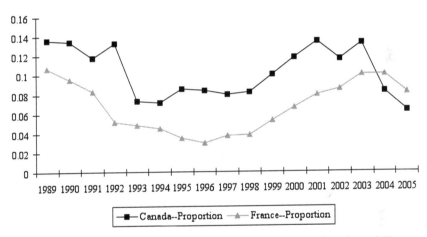

Figure 6.4 Percentage of asylum seekers in total population, Canada and France, 1989–2005.

that my study covers, the average percentage of asylum seekers in relation to the total population in Canada (0.103 percent) is more than 50 percent higher than in France (0.067 percent). Moreover, the lowest percentage of asylum seekers in the total population of Canada (in 2005) is more than 100 percent higher than the lowest percentage in France (in 1996), and the highest percentage in Canada (in 1989) is about 25 percent higher than the highest percentage in France (in 1989).

Furthermore, an important trend is discernible when the percentage of asylum seekers in the total population is discussed in relation to the number of world-wide refugees. That is, although the number of worldwide refugees increased at a rapid pace between 1989 and 1992, reaching a record high of 18 million in 1992, the percentage of asylum seekers in the total population was decreasing quickly in France. The percentage of asylum seekers in the total population of France decreased from 0.107 percent in 1989 to 0.051 percent in 1992, a 50 percent reduction in only four years. Numbers for Canada show a small decline in 1991, but a marked rise in 1992 to reach one of the highest percentages of the years studied. Actually, 1991's point in the case of Canada is 10 percent higher than the highest point in the case of France. The most important difference is found in 1992 when the percentage of asylum seekers in the total population is 150 percent higher in Canada than in France.

In sum, evidence suggests that "refugee pressure" is an inconclusive hypothesis to account for the variation in the level of securitization of migration found between Canada and France.

The terrorist attacks of 9/11

Another exogenous shock relevant in the context of this study is the terrorist attacks of September 11, 2001. Several scholars have highlighted the impact of 9/11 on the migration–security nexus; studies underline an increase in security practices such as detention, fingerprinting, and interdiction, and an increase in the use of biometric technology to identify potential threats in a post-9/11 world (Alexseev 2005; Andreas and Biersteker 2003; Faist 2004; Kruger *et al.* 2004; Rudolph 2006; Tirman 2004).

However, the view that the movement of people might have implications for security was established long before the events of September 11, 2001. Indeed, several enforcement measures structuring the migration–security nexus were actually developed and implemented before the attacks. For example, deportations and removals for security reasons existed in both Canada and France, and migration was listed as a national security concern in key official documents of the department in charge of foreign affairs and/or immigration before 9/11. In Canada, Bill C-11 (the Immigration and Refugee Protection Act) contains clauses related to the securitization of migration, such as provisions for condensing the security certificate protection procedure. These clauses were drafted before the terrorist attacks of 9/11, although the bill received Royal Assent on November 1, 2001 (Adelman 2002; Crépeau and Nakache 2006; Lyon 2006).

The attacks of 9/11 appear to have had a significant impact on the securitization of migration in Canada, though. In December 2001, Canada and the United States signed an agreement to tighten asylum procedures. Under the new procedures, foreigners will have to seek asylum in the first country they reach, thus ending the current pattern in which 60 percent of asylum seekers in Canada arrive from the United States. If a refugee claim is denied in the United States, Canada will also deny asylum. The agreement is credited with reducing the number of asylum seekers who crossed the U.S.–Canadian border and filed a refugee claim by 55 percent in 2005, according to a review of the Safe Third Country Agreement (Migration Dialogue 2002, 2005, 2007). The terrorist attacks also brought about, for instance, the creation of a new security agency, the Canadian Border Service Agency, of the

Canada–United States Smart Border Declaration, and of the Canadian Passenger Analysis Units—an advanced passenger information system to predetermine whether anyone on an air flight is cause for concern. Although several clauses of the Immigration and Refugee Protection Act were written before 9/11, the attacks undoubtedly gave an opportunity to harden the tone (Adelman 2004; Reitz 2004). The legislation "expedites the removal of people who are deemed to be security threats, imposes harsher penalties for migrant smuggling, and limits access to the Canadian refugee determination process" (Kruger *et al.* 2004: 77).

Furthermore, my evidence suggests that the linkage between migration and security became especially acute after 9/11 in several political agents' discourses. As we have seen in Chapter 4, Prime Minister Jean Chrétien did not hesitate to establish the linkage in his address during a special House of Commons debate in response to the terrorist attacks. The securitizing moves made by the Minister of Foreign Affairs also became acute after the attacks: immigration, security, terrorism, border controls, and security screening are fused into the same conceptual category in several of John Manley's speeches (2001a,b, 2002). Equally, Citizenship and Immigration Minister Elinor Caplan opted to send a strong message in one of the first speeches following 9/11: "Canadians are looking to us for reassurance that we can protect their health and safety, and the security of our society. I am proud to say that [the IPRA is a] very tough legislation for those who pose a threat to public security, and for those who do not respect our laws. . . . We will crack down on criminals and security threats" (Caplan 2001c). Throughout the months following 9/11, Caplan kept pushing for the securitization of migration. "In my own portfolio – immigration – we have acted quickly and firmly to deal with threats against the safety and security of Canada," she declared in November 2001 (Caplan 2001d). Her successor, Denis Coderre, also used the terrorist attacks as a rationale for the securitization of migration. He applauded security measures such as the introduction of immediate and in-depth security checks for refugee claimants, and the systematic fingerprinting and photographing of all refugee claimants.

I have also demonstrated that the terrorist attacks were responsible for shaking *La Presse*'s editorial position on the migration–security nexus while producing a profound turnaround in *The Globe and Mail*'s position. I have shown that, pre-9/11, *The Globe*'s editorialists saw the securitization of migration as unreasonable, unworthy, and creating a problem instead of offering a solution. In contrast, editorials post-9/11 were arguing that the securitization of migration was logical and reassuring, and that a wholesale rethinking of Canada's immigration laws was needed. Furthermore, evidence suggests that 9/11 did have a tremendous effect on the level of attention paid to migration by *The Globe and Mail*'s editorial team. *The Globe and Mail* published on average eleven editorials per year with migration as the main topic; about 45 percent of all their editorials in which migration was the main topic were written after the terrorist attacks. In comparison, *La Presse* published an average of nine editorials per year with migration as the main topic, *Le Figaro* published six, while *Le Monde* came in last with about four.

In France, my results suggest that the "9/11 effect" had a more limited impact. To be sure, an increase in restrictionist and repressive measures is observed: additional officers (about 750) were deployed to patrol France's borders, increased ID checks and forcible deportation occurred, and weekly charter flights were started in March 2003 to return illegal migrants. Similarly, the Sarkozy law, which increased the number of days that migrants could be held in detention from twelve to thirty-two days, was passed in 2003. The law also required applicants for three-month tourist visas to be fingerprinted—a measure that aimed to stop the practice of destroying documents after arrival, which made removal difficult because the identity of the migrant could not be proven (Migration Dialogue 2003).

However, the impact appears to be less significant in France than in Canada. Detailed analyses of France's immigration policy of the past decades reveal that no sign of major reversing policies were observed after 2001 and that no fundamental transformation has been undertaken (Hollifield 2004; Rudolph 2006). Also, the terrorist attacks had a limited impact on all political agents' speeches studied in my research. President Jacques Chirac, Prime Minister Lionel Jospin, and Interior Minister Sarkozy did not employ the terrorist attacks to push for the securitization of migration. Indeed, two months after 9/11, Chirac was stressing the elements of continuity in the assessment of France's national security. "The main threats to the security of France remain the same. They did not change," he declared in November 2001 (Chirac 2001a). Prime Minister Jospin not only made no securitizing attempt in his speech following 9/11 but also—and perhaps more importantly as it suggests a disconnection between immigration, 9/11, and security concerns—did not once mention the word "migration" or its derivatives (Jospin 2001). Likewise, even though Sarkozy made securitizing moves after 9/11, he did not justify them on the basis of the terrorist attacks, but rather in terms of domestic politics (such as delinquency and urban criminality) (Sarkozy 2002a,b, 2003).

Regarding the impact of 9/11 on editorialists of *Le Monde* and *Le Figaro*, I have shown that the attacks of September 11 are not the central event in the respective editorials with which migration is anchored in 2001 or 2002. Indeed, *Le Monde*'s editorialists rarely discussed the terrorist attacks in conjunction with migration in the weeks/months following the attacks. Similarly, the terrorist attacks of 9/11 have had almost no effect on *Le Figaro*'s editorialists: none of the securitizing moves made in 2001 and 2002 used the terrorist attacks as their rationale.

The important conclusion suggested by these results is that the impact of the terrorist attacks of September 11, 2001 on the migration–security nexus was interpreted in substantively different ways in Canada and in France. The terrorist attacks did not operate in an objective, deterministic way on the securitization of migration, as the securitization of migration is not simply an objective reaction to major external events. Rather, it is a continuously developing plan in which exogenous shocks such as 9/11 have to be read and interpreted as having security implications. Exogenous shocks acquire security meaning in the context of migration only if agents interpret these attacks accordingly. The attacks have certainly modulated several aspects of the securitization of migration and have served as a justification for many security practices touching migrants in Canada and to a lesser extent in France. In this way, the terrorist attacks have enabled securitizing agents to formulate securitizing moves—steps that the agents use to re-model immigration and security practices.

Regarding the question of variation between a weak securitization (Canada) and a strong securitization (France), the terrorist attacks of 9/11 appear to offer little guidance. To be sure, the effects of the attacks have been unequal: evidence suggests that they had a bigger impact in Canada than in France. As such, if 9/11 was a crucial factor explaining the variation of securitized migration, then we should observe a stronger securitized migration in Canada than in France. Yet we observe the opposite: a weak securitized migration in Canada and a strong securitized migration in France.

Domestic audiences

Electoral platforms

In Canada, there are no prominent anti-immigration political parties such as Jean-Marie Le Pen's Front National in France, the List Pim Fortuyn in the Netherlands, or Pauline Hanson's One Nation in Australia. Since 1945,[3] all parties have presented themselves to the electorate as supporting a selective immigration policy, largely based on the capacity—indeed the necessity—of the country to integrate immigrants without injury to a well-balanced economy. However, a significant change happened in the early 1990s, as major parties began to see migration through security lenses.

The Liberal Party of Canada has governed the country for forty-three of the last sixty years. Since 1945, the Liberals have been a major driving force in the pro-immigration camp in Canada's increasingly passionate debate about immigration. Despite this somewhat positive record on immigration, the party's establishment opted to prohibit "admission of people who pose a threat to public health, safety, order or national security" in their 1984 manifesto—an election that resulted in a debacle for the Liberals as their seat count fell from 135 to 40—a 95-seat loss, the worst performance in their history (The Liberal Party of Canada 1984). This particular position on immigration was somehow left out of the 1988 electoral platforms—a federal election that resulted in a second Progressive-Conservative majority government. In the red book *Creating Opportunity: The Liberal Plan of Canada* of 1993, the Liberal Party promises to pursue "strict enforcement of border controls to prevent false claimants from arriving in Canada" (The Liberal Party of Canada 1993: 13).

The electoral platforms of the Progressive-Conservative Party have remained silent on immigration issues for most of the second half of the twentieth century. Not once in all the federal elections since 1945 have the Conservatives linked migration and security in their manifestos. The only two electoral campaigns in which immigration was mentioned in the electoral platforms were in 1945 and 1957. In both, the party's position was cast in economic terms, that is, the selection of immigrants should be made in order to assure development of Canada's natural resources and to create employment.

The establishment of the Reform Party, a "spin-off" of the gradual collapse of the Progressive-Conservative Party in the late 1980s and early 1990s, worked toward the securitization of migration in the party electoral platform of 1993. While maintaining the Conservatives' focus on economic benefit for Canada as the primary criterion for the selection of immigrants, the Reform Party introduced new wording. For instance, the Reform Party would welcome "genuine" refugees—that is, refugees who qualified under the strict requirements of the UN Convention.[4] Furthermore, the Reform Party wanted to proceed to the "immediate deportation of bogus refugees and other illegal entrants" (The Reform Party of Canada 1993). In addition, the Constitution would have to be amended to ensure that the government could ultimately control entry into Canada; meanwhile, the "notwithstanding" provision of the Charter of Rights should be used to ensure such control. The Reform Party made a major breakthrough in 1993, inheriting nearly all of the Tories's support in the west (the party won all but four seats in Alberta and dominated British Columbia as well). In total, the Reform Party won fifty-two seats and came second across Canada with 18 percent of the popular vote. Its political power increased in the 1997 federal election, in which it won sixty seats and became the official opposition with nearly 20 percent of the popular vote.

The Reform's successor, the Canadian Alliance, kept most of the Reform Party's positions in the 2000 election, calling for immediate deportation of "bogus refugees and other illegal entrants" and promising to "severely penalize those who organize abuse of the system" (Canadian Alliance 2000).

Finally, the New Democratic Party, like its predecessor the Cooperative Commonwealth Federation, never made the linkage between migration and security. The NDP has endorsed, over the years, a "planned" immigration policy that would take into account several factors, such as employment opportunities, language training sessions, housing availability, and social services.

In a sharp contrast with the case of Canada, immigration has been a central issue in several French presidential elections.[5] In the 1974 presidential election, candidates from the major political parties—Valéry Giscard d'Estaing from the Independent Republicans-UFD and François Mitterand from the Socialist Party—touched on the question of immigration whereas Jean Marie Le Pen was silent on the subject. In the next electoral campaign for the presidency (1981), the platform of the Socialist Party did mention immigration in three of its 110 propositions: proposition 79 concerned the fight against discrimination; proposition 80 discussed the rights of immigrants and foreign workers; proposition 81 stated that the fight against clandestine traffic of immigrants would be strengthened (Weil 2005).

In the 1988 presidential election, the manifestos of all major candidates tackled the issue of immigration, albeit from a very different perspective. The manifesto of the First Secretary of the Socialist Party and incumbent President François Mitterand addressed the issue of immigrants mostly through a discussion of the Nationality Code. "We would honor ourselves by rendering the procedures [that a would-be immigrant has to fulfill] less humiliating: interminable waiting, rebuffs, excessive delays. I regret that the new citizen is welcomed in such a grimy way. I would prefer if they would be welcomed like a celebration, joyfully and solemnly, by the mayor where they live. We would breathe better in France" (Mitterand 1988). In contrast, the manifesto of the leader of the Rally for the Republic, Jacques Chirac, put the themes of security, criminality, and clandestine immigration at the forefront (Brechon 2002). In fact, the security–immigration nexus constituted one of the central points of the televised electoral debate between Mitterand and Chirac and certainly one of the central attacks of Chirac on Mitterand. "Concerning the question of immigration," Chirac strongly asserted, "we must stop it. Concerning clandestine immigration, we must fiercely fight against it. . . . Clandestine immigrants are by definition the natural pond of delinquents and even criminals; hence, we must expel them."[6] Finally, the manifesto of the Front National's candidate, Jean-Marie Le Pen, adopted a harsh security rhetoric on immigration.

In the first round of the 1995 presidential elections, the manifesto of Jean-Marie Le Pen unsurprisingly promised to stop immigration, to take seriously the "danger" threatening the nation and the people of France, and to expel a total of 3 million immigrants. The manifesto of the leader of the RPR, Jacques Chirac, and of the Socialist Party, Lionel Jospin, did not mention the question of immigration in either the first or second rounds. However, the theme of security, although absent in their respective platforms during the first round, was touched on by both candidates, but especially by Chirac in the second round.

Of course, the first round of the 2002 election came as a shock to many observers, almost all of whom had expected the second ballot to be between the incumbent President Chirac and the Socialist Jospin. However, Le Pen's unexpected appearance in the run-off election against Chirac did put the migration–security nexus at the forefront of the presidential campaign. The political platform of the Front National for the 2002 presidential election, *Pour un Avenir Français*, continued to put forward the overall ideology adopted in past years, which in the context of this study relates to the "expulsion of delinquent immigrants" and the cessation of the "immigration invasion." Furthermore, in the words of the general secretary of the Front National, Carl Lang, "integration [of immigrants] leads to national disintegration—that is, a multicultural, mosaicked, balkanized, and tribal France" (quoted in Brechon 2005: 37).

Pieces of legislation

In Canada, five pieces of legislation have considerable significance in the present context: Bills C-55, C-84, C-86, C-44, and the Immigration and Refugee Protection Act. Bill C-55, which came into effect in 1989, officially amended the *Immigration Act of 1976*. It provided a new structure and procedures for processing refugee claims; it also created an independent Immigration and Refugee Board. Also in 1989, Bill C-84 came into effect. It aimed to impose tougher immigration control measures, primarily directed at smugglers and illegal trafficking. Bill C-84, entitled the Refugee Deterrents and Detention Bill, introduced new detention measures, among them tougher criminal penalties for those who "smuggle" or aid the undocumented. The results of the vote in Parliament for both bills are telling in the context of this study. These bills were debated and passed through the House of Commons in 1986–1988. Bill C-55 passed on the third reading with 155 votes for and 48 against; Bill C-84 also passed on the third reading with 92 votes for and 52 against. However, the Senate amended them and they were both referred back to the House. In turn, the House of Commons did not accept all amendments and the bills died when Parliament was dissolved in 1988. The two bills were reintroduced in the subsequent parliament as Bill C-77. This bill was introduced, passed through all stages, and passed through the House of Commons in one day, June 14, 1990, without debate. It passed through the Senate without delay, and received Royal Assent on June 27, 1990. There were no recorded divisions for Bill C-77.

In 1992, the passage of Bill C-86 established tougher criteria for asylum, resettlement, and detention, including an expanded list of criteria by which an applicant might be determined inadmissible. The bill proposed revisions to the refugee determination system, mostly restrictive. The first-level screening process with the credible basis test was abandoned and "eligibility" determinations transferred in part to immigration officers. Other measures proposed were fingerprinting, harsher detention provisions, and making refugee hearings open to the public (these were amended as the bill passed through Parliament). New grounds of inadmissibility were added. The bill also included a provision requiring Convention refugees applying for landing in Canada to have a passport, valid travel document, or "other satisfactory identity document." Bill C-86, which "fundamentally altered the shape of immigration law" (Galloway 1997: 20), aimed at filling the perceived gaps in the existing legislation regarding migrants who threaten the security of Canada (Pratt 2005). The final vote in Parliament is a clear indication that an elite audience has facilitated the securitization of migration in Canada: the bill passed on the third reading with 115 in favor and 89 against.

Bill C-44, which was enacted in 1995, is clearly sensitive to concerns of national security. CIC's news release accompanying the legislation lists changes that the bill effected. One of them is that the bill "cancels the right of appeal to the Immigration Appeal Division by non permanent residents certified . . . to be a security risk" (quoted in Galloway 1997: 21). Bill C-44 sailed through Parliament with 152 votes for versus 84 votes against.

The last piece of legislation is the Immigration and Refugee Protection Act, which came into effect in June 2002. At the center of the IRPA are two bills. Bill C-31, tabled by then Minister Elinor Caplan on April 6, 2000, was intended to replace the 1976 Immigration Act, but the bill died when the November 2000 federal election was called. In February 2001, a slightly revised bill (Bill C-11) was introduced. This means that the core of what would become the IRPA, as well as most of the provisions, were in fact prepared and embedded in pieces of legislation well before the September 11 attacks. The IRPA presents a notable emphasis on security measures and illustrates the preoccupation with security, criminality and enforcement measures (Kruger *et al.* 2004; Pratt 2005). Like Bills

C-55, C-84, C-86, and C-44, the IRPA was passed with a comfortable majority: 135 in favor and 84 against.

In France, the repressive nature of the 1993 Pasqua law is well documented (Hollifield 2004; Rudolph 2006; Weil 2005). The Pasqua law sought, in the words of its architect, to "zero immigration" by seeing immigration primarily as a police matter and rolling back the rights of foreigners. As one of the leading specialists on France's immigration policy underscores, "equal protection and due process were denied to foreigners by cutting off possibilities of appeal for asylum seekers and by giving the police greater powers to detain and deport foreigners" (Hollifield 2004: 200). The Senate largely endorsed the law, voting with a proportion of 72 percent in favor. The National Assembly finally adopted the Pasqua law with a large majority: 480 votes for and 88 votes against. This means that 85 percent of the parliamentarians who took part in the vote were in favor of the Pasqua law.

On March 26, 1997, the new French immigration law, the Debré law, was approved by Parliament. The Debré law, designed to resolve the ambiguous status of some *sans-papiers*, proposes further draconian measures to limit the rights of foreigners in France as well as to crack down on illegal immigration. One of the provisions that received much attention concerns the requirement of all private citizens to notify local authorities whenever they received a non-European Union foreigner in their homes. Because of its Vichy-era similarity, the European Parliament passed a resolution condemning the Debré law. As for the Pasqua law, the Senate adopted the Debré law with a large majority (70 percent). National Assembly finally approved the Debré law with a majority (65 percent), but with significant modifications (most notably that foreigners themselves had to report their whereabouts to the authorities).

The recent law of February 2003—the Sarkozy law—focused mostly on security issues and aimed to reinforce measures against illegal migration and criminal phenomena tied to illegal migration. Among the most important provisions was the requirement for applicants for three-month tourist visas to be fingerprinted and the expansion of the number of days that foreigners could be held in detention from twelve to thirty-two days. The Sarkozy law was met with strong outcries and denouncements mostly from civil society groups and associations. However, the Senate adopted the law with nearly a 65 percent majority, and the National Assembly adopted the law with a show of hands.

Public opinion

Unfortunately, no poll has been conducted in Canada or France precisely on the question of the process of securitizing migration. In Canada, one way to tackle the question is to look at how Canadians perceive the number of immigrants accepted yearly, hypothesizing that if Canadians think migration is a security threat they will want to decrease this number. The Gallup poll has been asking the following question to Canadians since 1975: "If it were your job to plan an immigration policy for Canada at this time, would you be inclined to increase immigration, decrease immigration, or keep the number of immigrants at about the current level?"

As Figure 6.5 shows, nothing indicates that the Canadian mass audience perceives migration as a security concern. The only time that those who answered "decrease immigration" passed the threshold of 50 percent was during the economic recession of 1982. From 1991 to 1996, the level stays around 45 percent; after 1996, it falls to 40 percent of Canadian respondents wishing to decrease immigration.

One finding of this graph particularly worth emphasizing is the Canadian response after the terrorist attacks of September 11, 2001. Indeed, the lowest point in the proportion of Canadian respondents supporting a decrease in the number of immigrants in the last thirty years is after 9/11, in 2005, with 27 percent. This result suggests once again that the securitization of migration is not merely a function of objective reactions to material factors and exogenous shocks. Even one of the most influential events in the last decade did not operate in some objective way; 9/11 had to be interpreted and rendered meaningful along the migration–security nexus in order for the social construction of the securitization of migration to take place.

Canadian respondents remain hesitant to see migration as an existential threat, even when the question is framed in a more negative way. In the past decades, several pollsters have asked Canadians whether the government of Canada was letting in "too many immigrants." The results are consistent with the aforementioned

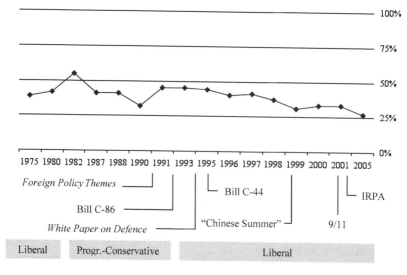

Figure 6.5 Percentage of Canadians supporting a decrease in the number of immigrants, 1975–2005. "Chinese Summer" refers to the arrival of four boats of Chinese would-be immigrants to British Columbia's shores; the grey horizontal line indicates which political party was in power (for the sake of simplicity I have omitted the Clark minority government—Progressive-Conservative—in power from June 1979 to March 1980). IRPA, Immigration and Refugee Protection Act.

Sources: Adapted from Reitz (2004), Gallup (2005).

findings. The only time in thirteen years that a majority of Canadian respondents have answered that Canada was letting in "too many immigrants" was in 1994 with 53 percent, as Figure 6.6 shows. The second lowest point between 1989 and 2002 is after the so-called "Chinese Summer of 1999," with 33 percent.

Mass audience was a particularly important limiting factor in the years 2000, 2001, and 2002, as Figure 6.7 shows. We have seen in Chapter 4 that a considerable proportion of securitizing moves made by the Prime Minister, the Minister of Foreign Affairs, and the Minister of Citizenship and Immigration were actually made in these three years. "We are facing new and complex security threats: including illegal migration, crime, terrorism, disease [. . .]," declared John Manley, Minister of Foreign Affairs, in October 2000 (Manley 2000). Citizenship and Immigration Minister Caplan was equally clear in January 2000: "We have had to adapt to this new phenomenon of sudden mass arrivals seeking to evade our detection. As always, [our fundamental] objectives include protecting the safety, security and health of Canadians" (Caplan 2000d). In April of the same year, she added that provisions for detention will be strengthened and that "front-end security screening and background checks will be initiated for all refugee claimants as soon as a protection claim is submitted" (Caplan 2000a). Yet the proportion of those agreeing that Canada is letting in "too many immigrants" dropped to 30 percent in these three years.

Hence, evidence suggests that the power of the Canadian mass audience has not been merely in approving securitizing agents' moves, as ST currently posits. The role of the Canadian mass audience has been more complex than that, and one feature of that complex role is that of a constraining force throughout the years that my study covers.

In France, the situation is strikingly different. Already in 1984, 58 percent of respondents answered that there were "too many immigrants" in France, as Figure 6.8 shows.[7] The anti-immigrant sentiment reached a record high of 78 percent in 1993. An average of 64 percent of French respondents answered that there were too many immigrants in France between 1984 and 2005. The percentage of French respondents answering that there were too many immigrants never dropped below 58 percent for the time period that this study covers.

The sharp difference between Canada and France is made even clearer when securitizing moves made by French political agents are juxtaposed with the proportion of French people agreeing that there are "too many immigrants" in France, as Figure 6.9 shows. When the number of securitizing moves made by political agents reached a record high of thirty in 1993, the anti-immigrant feeling reached a record high, with 78 percent answering that there were too many immigrants in France.

These polls have been asking Canadians and French people the same questions over the last two decades; they represent robust evidence. They not only permit us to control for the effect of idiosyncratic events on public opinion, such as the 1999 arrival of the refugee boats in Canada, but also give a clear indication of the evolution of Canadian and French public opinion on the issue. Furthermore, a comparative analysis of these polls highlights that, although Canadian respondents advocating a decrease in immigration in 1991 were more numerous than in

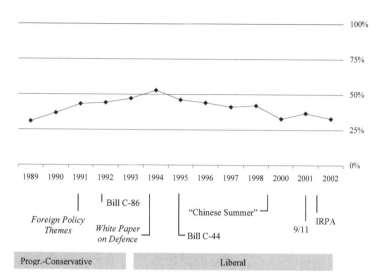

Figure 6.6 Percentage of Canadians agreeing that Canada is letting in "too many immigrants," 1989–2002.

Sources: Angus Reid/Southam News, Longwoods International Inc, Ekos, Leger Marketing, CIC, Environics, Angus Reid.

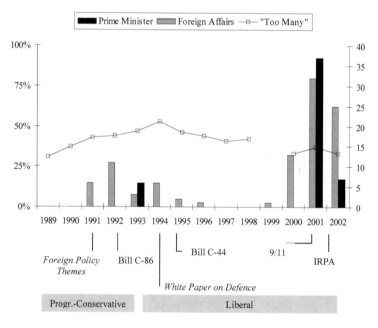

Figure 6.7 Political agents' securitizing moves and the percentage of Canadians agreeing that Canada is letting in "too many immigrants," 1989–2002.

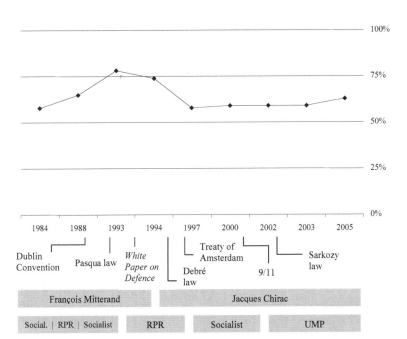

Figure 6.8 Percentage of French people agreeing that there are "too many immigrants" in France, 1984–2005.

Sources: Sofres (1996, 1998); TNS-Sofres (2006).

Note: The upper grey horizontal line indicates who the President was at a particular point in time; the lower grey horizontal line indicates which political party was controlling the government. RPR, Rally for the Republic; UMP, Union for Popular Movement.

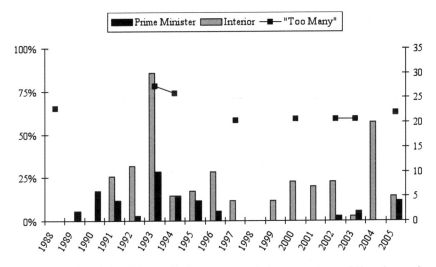

Figure 6.9 Political agents' securitizing moves and the percentage of French people agreeing that there are "too many immigrants" in France, 1989–2005.

previous years, they still represented a minority, whereas in France nearly four out of five respondents agreed that there were too many immigrants in 1993. These polls also underscore the enduring continuity in Canadian and French attitudes toward immigration. Whereas an average of 39 percent of Canadian respondents answered that they wanted to decrease immigration between 1975 and 2005, an average of 64 percent of French respondents answered that there were too many immigrants in France between 1984 and 2005.

Seen through the prism of a constructivist understanding of power, these polls suggest that the Canadian mass audience has been reluctant to see migration as an existential security threat and, consequently, has been a constraining factor in the process of securitizing migration. In France, evidence suggests that the mass audience has been an inducing force in the securitization process throughout the years that my study covers.

Even more, this strong cultural factor finds an echo in other vectors of public opinion in Canada and France. A series of polls conducted in 1989 showed that most Canadians felt that immigrants make a positive contribution to Canada's economy and culture (Malarek 1990). By the end of the 1990s the positive sentiment toward immigrants was even stronger. When Canadians were asked whether they agreed or disagreed with the statement "Immigration has a positive impact on Canada," a clear majority of respondents agreed with the statement. Whereas more than 65 percent of respondents agreed with the statement in 1997, this increased by more than 10 percent three years later to reach 77 percent, as Table 6.1 shows. Furthermore, this additional 12 percent was added to the vast majority in the category "strongly agree," at the same time reducing the percentage of respondents who "strongly disagree" to less than 4 percent in 2000. In 2006, an international Ipsos MORI study confirmed Canadians' positive attitudes toward immigration. To the question, "Overall, would you say immigrants are having a good or bad influence on the way things are going in [Canada]?," a solid 75 percent answered that immigrants have an overall positive influence on the country (Adams 2007).

In addition, Canadians remain strikingly consistent in their views of immigration's impact on Canadian culture. In 1991, 63 percent of Canadian respondents said that the fact that there are people from different races in Canada adds to what is good about Canada; in 2004 and 2005, the majority of Canadians also felt that the presence of immigrants in Canada from several cultures serves to strengthen Canadian culture (*The Globe and Mail* 1991). Indeed, in 2004, to the

Table 6.1 Canadians and the contribution of immigrants

	Immigration has a positive impact on Canada (%)			
	Strongly agree	*Agree*	*Disagree*	*Strongly disagree*
1997	15	52	16.1	6.2
2000	26	50.6	12.1	3.7

Sources: CROP (1997, 2000).

question "Does the fact that we accept immigrants from many different cultures make our culture stronger or weaker?," 61 percent of Canadians respondents said that immigrants from many different cultures make Canadian culture stronger (Ipsos-Reid 2006).

By contrast, in France, a public opinion poll commissioned in 1990 as part of an investigation launched by Prime Minister Michel Rocard's office concluded that the French were becoming increasingly intolerant of ethnic minorities. According to the poll, 76 percent of French respondents thought that there were too many Arabs living in France. In total, 39 percent of those surveyed openly said that they did not like the Arab immigrants; 24 percent of those surveyed thought that there were too many Jews as well. In April 1990, a new opinion survey showed that an overwhelming majority of respondents (85 percent) thought that the country had reached what President Mitterand once called "*le seuil de tolérance*"—the saturation point—beyond which welcoming more immigrants was no longer possible or acceptable (Morier 1990; Reuter 1990).

In another poll by Sofres conducted in August 1991 Jean-Marie Le Pen (leader of the hard-line Front National) came first (22 percent of respondents) among the politicians "who propose [a] satisfactory solution to the problem of immigration," an increase of 7 percent from 1985 (*Le Monde* 1991). Similarly, Le Pen's ideas on immigration also hit a record high of approval in 1991. Asked the question, "Do you approve or disapprove of Le Pen's positions on immigrants," 38 percent of French respondents approved his ideas. As Figure 6.10 shows, this represented a gain of 14 percent from 1988.

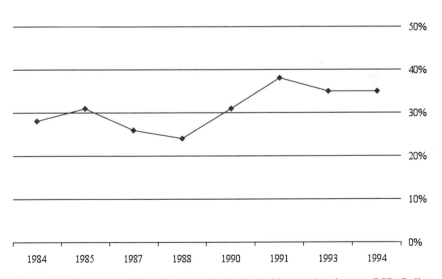

Figure 6.10 Percentage of French approving Le Pen's ideas on immigrants. RPR, Rally for the Republic.

Sources: Sofres (1996, 1998); TNS-Sofres (2006).

A poll conducted in 1992 to assess Mitterand's presidency, which was celebrating its tenth anniversary, confirmed French opinion on the topic. To the question, "According to you, what was [Mitterand's] biggest failure?," the rise in the number of immigrants came second (41 percent), after the rise of unemployment (49 percent).

Tellingly, the French concerns about the movement of people are not a function of fear of unemployment or the loss of a job for a "Frenchman." Rather, concerns are framed as fear of the loss of national identity, as Table 6.2 shows. In 1989, nearly three out of four French citizens feared that France would lose its national identity if immigration was not limited. In 1993, 67 percent thought the same. Furthermore, almost half of French respondents agreed in 2005 with the statement, "We don't feel at home anymore in France," a increase of 4 percent from 2003 (Sofres 1996, 1998; TNS-Sofres 2006).

Differences between Canada and France can also be observed when the two countries are directly compared—that is, when a public opinion poll has asked the same question across countries. For instance, Canadians sees immigrants' impact on their society and culture in a much more positive light than their French counterparts. A total of 67 percent of Canadian respondents answered "yes" to the question "Do immigrants improve your society by bringing new ideas and cultures?" compared with 41 percent of French respondents (Carleton University Survey, in Jedwab 2006). Perhaps the most striking finding is the percentage of those who disagreed with the statement: at 34 percent, French respondents who disagreed were nearly three times as many as their Canadian respondents (12 percent). Additionally, 52 percent of French respondents, just over half, said that it is better if almost everyone in a country shares the same customs and traditions (Associated Press-Ipsos-Reid, 2004). These results suggest that international

Table 6.2 French attitudes toward national identity and safety

If something isn't done to limit the number of immigrants, France risks losing its national identity (%)

	Agree	*Disagree*	*Don't know*
1985	68	27	5
1989	74	24	2
1993	67	32	1

In areas where there are many immigrants, one doesn't feel safe (%)

	Agree	*Disagree*	*Don't know*
1985	75	17	8
1989	69	23	8
1993	75	17	8

Source: Lynch and Simon (2003).

migration does not by itself threaten collective identity and national security. Rather, the movement of people has to be socially constructed and understood as having security implications for international migration to have security consequences.

When the crime vector is factored in, the difference between Canada and France is striking; compared with the French, Canadians reject associating immigrants with negative stereotypes. Table 6.3 underscores that Canada came first among several countries in rejecting the statement that immigrants increase crime rates. Whereas almost 50 percent of French respondents agreed that immigrants increase crime rates, only 27 percent of Canadian respondents concurred with the link between crime and migration.

Moreover, a poll of nine Western countries published in May 2004 by Ipsos-Public Affairs also underscored the difference in attitudes toward immigration. In the United States and in the European countries polled—France, Britain, Germany, Italy, and Spain—people were more likely to have negative views of the influence of immigrants. More than half of French respondents, 53 percent, said that immigrants are a bad influence on their country. Of the nine countries polled, only the Canadians had a positive view of the influence of immigrants; almost two-thirds of Canadian respondents, 73 percent, said that immigrants are a very good or somewhat good influence (Associated Press-Ipsos-Reid 2004).

Table 6.3 Perception of the link between crime and migration

Do immigrants increase crime rates?

	Agree (%)
Canada	27
United States	27
Great Britain	40
France	44

Generally, do you think that immigrants are more likely to be involved in criminal activity than people born here or less likely, or isn't there much difference?

	More likely (%)
Italy	41
Germany	35
France	26
Great Britain	25
Australia	22
United States	19
Canada	15

Sources: Carleton University Survey in Jedwab (2006); Ipsos-MORI (2006).

Does a popular/mass audience constrain or induce the securitization of migration? Findings suggest that the mass audience in Canada, by systematically and repeatedly not seeing migration as an existential threat throughout the years that my study covers, has been a constraining force in the securitization process. Between 1989 and 2005, the proportion of Canadians wishing to decrease the level of intake of immigrants never passed the threshold of 50 percent. The lowest point in the last thirty years was after 9/11, in 2005, with 27 percent of Canadians wishing to decrease the level of intake of immigrants. The Canadian mass audience feels that the presence of immigrants from different cultural backgrounds in Canada serves to strengthen Canadian culture rather than representing an existential threat to Canadian cultural identity. On the other hand, the French mass audience, in systematically and repeatedly seeing migration as an existential threat throughout the years that my study covers, appears to have been an inducing force in the process of securitizing migration. An average of 64 percent of French respondents answered that there were too many immigrants in France between 1984 and 2005. The anti-immigrant tendency reached a record high of 78 percent in 1993. In 1991, 38 percent of French respondents approved extreme-right leader Jean-Marie Le Pen's ideas on immigration. Two out of three French citizens feared that France would lose its national identity if immigration was not limited. In 2005, almost half of French respondents felt that they "do not feel at home anymore in France."

As such, evidence suggests that a mass audience offers useful guiding principles to account for the variation in levels of securitized migration between a weakly securitized migration (Canada) and a strongly securitized migration (France). To be sure, detailed process tracing of the deliberations of politicians would be necessary to prove more definitively the role that public opinion on immigration played in discouraging or encouraging securitizing attempts, but the results here certainly suggest that the public audience has been more of a limiting factor for the securitization of immigration in Canada than in France.

Conclusion

In the search to better understand the process of securitizing international migration in Canada and France, this chapter has found some answers. The magnitude of the "refugee crisis" in the early 1990s, as well as the powerful image of massive flow and potential spillover that it carries, were vectors of anxiety and apprehension in the particular context of this study. The attacks of 9/11 appear to have had a significant impact on the securitization of migration in Canada and a more limited impact in France. Both exogenous shocks have offered securitizing agents "windows of action" to pursue their objectives of securitizing migration. Some agents have chosen to interpret these contextual factors as having security implications; others have been more reluctant to do so. However, these two exogenous shocks, despite being important social constituents of the securitization process, have not provided convincing guiding principles to account for the variation in levels of securitized migration found between my two cases.

My study of domestic audiences appears to be useful in this context. My analysis of electoral platforms as a site of an elite audience's involvement in the process of securitizing migration suggests that elite audiences constitute a social constituent of the securitization process in both Canada and France. Although no Canadian political parties have made immigration their leitmotif in an electoral campaign, the early 1990s saw a rupture nevertheless. In France, although the Socialist Party under the leadership of Mitterand mostly refrained from perceiving migration as a security threat, Chirac's political party tapped into the linkage between migration and security as one of its electoral leitmotifs. An analysis of important pieces of legislature also suggests that elite audiences in both Canada and France have enabled and facilitated the securitization of migration. In Canada, some pieces of legislation were passed without debate whereas others obtained an overwhelming Parliamentary majority. None came close to being defeated. The situation is quite similar in France. All three important pieces of legislation for this study sailed through Parliament. In addition, the mass audience appears to have been a constraining and a facilitating force in the securitization process in both Canada and France. A host of public opinion polls show that Canada's mass audience has been reluctant to see the movement of people predominantly as a security concern; it also demonstrates that the mass audience has behaved in a consistent way throughout the years that this study covers. On the contrary, several public opinion measures show that France's mass audience has seen migration through security lenses; polls also show that the mass audience has done so continually between 1989 and 2005.

This chapter directly speaks to Barnett and Duvall's (2005) argument that power should be understood in terms of the *kinds* of social relations through which power works and the *specificity* of social relations through which power's effects are produced. Regarding the former dimension, this chapter underlines how structural/contextual factors are empowered in the process of securitizing migration. In particular, I have shown the enabling and constraining power capability of the so-called "refugee crisis," the terrorist attacks of 9/11, and domestic audiences in the securitization process. Regarding the latter dimension, my study underlines that power operates through diffuse processes embedded in the historically contingent and multifaceted cultural settings. In particular, I have demonstrated that the power of contextual factors within the securitization process does not function in a binary, direct, and almost mechanical way (contra ST). The power of audience, to take one example, is not merely to "approve" or "disapprove" of securitizing agents' moves. Rather, this chapter has established that the power of contextual factors works in a diffuse yet tangible way and within a continuum of power ranging from enabling to constraining capacities.

Evidence amassed in my study which suggests that audiences offer useful guiding principles to account for the variation in levels of securitized migration between a weakly securitized migration (Canada) and a strongly securitized migration (France) does not deny the existence of other hypotheses. I am not arguing that domestic audience is the sole determinant of the variation in levels of securitized migration. Rather, my goal in this chapter was to inductively gain a better understanding of several structural/contextual factors in the process of securitizing international migration. Seen in this light, the analytical framework for studying the securitization process that I propose speaks to the embedded liberalism model developed in migration studies (Guiraudon 2000b; Guiraudon and Joppke 2001; Hollifield 1992, 2000; Joppke 1998, 2001). To be sure, we are not asking the same question. I seek to gain a better understanding of the process by which an issue—here international migration—enters the realm of security, whereas the embedded liberalism model seeks to explain why states cannot move freely in adopting restrictionist migration policy. Yet, my stress on contextual factors as a site of potential explanation for the variation in levels of securitized migration is compatible with the embedded liberalism model. Emphasizing the role of ideational and legal-domestic factors, the embedded liberalism model argues that liberal ideas and domestic courts act in various ways as a constraint on states' intentions to adopt restrictionist policies. By extension, the embedded liberalism model's findings obtained in the context of the debate on controlling the migration flow would suggest that legal-domestic courts could have constraining powers in the process of securitizing migration in liberal states, although the role and influence of courts in the matter of national security might be less clear than in issues of family reunification and refugees policies. This would echo my argument that contextual factors can have constraining powers in the securitization process.

However, my analytical framework indirectly challenges the liberalism model's understanding of the relationship between securitizing agents and contextual factors in that it highlights that the liberal model looks only at factors that act as a constraining force. Indeed, by underscoring factors limiting states' intentions, the embedded liberalism model tends to see only half of the story. By contrast, my emphasis on the dual powers of contextual factors allows for the study of contextual factors that constrain agents and of contextual factors that enable agents. It is important that an analytical framework for the study of the securitization process contains theoretical and empirical space to investigate factors inducing the process as well as factors limiting the process. My findings suggest that mass audiences have been a constraining force in one context and a facilitating force in another context, and that they have systematically acted in this way throughout the years that my study covers. Seen in this way, further research on the interconnections between my findings and the embedded liberalism model would be a relevant follow-up project and, potentially, a welcome contribution to both migration studies and securitization research.

7   Conclusion

Movement and order: contributions to the field

This book is about the process of integrating, discursively and institutionally, the international movement of people into security frameworks that emphasize policing and defense. This study of the securitization process reveals the values of a constructivist perspective in trying to refine Securitization Theory (ST). I do not want to suggest that ST should find its "home" in constructivism or to propose that the analytical framework developed in this book should stand in opposition to ST. Rather, my aim is to demonstrate that constructivism offers useful correctives to ST and that these correctives can be integrated within ST without distorting the theory.

My study makes three theoretical contributions to the securitization research literature. First, I argue that a constructivist approach stressing the importance of multifaceted contexts and the mutual constitution of agents and structural/contextual factors is useful. My analytical framework understands the relationship between agents and contextual factors as mutually constituted, durable but not static, generative, and structured. Doing so renders possible the inclusion of time in the framework by opting to use, to borrow a forceful image from Paul Pierson (2004), a "moving pictures" approach to the phenomenon of securitized migration instead of taking merely a "snapshot" view of the phenomenon.

Second, I integrate a polymorphous understanding of power into the analytical framework in postulating that power operates through diffuse processes embedded in the historically contingent and multifaceted cultural settings, and within a continuum of power ranging from enabling to constraining capacities. I contend that ST's understanding of power—which sees the power of agents merely in terms of their *ability to convince* the audience and the power of the audience only in terms of its *capacity to approve* agents' securitizing moves—does not match the complexity of contemporary social dynamics of security. In contrast, I argue that power operates through diffuse processes embedded in the historically contingent and multifaceted cultural settings, and within a continuum of power ranging from enabling to constraining capacities.

Third, my analytical framework, in understanding security as a continuum, possess the theoretical space to address the question of levels of securitized migration. The issue of variation in levels is particularly problematic for ST because ST treats security as a binary notion, and consequently, cannot recognize levels of securitized migration or provide adequate guidance for the suggestion of hypotheses explaining the variations. In contrast, I propose empirical measurements and "thick" descriptions of levels or intensities of the securitization of migration across time and across cases—as I have shown in Chapter 2, although the securitization of migration can be observed in both Canada and France, a considerable variation in the level of securitization exists. I further suggest that contextual factors, particularly domestic audiences, are a site of potential explanation for the variation in levels of securitized migration.

The findings amassed in the previous chapters underline this set of arguments and make steps in gaining a better understanding of the pattern of engagement of several agents and contextual factors with the phenomenon of securitized migration.

In Canada, my investigation reveals that the role of the Minister of Foreign Affairs has been paramount in initiating the securitization process. Barbara McDougall made numerous and repeated securitizing moves in the crucial year of 1991, as well as in 1992 and 1993. Several years later, John Manley and Bill Graham repeatedly and fervently made several securitizing moves in the context of migration. Although the securitization of migration could hardly have occurred without the Prime Minister's engagement or tacit accord, my findings suggest that the Prime Minister has participated only in an active way, and for a short period of time, in the securitization process after the terrorist attacks of September 11, 2001. Finally, from Caplan onward, Ministers of Citizenship and Immigration have all been important agents in the securitization process, as Figure 7.1 summarizes.

In France, Ministers of the Interior have been without doubt central players in the securitization of migration. Ministers of the Interior have made 60 percent of all securitizing moves in the context of migration. Ministers Philippe Marchand, Charles Pasqua, Jean-Louis Debré, and Nicolas Sarkozy have been the most influential in the securitization process. Prime Minister Michel Rocard was already making securitizing moves in 1989, thereby setting in motion the securitization process. As well, Prime Minister Édouard Balladur appears to have been an important securitizing agent in the context of migration. Although he has not actively and directly participated in the process, President Jacques Chirac made several securitizing attempts in the context of migration in the first two years of his first presidential mandate, and shortly after the terrorist attacks of September 11, 2001, which has given him a role in the context of this study. Finally, no French Minister of Foreign Affairs has been an important agent in the securitization of migration, as Figure 7.2 shows.

My study of the role of editorialists in the securitization of international migration highlights some counterintuitive conclusions. My analysis of editorialists of *The Globe and Mail* establishes that in the first few years that this study covers they did not understand and perceive international migration as a threat to Canada's national security and collective identity. However, it is not as if editorialists had no interest in migration issues or no opportunity to induce them to formulate securitizing moves, as we have seen. My investigation also demonstrates that the

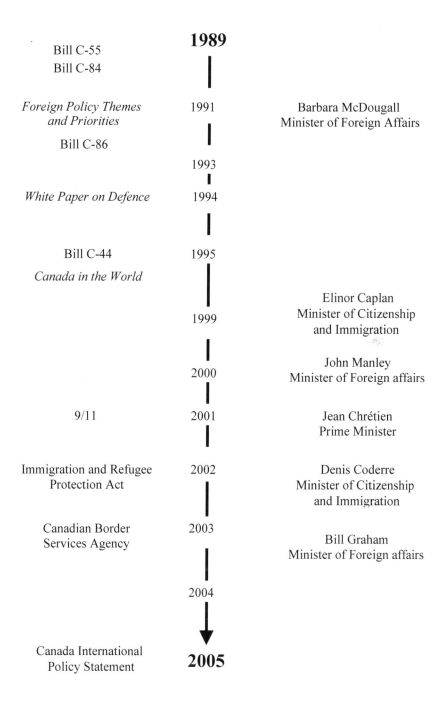

	1989	
Bill C-55		
Bill C-84		
Foreign Policy Themes *and Priorities*	1991	Barbara McDougall Minister of Foreign Affairs
Bill C-86		
	1993	
White Paper on Defence	1994	
Bill C-44	1995	
Canada in the World		
	1999	Elinor Caplan Minister of Citizenship and Immigration
	2000	John Manley Minister of Foreign affairs
9/11	2001	Jean Chrétien Prime Minister
Immigration and Refugee Protection Act	2002	Denis Coderre Minister of Citizenship and Immigration
Canadian Border Services Agency	2003	Bill Graham Minister of Foreign affairs
	2004	
Canada International Policy Statement	**2005**	

Figure 7.1 Securitized migration and the role of principal political agents, Canada, 1989–2005.

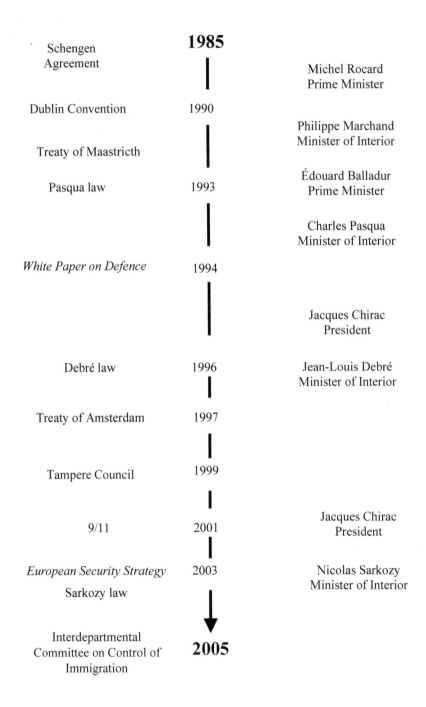

	1985	
Schengen Agreement		
	$\vert$	Michel Rocard Prime Minister
Dublin Convention	1990	
	$\vert$	Philippe Marchand Minister of Interior
Treaty of Maastricth		
		Édouard Balladur
Pasqua law	1993	Prime Minister
	$\vert$	Charles Pasqua Minister of Interior
White Paper on Defence	1994	
		Jacques Chirac President
Debré law	1996	Jean-Louis Debré Minister of Interior
Treaty of Amsterdam	1997	
Tampere Council	1999	
9/11	2001	Jacques Chirac President
European Security Strategy Sarkozy law	2003	Nicolas Sarkozy Minister of Interior
Interdepartmental Committee on Control of Immigration	**2005**	

Figure 7.2 Securitized migration and the role of principal political agents, France, 1985–2005.

terrorist attacks of 9/11 constituted the source of a profound rupture—if not a complete contradiction—in the way that the editorialists saw the movement of people. My investigation of *La Presse*'s editorials reveals that editorialists generally rejected the securitization of migration between 1989 and 2005.

In France, my analysis of *Le Monde*'s editorials demonstrates that this particular media agent was not a significant securitizing agent in the context of migration. Not only was migration not understood to be an existential threat to France's cultural identity for the entire period under study, but also the terrorist attacks of 9/11 also provoked no significant change in the position of editorialists of *Le Monde*. My analysis also shows that this was an altogether different picture in the case of *Le Figaro*. Editorialists of *Le Figaro* systematically and repeatedly made several securitizing moves throughout the years that my study covers.

My analysis of contextual factors in the securitization of migration in Canada and in France also reveals important insights. Both the image of "massive flow" and "potential spillover" associated with the rise in the proportion of refugees accepted by Western countries and the terrorist attacks of 9/11 have been important contextual factors in the securitization process. Both exogenous shocks offered securitizing agents "windows of action" to pursue their objectives of securitizing migration. Evidence suggests, however, that neither the "refugee crisis" nor the terrorist attacks of 9/11 offers guidance in explaining the variation in the levels of securitized migration.

My study of electoral platforms and pieces of legislation as sites of the elite audience's involvement in the process of securitizing migration suggests that the elite audience constitutes a social constituent of the securitization process in both Canada and France. Although no Canadian political parties have made immigration their leitmotif in an electoral campaign, the early 1990s saw a rupture nevertheless. The two biggest political parties started to link migration and security in their manifestos. In France, although the Socialist Party under the leadership of Mitterand mostly refrained from perceiving migration as a security threat, Chirac's political party, from the 1988 election onward, tapped into the linkage between migration and security as part of its electoral leitmotif. An investigation of important pieces of legislation also suggests that elite audiences in both Canada and France have enabled and facilitated the securitization of migration. In Canada, five pieces of legislation have had considerable impact in the present context: Bills C-55, C-84, C-86, C-44, and the Immigration and Refugee Protection Act. Some pieces of legislation were passed without debate whereas others obtained an overwhelming Parliamentary majority. None came close to being defeated. In France, the Pasqua law, the Debré law, and the Sarkozy law sailed through Parliament.

With regard to popular/mass audiences, my findings suggest that the mass audience in Canada has been a constraining force in the securitization process, whereas the mass audience in France has been a facilitating force in the process of securitizing migration. A host of public opinion polls show that Canada's mass audience has indeed been reluctant to see the movement of people predominantly as a security concern. These polls also demonstrate that the mass audience has behaved in a consistent way throughout the years that this study covers. On the contrary, several public opinion polls show that France's mass audience has largely facilitated the securitization process, and that it did so continually between 1989 and 2005. Evidence amassed in my study suggests that, when the mass audience represents a relatively constant constraining and limiting force on agents' securitizing moves, as in Canada, the outcome is a weak securitization. When the mass audience represents an enabling and facilitating force on agents' securitizing moves, as in France, the outcome is a strong securitization.

The politicization and the securitization of migration

My emphasis in this book was on the securitization of migration and not on the politicization of migration. Politicization of migration refers here to the process of taking an issue *out* of restricted networks and/or bureaucracies and bringing the issue *into* the public arena (Guiraudon 1998; Huysmans 2006). Defined as such, the politicization of migration is a neutral process. It encompasses both the positive and the negative points of view on the issue, even though anti-immigration political actors have been keen to voice their message in a particularly strong way in recent years.

In the context of this study, the distinction between the politicization and the securitization of migration is an important one for several reasons. A politicization of migration does not necessarily equate with a securitization of migration; an agent can politicize an issue without securitizing it. When the Prime Minister of Canada stresses the benefits of multiculturalism as an umbrella policy for immigration, he is making a politicizing move, albeit with positive overtones. When the Minister of Citizenship and Immigration highlights the contribution of immigrants to Canadian history and cultural identity, she is positively politicizing migration. Along the same lines, it is one thing to question the efficiency of the refugee recognition process, the overconcentration of migrants in large urban agglomerations, refugee adjudication, the adequacy of settlement services, and the failure to recognize overseas professional credentials. It is an altogether different thing to declare that migration is a national security threat.

Nonetheless, critics might indeed argue that my indicators of a securitized migration developed in Chapter 2 leave out the fact that immigrants have increasingly become the subjects of harsh political discourses and are singled out as convenient scapegoats for political parties wanting to offer an image of robustness and control. Still, I argue that the evidence amassed here underscores the validity and necessity of distinguishing between politicization and securitization. My quantitative results demonstrate, for example, that Canada's Prime Ministers have markedly politicized the issue of migration in the years that my study covers. Among the migratory questions touched on by Prime Minister Chrétien are the category of immigrants accepted, multiculturalism, and the positive contribution of immigrants to Canadian society—to name just a few. The key point, however, is that Chrétien's focus on migration does not always translate into securitizing moves. A telling example is Chrétien's series of speeches following the arrival of almost 600 would-be Chinese immigrants near Vancouver in 1999. The arrival, and the media coverage that it produced, could have easily induced bold statements to the effect that mass migration was disturbing Canada's security. Notwithstanding, Chrétien made no declaration of that nature.

In addition, a detailed content analysis of the complete set of political agents' speeches underlines the benefit of distinguishing between politicization and securitization. There were a limited number of powerful speeches using immigrants as scapegoats for social problems. These speeches are especially rare in the case of Canada; in France, they are almost limited to Charles Pasqua and Jean-Louis Debré. In fact, harsh rhetoric about immigration seems to be the political turf of leaders of the opposition in Canada (e.g. the Reform Party), and, in the case of France, of leaders of far-right political parties (e.g. Jean-Marie Le Pen and Philippe de Villiers). Actually, this might be a logical consequence of the politicization of migration. As Guiraudon (1998) and Huysmans (2006) highlight, bringing an issue into the public arena, that is, politicizing an issue, allows the participation of political agents, especially leaders of far-right political parties.

Furthermore, my study of media agents is helpful in looking at the politicization/securitization debate. Between 1989 and 2005, *The Globe and Mail* has published on average more than ten editorials per year with migration as the main topic. Among the migratory issues discussed in these editorials are the discretionary power of the Minister, immigration and refugee selection, the economic contribution of immigrants, and the "Chinese Summer." Yet *The Globe and Mail* made no securitizing moves in these crucial years. We also have seen that some of *La Presse*'s editorialists have strongly politicized the issue of the refugee determination process. In particular, Dubuc has contended that refugee advocacy groups are responsible for portraying Canada as a closed and unjust country and has asked whether it is normal that an accepted refugee become automatically an immigrant when the right of asylum is temporary and should stop when the situation in the home country goes back to normal. Undoubtedly, this is a strong politicization of migration. Yet, no securitizing moves were made.

The logic of exception and the logic of unease

In constructivist security studies, two logics of security are emerging: the logic of exception and the logic of unease. The logic of exception, best represented by ST, focuses on speech acts legitimizing exceptional policies and practices in the face of a security threat. Building on Carl Schmitt's (1985 [1922], 1996 [1932]) and Giorgio Agamben's (1998, 2005) notion of the state of exception, this logic postulates that security is about the fight against an existential threat that necessitates exceptional measures (Buzan *et al.* 1998; Doty 2007; Landau 2006; Wæver 2009; Williams 2003). The logic of unease, building on Michel Foucault's systems of thought, sees securitization as a process of establishing and inscribing meaning through practices of professionals of security. It proposes an understanding of securitization as routine practices of bureaucracies and security professionals in which technology and technocratic practices come to hold a prominent place.

It identifies an overarching system of unease and insecurity that contributes to a governmentality of unease (Aradau and van Munster 2007; Bigo 1992, 2002; Bigo and Tsoukala 2008; Ceyhan and Tsoukala 2002; Doucet and de Larrinaga 2010; Walters 2002).

Against the current standpoint in the literature to understand the two logics as opposing and competing models, I argue that scholars should refrain from seeing the two logics as competing views of the securitization process. In fact, it is not clear that they can compete, for it is not clear that they are mutually exclusive. I contend that presenting the two logics as regulated by a zero-sum game in which scholars have to prove the predominance of one logic over the other, or seeking to incorporate central elements of a logic into the framework of another logic, limits more than it reveals.

In fact, the parameters of both logics are relatively well known and well documented—both in theoretical and empirical terms. What is needed at this point is research on the complementarity and/or on the simultaneity of the two logics. The usefulness of seeing the logic of exception and the logic of unease as complementary ones rather than competing ones would not only move the scholarship away from potential contradictions but also put the emphasis on the dynamic and multifaceted relationship between the two logics.

Furthermore, my results show that both logics of security are present in Canada and in France, suggesting in fact that the two logics might be cohabiting. Indeed, my findings show that, although the logic of exception has been primarily at play in Canada, elements of the logic of unease have recently gained both intensity and frequency. Immigration is a fundamental defining aspect of Canada's identity as a nation-state, and discourses did present international migration as a particularly salient security issue for Canada in order to justify the introduction of security policies aimed at the movement of people, as seen in Chapter 4. In addition, the detention center, like the camp, exemplifies the sovereign power to rule on the exception. The detention center is indeed an exceptional space governed by exceptional measures. At the same time, notions of insecurity, discomfort, and unease have gained relative popularity in Canada in the past few years. An important example is the first pillar of the 2001 Smart Border Declaration's action plan, which defined the movement of people across borders as follows: someone is either a security "risk" or a "low risk" migrant. Tellingly, the category "not a risk" or "not a threat" is absent from the Declaration. Since 2001, immigration, security, terrorism, border controls, and security screening are increasingly fused into the same conceptual category. One could observe a trend in governing through a crime–security–immigration triangle nexus. The systematic fingerprinting of all refugee claimants in Canada and the entry of this biometric data into the Royal Canadian Mounted Police's Automatic Fingerprint Identification System, which contains more than 3 millions fingerprints and checks for criminal histories, is a prime example.

Similarly, both logics are present in France. Several political and media agents have made speech acts attempting to securitize migration through emergency and exceptional measures. The security threat that mass migration flow posed to France's social cohesion in the early 1990s was for Prime Minister Édouard Balladur the most difficult period since the Second World War, a situation that required all political parties to work together to ensure that France—as a nation and a society—would not be in peril of disappearing. In the same way, Charles Pasqua, in his first speech as Minister of the Interior, has argued that clandestine immigration is a new phenomenon that France urgently needs to combat if it does not want to see its national cohesion explode. Editorialists of *Le Figaro* also urged the governments to see the "problem" of migration flow and migration control as "a new form of war." In addition, a general sense of insecurity and unease is hard to miss in France. Already in 1991, Prime Minister Édith Cresson was recognizing that feelings of "insecurity," individual and collective, were influential in forcing the government to gain full control of migratory flux and in promoting a neighborhood-oriented police service. The near total absence of positive dispositions toward the issue of immigration in *Le Figaro* editorials is also telling. When the topic of migration has managed to reach the top of an editorialist's agenda, it has been for its negative, dangerous, and threatening aspects. A clear sense of bitterness, unease, and aggressiveness toward the phenomenon of the movement of people seems particularly strong.

In sum, I argue that sophisticated theoretical and empirical studies, which have demonstrated that the securitization process includes elements of both logics, calls for a complementary understanding of the two logics. A multifaceted discussion on the relationship between the logic of exception and the logic of unease would not only bolster our understanding of the securitization process but would also take securitization research into novel, insightful, and important directions.

Avenues for future research

Although the purpose of this book was to gain a better understanding of the process of securitizing the movement of people as well as to propose guiding principles for explaining the variation in levels of securitized migration between Canada and France, my study suggests broader conclusions and avenues for future research worth emphasizing.

As we have seen in this concluding chapter, my study speaks to two broad comparisons currently at the heart of security studies and securitization research: (1) the politicization process and the securitization process and (2) the logic of exception and the logic of unease. My analysis has indeed made a few steps in gaining a better understanding of the inter-relationship between the politicization process and the securitization process. In addition, my study has offered a novel perspective in arguing that the logic of exception and the logic of unease should not be seen as mutually exclusive.

My study also highlights that the undifferentiated quality of the national security interests associated with some models trying to explain the securitization process is unwarranted. States are not unitary and autonomous actors. Treating states as autonomous actors having objectively known security interests limits more than it reveals in the context of a study about the social mechanisms of

the securitization process. For instance, "the" Canadian position on the migration–security nexus significantly varied depending on who was the Minister of
Foreign Affairs, even when Ministers came from the same political party. Indeed,
the Department of Foreign Affairs has not spoken in a unified voice during the
time period of my study. The same is equally true for Prime Ministers of France.

Seen in this way, a follow-up research project would be to expand the securitizing agents under study. This could take multiple forms. The category "political
agents" could be expanded to include leaders of all major political parties and
not only those who were in power, as in the present study. Mayors of both small
and large cities could also be included. The category "media agents" could also
include key columnists and prominent journalists, not to mention other media
sources such as television, talk radio, and the Internet. Finally, other categories of
agents could also be included, such as the judiciary, leaders of interests groups,
academics, and the migrants themselves. Gaining a better understanding of agents
involved in the securitization of international migration is only in its infancy and
further research is definitely needed to map out the social interactions between
dominant and dominated narratives.

Against the idea that everything is built anew after an exogenous shock such
as the terrorist attacks of September 11, 2001, my study suggests that time and
history are significant in the securitization of migration. The attitude of mass
audiences toward immigration has not been created overnight. Of course, idiosyncratic events that mark collective memory influence the attitude of mass
audiences; however, one should also take into account the power of time and
legacy on a mass audience's inclination toward the movement of people.

The question of time brings the issue of whether within-case variation in the
levels of securitization exists. To be sure, I have investigated variation in the level
of securitization of migration *across cases*. Further research is needed to examine the issue of variation in intensity of securitized migration within cases but
across time. Is the securitization of migration stronger in the post-Cold War era
than in the period following the First World War or the Second World War? What
are the consequences of a within-case variation of security concerns for security
studies and securitization research? How has the securitization process evolved
over a large period of time in one country? Do we observe, over time, periods
of de-securitization followed by periods of securitization? Or is it the reverse:
securitization moments leading to de-securitization moments?

Understanding the phenomenon of securitized migration as a socially, historically, and discursively constructed phenomenon, as this book does, allows us to
critically examine the nature, the origin, and the durability of the relationship
between the movement of people and the system of order underpinning the movement. Opting for a sociological approach to studying the securitization process
also brings to the forefront fundamental issues such as path-dependence, self-
reinforcing dynamic, resilience to change, enduring consequences of history and
legacy, and the importance of imprints left by institutions and social norms—
concepts and notions that open new research avenues for securitization research,
security studies, and international relations.

Notes

1 Introduction

1 See Adamson (2006); Akaha and Vassellieva (2006); Alexseev (2005); Andreas (2000); Bigo (2002); Dauvergne (2008); Doty (1998); Guild and van Selm (2005); Huysmans (2006); Loescher (1992); Newman and van Selm (2003); Pratt (2005); Tirman (2004); Weiner (1993); Whitaker (1998).

2 See also Aradau (2004); Balzacq (2005); Behnke (2006); Curley and Wong (2008); Emmers (2003); Eriksson (1999); Hansen (2000); Huysmans (1998); Jackson (2006); Kennedy-Pipe (2004); McSweeney (1996); Roe (2004); Stritzel (2007); Taureck (2006); Wilkinson (2007); Williams (2003).

3 Obviously numerous other agents could be said to be political and contribute to the securitization of migration. I am simply confining my analysis for purposes of feasibility to an exhaustive analysis of a particular set of agents that are undeniably powerful and, indeed, I contend, the most powerful set of political agents involved in these processes, without discounting that others play roles as well. Because these agents I focus upon display the kinds of differences that are at the heart of this study, they serve the analytical purposes of explaining variation well.

4 Demonstrating that international migration is securitized and seeking to better understand the securitization process across cases (like I do) is not to argue that security is the defining logic of immigration in Western states.

2 Securitized migration

1 For more details, see the heartbreaking account narrated by Pratt (2005), the Inter-American Commission on Human Rights (2000), and Amnesty International (1997).

2 Interviewee #3, Department of Foreign Affairs, Canada, November 2, 2005.

3 Children born per woman, 2003 estimate.

4 See Dauvergne (2006) for Canada; see http://www.contreimmigrationjetable.org/article.php3?id_article=7 (last accessed November 18, 2010) for France.

5 See also Feldblum (1999); Wahnich (1997); Weil (2005); Wihtol de Wenden (1987).

6 With perhaps the notable exception of Nicolas Sarkozy when he was the Minister of the Interior.

7 See Baldwin (1997); Booth (1991, 2005b); Campbell (1992); Dalby (1992); Dillon (1996); Eisenhower Institute (2004); Enloe (1989); Homer Dixon (1991); Katzenstein (1996); Klein (1998); Krause and Williams (1997); Mack (2002); Matthews (1989); Mutimer (1997); Tickner (1992, 1995); Ullman (1983).

8 To help clarify these issues I do not argue that the integration of constructivism permits the development of better indicators of the phenomenon of securitized migration. Measurement, indicators, and variables are not necessarily associated with constructivism. I recognize that these are clearly complicated methodological issues on which

there is substantial disagreement. However, it is beyond the scope of this study to enter into methodological debates about these questions. For my purpose, I think that gaining a better understanding the phenomenon that I intend to study (securitized migration) is a necessary step before investigating the process of securitizing international migration in Canada and France between 1989 and 2005.

9 One major exception is the recent work of Jef Huysmans who, without directly providing criteria, has offered some guiding principles for further research.

10 Until December 2003, the Department of Citizenship and Immigration was responsible for immigration detention. Since then this responsibility has been assigned to the Canada Border Services Agency (CBSA), an agency created in 2003 within the Department of Public Safety and Emergency Preparedness. The decision to order immigration detention accordingly now lies with CBSA officers.

11 The previous *White Paper on Defence* was published in 1972.

12 See Ministère des Affaires Étrangères, (2002) "Rapport d'activité 2002." Paris, République française. Available at http://www.diplomatie.gouv.fr/fr/IMG/pdf/ram2002-2.pdf (last accessed November 18, 2010).

13 The Foreigner Code, officially known as the "Code de l'entrée et du séjour des étrangers et du droit d'asile," lists all legislative dispositions relating to foreigner/immigrant rights.

3 Constructivism, security, and the movement of people

1 Pierre Bourdieu's ideas are beginning to generate interest among IR theorists (particularly within the constructivist "family"); see Bigo (2005); Guzzini (2000); Jackson (2008); Pouliot (2008); Williams (2007).

2 See among many others Aleinikoff and Chetail (2003); Brettell and Hollifield (2000); Castles and Miller (1993); Clifford (1994); Cohen (2008); Geddes (2003); Hall (1990); Jacobson (1997); Ong and Nonini (1996); Sassen (1996).

3 Actually, one could hypothesize that the gap is rather small between policies and outcomes in the context of the securitization of migration, as Chapter 2 has shown that the phenomenon of securitized migration scores on both the institutional and the security practices sets of indicators.

4 The relationship between the governmentality of unease model and the model proposed by ST will be discussed further in the conclusion.

5 See Abrahamsen (2005); Alker (2006); Aradau (2004, 2008); Balzacq (2005); Behnke (2006); Booth (2005a,c); Curley and Wong (2008); Elbe (2005); Emmers (2003); Eriksson (1999); Hansen (2000); Higashino (2004); Huysmans (1998, 2006); Jackson (2006); Kennedy-Pipe (2004); McDonald (2008); McSweeney (1996); Roe (2004); Sasse (2005); Smith (2005); Stritzel (2007); Taureck (2006); Wilkinson (2007); Williams (2003); Wyn Jones (2005).

6 Recent works on how ST should incorporate contexts into its analytical framework have developed in a number of directions. In a provocative article, Holger Stritzel (2007: 358) argues that "too much weight is put on the semantic side of the speech act articulation at the expense of its social and linguistic relatedness and sequentiality." Instead, however, of seeking refinements or correctives to ST, Stritzel contends that ST simply cannot integrate the notion of context into its analytical framework. He appears to argue that ST is marred with flaws, internal tensions, and contradictions to the point where it cannot be refined. Therefore, a new analytical framework has to be elaborated and this new model (he calls it a "comprehensive theory") would stand in opposition with ST. In a related way, Matt McDonald (2008) contends that the context of the act in ST is narrowly defined, with the focus on the moment of intervention only. Criticizing ST for being too narrow analytically, he suggests adopting a "broader approach" and moving beyond the depiction through speech act of issues as existential security threats. He further contends, with a negative tone, that scholars have been attracted to

ST in part because of the desire "to simply apply a set of universal and ready-made tools to different social, historical and political contexts" (McDonald 2008: 582).

However, Stritzel fails to demonstrate convincingly why ST cannot integrate any notions of context within its analytical framework, and there are good reasons to avoid being too quick to announce the demise of ST on the basis of its incapacity to integrate contextual factors in a meaningful and cogent way. In addition, I think McDonald's understanding of the importance that ST has had in security studies in the last decade is a simplified one. More importantly, I think that McDonald also fails to convincingly demonstrate that ST is not capable of including contextual factors into its analytical framework before moving on to propose his model, which provides little insight into how precisely contextual factors work within the securitization process, what kind of power contextual factors possess, how this power is expressed, and how the power of contextual factors interacts with securitizing actors. Although ST's architects have so far proposed an underdeveloped understanding of contextual factors' importance in the securitization process, the analytical framework contains enough fluidity to permit refinements in the inclusion of contextual factors. As Alker (2006) summarizes it, ST as a de-essentializing and discursive approach suggests illuminating ways of analyzing perceptions, representations, strategies, and practices supposedly enhancing or undermining the identities, integrities, relationships, resources, and other features of various individuals, groups, communities, states or societies. In my reading, many of these elements do in fact relate to context.

7 Echoing Bourdieu's (1982) criticism that Austin's speech act theory neglects the social conditions for the possibility of the speech act, Bigo argues that securitizing actors' speech acts are not decisive but the result of structural competition between agents with different forms of capital and legitimacy. Although this aspect of ST is not the focus of my study, it is not at all clear to me that ST cannot incorporate competition among agents within its analytical framework. Even though ST's focus is on securitizing agents' speech acts, it does not mean that ST is blind to the rivalry among agents for defining security. In fact, advocates of ST would find little disagreement with Bigo and Tsoukala's (2008: 6) argument that the result of the securitization process "cannot be assessed from the will of an actor, even a dominant one." ST's objective is not to identify the authors of the securitization—if such a role exists.

8 See also Wæver (2000).

4 Political agents and their security speech acts

1 I acknowledge that the actual name of the department in charge of foreign affairs has changed over time in Canada; however, for the sake of simplicity, I have used the most recent denomination.

2 I acknowledge that the actual name of the department in charge of the immigration portfolio has changed over time in Canada; however, for the sake of simplicity, I have used the most recent denomination.

3 A note is required at this point. I have been able to retrieve and collect the complete set of speeches made by all political agents with one exception: the Ministers of Citizenship and Immigration of Canada. I have worked with several archivists and librarians of Library and Archives Canada to collect as many speeches as possible; however, the collection of speeches by Ministers Bernard Valcourt, Sergio Marchi, and Lucienne Robillard are partially closed to the public. Some speeches from Minister Barbara McDougall are closed to the general public until 2017. I have also made a request under the Access to Information Act for all speeches by all Ministers of Citizenship and Immigration of Canada between 1989 and 2005. I have received an incomplete set of speeches: for example, I received seventeen speeches for 1999 (for comparison, the Minister of Foreign Affairs on average makes thirty speeches per year), seven speeches for 1992, but none for 2004. Hence, my conclusions concerning the role of Ministers

of Citizenship and Immigration are not as robust as with the other Canadian and French political agents.

4 Because only ten Speeches from the Throne were made within the time frame of my study (1989–2005), I have also investigated all Speeches from the Throne (fifty-seven speeches) since the end of the Second World War. The analysis reveals that no securitizing moves were made in regards to migration between 1945 and 1989.

5 Despite the fact that until 1993 the post was known as Secretary of State for External Affairs, I use the title of Minister of Foreign Affairs for the sake of simplicity.

6 Interview, Department of Foreign Affairs, Canada, November 3, 2005.

7 Unless otherwise indicated, all translations are mine.

8 To be sure, migration was not the only aspect of the center-right enterprise of *"redressement"* (Balladur takes good care to include Jacques Chirac within the movement just two years before the presidential election), but it certainly holds a prominent place. Indeed, three of the eight elements justifying such an enterprise of *"redressement"* concern migration (the others being, for example, budget deficit and the justice crisis).

9 The "Debré" law, adopted on April 24, 1997 (i.e. two months before the legislative election), increases the repressive measures on migration (e.g. confiscation of passports of foreigners found in irregular situations).

10 That responsibility was transferred in 1998 (with the Chevènement law) to the Department of the Interior.

11 Interview #37, Department of Interior, June 13, 2006.

5 Media, migration, and security: an obvious link?

1 As such, editorialists are not detached from a population's concern at a given time. For example, concern about Canada's immigration policy subsided in November 1999 after shooting upward in September 1999 when polling showed that 20 percent of respondents cited it as the most important issue (compared with 34 percent for health care), that is, after the "Chinese Summer crisis" of 1999. In November 1999, concern over the issue had fallen back to normal levels, with 7 percent of Canadians citing it as the country's most pressing issue.

2 For example, when a new cabinet shuffle was discussed and the new minister in charge of the immigration portfolio was simply named, I have not considered this as an editorial in which migration was the main topic.

3 In French, "Disparaître: Le sort inévitable de la nation française d'Amérique." The documentary is a co-production of Radio-Canada and the National Film Board of Canada.

4 See *The Globe and Mail* (1994, 2004, 2005).

5 See *The Globe and Mail* (2001a).

6 Contrary to Dubuc's description, we do not have to go back twenty-five years.

7 When the Canadian government granted immigrant status to the former Iraqi Ambassador to the United States, Mohammad al-Mashat, in an unusually short processing period, it sparked intense media and public debate. Stories about al-Mashat dominated the news for days and weeks.

6 The powers of contextual factors

1 I further argue that it is important to move away from conceptualizing the role of contextual factors as "blocking" the securitization process for it would suggest that contexts would have no influence on the process of elaborating a security speech act and that contextual powers would be important only after an agent made a securitizing move. Feedback and multidirectionality in the interaction between agents and contextual factors are important elements of the analytical framework for the study of the securitization process that I develop.

2 Many scholars have followed the Weiner and Loescher path; see Kenyon Lischer (2005); Lohrmann (2000); Newman and van Selm (2003); Salehyan and Gleditsch (2006). One could argue that they have been heard. As Roberts (1998) highlights, the UN Security Council, which has a long record of involvement in refugee issues, has been far more preoccupied with them in the 1990s than in any previous period. He points out that, in resolutions concerning at least five major crises, the Security Council has identified the fear of refugee flows and the actual flow as constituting threats to international security.

3 I have broken with the general structure of the study (1989–2005) and included political parties' manifestos since the end of the Second World War for two reasons: (1) it gives a better overview of each political party's position on the migration–security nexus; and (2) it permits and strengthens my analysis of rupture and continuity in how the movement of people is seen by the political party.

4 What this means is that most Indo-Chinese refugees would not have been allowed into Canada in the late 1970s and early 1980s. They did not in fact fit the definition of the 1951 UN Convention and had to enter Canada under the "designated class" provisions of the 1976 Act.

5 Despite being an individual election (as president), candidates are usually supported by a political party. Indeed, the candidate is generally seen as the leader or the representative of a political party or a coalition of political parties. In that sense, even though the manifestos take an individual form presenting the policy program of the presidential candidate, one should not underestimate the influence of the organization behind each candidate. Furthermore, presidential candidates usually have to go through an investiture process in order to be nominated as the political party's presidential candidate. This process contextualizes the power of the candidate on the one hand, and underlines the influence of the political party on the other hand.

6 A complete transcript of the debate can be found at http://www.leboucher.com/pdf/president/xdebat.pdf (last accessed November 18, 2010).

7 One should also note the difference in wording between the question asked in Canada (whether Canadians agree that Canada is *letting in* too many immigrants) and the one asked in France (whether the French agree that *there are* too many immigrants in France). Although the difference means that we cannot directly compare the responses given to these questions, it does not prevent a comparative analysis of the role of mass audiences in the securitization of migration.

References

Abrahamsen, Rita. (2005). "Blair's Africa: The politics of securitization and fear." *Alternatives* 30(1): 55–80.

Adams, Michael. (2007). *Unlikely Utopia. The Surprising Triumph of Canadian Pluralism.* Toronto, Penguin.

Adamson, Fiona. (2006). "Crossing borders: International migration and national security." *International Security* 31(1): 165–99.

Adelman, Howard. (2002). "Canadian borders and immigration post 9/11: Perspectives from around the world." *International Migration Review* 36(1): 15–28.

Adelman, Howard. (2004). "Governance, immigration policy, and security: Canada and the United States post-9/11." In *The Maze of Fear. Security and Migration after 9/11*, edited by John Tirman, pp. 109–31. New York, The New Press.

Adler, Emanuel. (1997). "Seizing the middle ground: Constructivism in world politics." *European Journal of International Relations* 3(3): 319–63.

Adler, Emanuel. (2002). "Constructivism and international relations." In *Handbook of International Relations*, edited by Walter Carlsnaes, Thomas Risse and Beth A Simmons, pp. 95–118. London, Sage.

Adler, Emanuel and Michael N. Barnett. (1998). *Security Communities*. Cambridge, Cambridge University Press.

Agamben, Giorgio. (1998). *Homo Sacer: Sovereign Power and Bare Life.* Trans. Daniel Heller-Roazen. Stanford, Stanford University Press.

Agamben, Giorgio. (2005). *State of Exception.* Trans. Kevin Attell. Chicago, University of Chicago Press.

Akaha, Tsuneo and Anna Vassellieva, eds. (2006). *Crossing National Borders. Human Migration Issues in Northeast Asia.* Tokyo, United Nations University Press.

Albert, Mathias, Jacobson, David and Lapid, Yosef. (2001). *Identities, Borders, Orders: Rethinking International Relations Theory.* Minneapolis, MN, University of Minnesota Press.

Aleinikoff, Alexander T. and Vincent Chetail, eds. (2003). *Migration and International Legal Norms.* Geneva, International Organization for Migration.

Alexseev, Mikhail A. (2005). *Immigration Phobia and the Security Dilemma: Russia, Europe and the United States.* Cambridge, Cambridge University Press.

Alker, Hayward. (2005). "Emancipation in the critical security studies project." In *Critical Security Studies and World Politics*, edited by Ken Booth, pp. 189–214. London, Lynne Rienner.

Alker, Hayward. (2006). "On securitization politics as contexted texts and talk." *Journal of International Relations and Development* 9(1): 70–80.

Amnesty International. (1997). *Human Rights Report.* London, Amnesty International.

Andreas, Peter. (2000). *Border Games: Policing the U.S.–Mexico Divide*. Ithaca, Cornell University Press.

Andreas, Peter and Thomas J. Biersteker. (2003). *The Rebordering of North America: Integration and Exclusion in a New Security Context*. New York, Routledge.

Aradau, Claudia. (2004). "Security and the democratic scene: desecuritization and emancipation." *Journal of International Relations and Development* 7(4): 388–413.

Aradau, Claudia. (2006). "Limits of security, limits of politics? A response." *Journal of International Relations and Development* 9(1): 81–90.

Aradau, Claudia. (2008). *Rethinking Trafficking in Women. Politics out of Security*. Basingstoke, Palgrave.

Aradau, Claudia and Rens van Munster. (2007). "Governing terrorism through risk: Taking precautions, (un)knowing the future." *European Journal of International Relations* 13(1): 89–115.

Arendt, Hannah. (1958). *The Human Condition*. Chicago, University of Chicago Press.

Associated Press-Ipsos-Reid. (2004). "AP-Ipsos immigration highlights." *Associated Press*, May 26.

Auditor General of Canada. (2008). *Report to the House of Commons*, Ottawa, Office of the Auditor General of Canada.

Axworthy, Lloyd. (1999). *Notes for an Address by the Honourable Lloyd Axworthy, Minister of Foreign Affairs, to the Atlantic Diplomatic Forum*. Ottawa, Department of Foreign Affairs, November 5.

Axworthy, Lloyd. (2000). *Notes for an Address by the Honourable Lloyd Axworthy, Minister of Foreign Affairs, to the Middlebury College 200th Anniversary Symposium on International Affairs*. Ottawa, Department of Foreign Affairs, March 30.

Badie, Bertrand and Catherine Wihtol de Wenden. (1994). *Le defi migratoire: questions de relations internationales*. Paris, Presses de la Fondation Nationale des Sciences Politiques.

Baldwin, David. (1997). "The concept of security." *Review of International Studies* 23(1): 5–26.

Balladur, Édouard. (1993a). *Déclaration de politique générale de M. Édouard Balladur, Premier Ministre, à l'Assemblée nationale*. Paris, Bureau du Premier Ministre, 8 avril.

Balladur, Édouard. (1993b). *Déclaration de M. Edouard Balladur, Premier ministre, sur le bilan des réformes du gouvernement, aux journées parlementaires du RPR, La Rochelle*, Paris, Bureau du Premier Ministre, 26 septembre.

Balzacq, Thierry. (2005). "The three faces of securitization: Political agency, audience and context." *European Journal of International Relations* 11(2): 171–201.

Barnett, Michael and Raymond Duvall. (2005). "Power in global governance." In *Power in Global Governance*, edited by Michael Barnett and Raymond Duvall, pp. 1–32. Cambridge, Cambridge University Press.

Beare, Margaret E. (1997). "Illegal migration: Personal tragedies, social problems or national security threats?" *Transnational Crime* 3(4): 11–41.

Behnke, Andreas. (2006). "No way out: Desecuritization, emancipation and the eternal return of the political. A reply to Aradau." *Journal of International Relations and Development* 9(1): 62–9.

Bigo, Didier, ed. (1992). *L'Europe des polices et de la sécurité intérieure*. Bruxelles, Editions Complexe.

Bigo, Didier. (1996). *Polices en réseaux: L'expérience europeenne*. Paris, Presses de Sciences Po.

Bigo, Didier. (1998a). "Sécurité et immigration: Vers une gouvernementalité par l'inquiétude." *Cultures & Conflits* 31–32: 13–38.

Bigo, Didier. (1998b). "L'Europe de la securite interieure: Penser autrement la securite." In *Entre unions et nations*, edited by Anne-Marie Le Gloannec. Paris, Presses de Sciences Po.

Bigo, Didier. (2002). "Security and immigration: Toward a critique of the governmentality of unease." *Alternatives* 27: 63–92.

Bigo, Didier. (2005). "La mondialisation de l'insécurité? Réflexions sur le champ des professionnels de la gestion des inquiétudes et analytique de la transnationalisation des processus d'insécurisation." *Cultures & Conflits* 58: 53–100.

Bigo, Didier. (2008). "Globalized (in)security. The field and the ban-opticon." In *Terror, Insecurity, and Liberty*, edited by Didier Bigo and Anastassia Tsoukala, pp. 10–49. London, Routledge.

Bigo, Didier and Elspeth Guild. (2003). "La mise à l'écart des étrangers: Le visa Schengen." *Cultures & Conflits* 49–50.

Bigo, Didier and Elspeth Guild. (2005). *Controlling Frontiers. Free Movement Into and Within Europe*. Burlington, Ashgate.

Bigo, Didier and Anastassia Tsoukala. (2008). "Understanding (in)security." In *Terror, Insecurity, and Liberty*, edited by Didier Bigo and Anastassia Tsoukala, pp. 1–10. London, Routledge.

Booth, Ken. (1991). "Security and emancipation." *Review of International Studies* 17(4): 313–27.

Booth, Ken. (2005a). "Critical explorations." In *Critical Security Studies and World Politics*, edited by Ken Booth, pp. 1–20. London, Lynne Rienner.

Booth, Ken, ed. (2005b). *Critical Security Studies and World Politics*. London, Lynne Rienner.

Booth, Ken. (2005c). "Beyond critical security studies." In *Critical Security Studies and World Politics*, edited by Ken Booth, pp. 259–78. London, Lynne Rienner.

Borowski, Allan and Derrick Thomas. (1994). "Immigration and crime." In *Immigration and Refugee Policy. Vol. 2*, edited by Howard Adelman, Allan Borowski, Meyer Burstein, and Lois Foster, pp. 631–53. Toronto, University of Toronto.

Boswell, Christina. (2006). "Migration in Europe." In *The Politics of Migration. A Survey*, edited by Barbara Marshall, pp. 91–111. London, Routledge.

Bourdieu, Pierre. (1982). *Ce que parler veut dire: L'economie des echanges linguistiques*. Paris, Fayard.

Bourdieu, Pierre. (1990). *The Logic of Practice*. Stanford, Stanford University Press.

Bourdieu, Pierre. (1991). *Language and Symbolic Power*. London, Polity Press.

Brechon, Pierre, ed. (2002). *Les élections présidentielles en France. 40 ans d'histoire politique*. Paris, La Documentation Française.

Brechon, Pierre, ed. (2005). *Les partis politiques français*. Paris, La Documentation Française.

Brettell, Caroline and James Frank Hollifield. (2000). *Migration Theory: Talking across Disciplines*. New York, Routledge.

Brézet, Alexis. (2001). "Éditorial." *Le Figaro*, 27 novembre: 16.

Brézet, Alexis. (2005). "Éditorial." *Le Figaro*, 4 novembre: 19.

Brochmann, Greta and Thomas Hammar, eds. (1999). *Mechanisms of Immigration Control: A Comparative Analysis of European Regulation Policies*. Oxford, Berg.

Brubaker, Rogers. (1992). *Citizenship and Nationhood in France and Germany*. Cambridge, Harvard University Press.

Brubaker, Rogers. (1995). "Comments on 'modes of immigration policies in liberal democratic states'." *International Migration Review* 29(4): 903–8.

Butler, Judith. (1997). *Excitable Speech: A Politics of the Performative*. London, Routledge.

Butler, Judith. (1999). "Performativity's social magic." In *Bourdieu. A Criticial Reader*, edited by Richard Shusterman, pp. 113–28. London, Blackwell.

Buzan, Barry, Ole Wæver, Jaap de Wilde. (1998). *Security: A New Framework for Analysis*. Boulder, CO, Lynne Rienner.

Caloz-Tschopp, Marie-Claire. (2004). *Les étrangers aux frontières de l'Europe et le spectre des camps*. Paris, La Dispute.

Caloz-Tschopp, Marie-Claire and Pierre Dasen, eds. (2007). *Mondialisation, migration et droits de l'homme: un nouveau paradigme pour la recherche et la citoyenneté*. Genève, Bruylant.

Campbell, David. (1992). *Writing Security: United States Foreign Policy and the Politics of Identity*. Minneapolis, University of Minnesota Press.

Campbell, Kim. (1993). *Notes for a Statement by Prime Minister Kim Campbell*. Ottawa, Office of the Prime Minister, June 25.

Canadian Alliance. (2000). *Your Principles: Policy Declaration*. Calgary, Canadian Alliance.

Caplan, Elinor. (1999a). *Remarks by the Honourable Elinor Caplan, Minister of Citizenship and Immigration, to the Canadian Club*. Ottawa, Department of Citizenship and Immigration, September 9.

Caplan, Elinor. (1999b). *Notes for an Address by the Honourable Elinor Caplan, Minister of Citizenship and Immigration, to the Annual Meeting of the Canadian Council for Refugees*. Ottawa, Department of Citizenship and Immigration, December 3.

Caplan, Elinor. (1999c). *Statement by the Honourable Elinor Caplan, Minister of Citizenship and Immigration, on Illegal Human Smuggling to Canada*. Ottawa, Department of Citizenship and Immigration, August 11.

Caplan, Elinor. (2000a). *Notes for an Address by the Honourable Elinor Caplan, Minister of Citizenship and Immigration, to the Canada China Business Council*. Ottawa, Department of Citizenship and Immigration, April 25.

Caplan, Elinor. (2000b). *Notes for an Address by the Honourable Elinor Caplan, Minister of Citizenship and Immigration, to the European Union Seminar on Illegal Migration*. Ottawa, Department of Citizenship and Immigration, July 20.

Caplan, Elinor. (2000c). *Notes for an Address by the Honourable Elinor Caplan, Minister of Citizenship and Immigration, to the Fourth National Metropolis Conference*. Ottawa, Department of Citizenship and Immigration, March 25.

Caplan, Elinor. (2000d). *Notes for an Address by the Honourable Elinor Caplan, Minister of Citizenship and Immigration, to the Maytree Foundation Trends in Global Migration Forum*. Ottawa, Department of Citizenship and Immigration, January 12.

Caplan, Elinor. (2001a). *Notes for an Addess by the Honourable Elinor Caplan, Minister of Citizenship and Immigration, to the Standing Committee on Citizenship and Immigration on Bill C-11 The Immigration and Refugee Protection Act*. Ottawa, Department of Citizenship and Immigration, March 1.

Caplan, Elinor. (2001b). *Notes for an Address by the Honourable Elinor Caplan, Minister of Citizenship and Immigration, to the House of Commons Standing Committee on Citizenship and Immigration on Bill C-11 The Immigration and Refugee Protection Act*. Ottawa, Department of Citizenship and Immigration, March 8.

Caplan, Elinor. (2001c). *Notes for Remarks by the Honourable Elinor Caplan, Minister of Citizenship and Immigration, to the Senate Standing Committee on Social Affairs, Science and Technology*. Ottawa, Department of Citizenship and Immigration, October 4.

Caplan, Elinor. (2001d). *Notes for an Addess by the Honourable Elinor Caplan, Minister of Citizenship and Immigration, to the Canadian Arab Federation*. Ottawa, Department of Citizenship and Immigration, November 9.

Castles, Stephen and Alastair Davidson. (2000). *Citizenship and Migration: Globalization and the Politics of Belonging*. New York, Routledge.

Castles, Stephen and Mark J. Miller. (1993). *The Age of Migration: International Population Movements in the Modern World*. New York, Guilford Press.

CBSA. (n.d.). "About us. Mandate and mission". Available online at http://www.cbsa-asfc. gc.ca/agency-agence/who-qui-eng.html (last accessed November 18, 2010).

Cederman, Lars-Erik. (1997). *Emergent Actors in World Politics. How States and Nations Develop and Dissolve*. Princeton, Princeton University Press.

Ceyhan, Ayse and Anastassia Tsoukala. (2002). "The securitization of migration in Western societies: Ambivalent discourses and policies." *Alternatives* 27(Supplement S): 21–39.

Chirac, Jacques. (1996). *Discours de M. Jacques Chirac, Président de la République, devant le Congrès des Etats-Unis d'Amérique*. Paris, Présidence de la République, 2 janvier.

Chirac, Jacques. (2001a). *Discours de M. Jacques Chirac, Président de la République, lors de la visite de la marine (Toulon)*. Paris, Présidence de la République, 8 novembre.

Chirac, Jacques. (2001b). *Discours de M. Jacques Chirac, Président de la République, au forum régional sur l'avenir de l'Europe*. Paris, Présidence de la République, 4 octobre.

Chirac, Jacques. (2005). *Discours de M. Jacques Chirac, Président de la République, lors du 50e anniversaire de la Chambre Franco-Allemande de commerce et d'industrie*. Paris, Présidence de la République, 26 avril.

Cholewinski, Ryszard. (2000). "The EU acquis on irregular migration: Reinforcing security at the expense of rights." *European Journal of Migration and Law* 2(3–4): 361–405.

Chrétien, Jean. (2001). *Address by Prime Minister Jean Chrétien on the Occasion of a Special House of Commons Debate in Response to the Terrorist Attacks in the United States on September 11, 2001*. Ottawa, Office of the Prime Minister, September 17.

CIC. (1996). *Citizenship and Immigration Detention Policy*. Ottawa, Citizenship and Immigration Canada.

CIC. (2002a). *Immigration Manual. Inadmissibility*. Ottawa, Citizenship and Immigration Canada.

CIC. (2002b). *Immigration Manual. Detention*. Ottawa, Citizenship and Immigration Canada.

CIC. (2006). *Facts and Figures 2005*. Ottawa, Government of Canada.

Cimade (2006) *Rapport 2005*. Paris, Cimade.

Clifford, James. (1994). "Diasporas." *Cultural Anthropology* 9(3): 302–38.

Coderre, Denis. (2003a). *Notes for an Appearance by the Honourable Denis Coderre, Minister of Citizenship and Immigration, before the Standing Committee on Citizenship and Immigration*. Ottawa, Department of Citizenship and Immigration, March 20.

Coderre, Denis. (2003b). *Notes for an Address "Document Integrity and Biometrics: Exploring the Options for our Future" by the Honourable Denis Coderre, Minister of Citizenship and Immigration*. Ottawa, Department of Citizenship and Immigration, September 19.

Coderre, Denis. (2003c). *Notes for an Address by the Honourable Denis Coderre, Minister of Citizenship and Immigration, to the Meeting of the Canadian Bar Association*. Ottawa, Department of Citizenship and Immigration, May 3.

Coderre, Denis. (2003d). *Notes for an Address by the Honourable Denis Coderre, Minister of Citizenship and Immigration, in the House of Commons in Response to a Motion Opposing a National Identity Card*. Ottawa, Department of Citizenship and Immigration, February 13

Coderre, Denis. (2003e). *Notes for an Address by the Honourable Denis Coderre, Minister of Citizenship and Immigration, to a Forum on Biometrics: Applications and Implications for CIC*. Ottawa, Department of Citizenship and Immigration, October 8.

Cohen, Robin. (2008). *Global Diasporas*. London, Routledge.

Coleman, David A. (1997). "Europe under migration pressure: some facts on immigration." In *Immigration into Western Societies. Problems and Policies*, edited by Emek M. Uçarer and Donald J. Puchala, pp. 121–46. London, Pinter.

Comité Interministériel de Contrôle de l'Immigration (CICI). (2006). *Les orientations de la politique de l'immigration. Rapport au Parlement*. Paris, République Française.

Commissioner for Human Rights. (2006). *Report by Mr. Alvaro Gil-Robles, Council of Europe Commissioner for Human Rights, on the Effective Respect for Human Rights in France Following his Visit from 5 to 21 September 2005*. Strasbourg, Council of Europe.

Connelly, Matthew and Paul Kennedy. (1994). "Must it be the rest against the West?" *Atlantic Monthly* 274(6): 61–91.

Cornelius, Wayne A., Philip L. Martin and James F. Hollifield, eds. (1994). *Controlling Immigration: A Global Perspective*. Stanford, Stanford University Press.

Cornelius, Wayne A., Takeyuki Tsuda, Philip L. Martin and James F. Hollifield. (2004). *Controlling Immigration: A Global Perspective*. Stanford, Stanford University Press.

Crépeau, François and Delphine Nakache. (2006). "Controlling irregular migration in Canada. Reconciling security concerns with human rights protection." *Choices. Institute for Research on Public Policy* 12(1): 1–42.

Cresson, Édith. (1991). *Déclaration de politique générale de Mme Édith Cresson, Premier Ministre, sur le programme du gouvernement*. Paris, Bureau du Premier Ministre, 22 mai.

CROP. (1997). *Political Surveys*. In Canadian Opinion Research Archive. Available at http://www.queensu.ca/cora/ (last accessed November 18, 2010).

CROP. (2000). *Political Surveys*. In Canadian Opinion Research Archive. Available at http://www.queensu.ca/cora/ (last accessed November 18, 2010).

Curley, Melissa and Siu-lun Wong, eds. (2008). *Security and Migration in Asia: The Dynamics of Securitisation*. London, Routledge.

Dalby, Simon. (1992). "Security, modernity, ecology: The dilemmas of post-Cold War security discourse." *Alternatives* 17(1): 95–134.

Dauvergne, Catherine. (2006). *Humanitarianism, Identity, and Nation: Migration Laws of Australia and Canada*. Vancouver, University of British Columbia Press.

Dauvergne, Catherine. (2008). *Making People Illegal: What Globalization Means for Migration and Law*. Cambridge, Cambridge University Press.

Davidson, Robert A. (2003). "Spaces of immigration "prevention": Interdiction and the nonplace." *Diacritics* 33(3/4): 3–18.

de Charette, Hervé. (1995). *Intervention du Ministre des Affaires Étrangères, M. Hervé de Charette, lors du débat sur la politique europénne de la France à l'Assemblée nationale*. Paris, Ministère des Affaires Étrangères, 20 juin.

de Villepin, Dominique. (2003). *Déclaration de M. Dominique Galouzeau de Villepin, Ministre des Affaires Étrangères, sur la préparation de la Convention européenne et la réforme des institutions*. Paris, Ministère des Affaires Étrangères, 5 juin.

de Villepin, Dominique. (2004). *Déclaration de M. Dominique Galouzeau de Villepin, Ministre de l'Intérieur, sur les résultats obtenus en matière de sécurité publique et sur les moyens engagés pour poursuivre l'action de la police*. Paris, Ministère de l'Intérieur, 29 novembre.

DEA. (1991). *Foreign Policy Themes and Priorities, 1991–92 Update*. Ottawa, Department of External Affairs and International Trade, Government of Canada. Reprinted in Granatstein, J.L., ed. (1993) *Canadian Foreign Policy. Historical Readings*, Toronto, Copp Clark Pitman.

Debré, Jean-Louis. (1996). *Déclarations de M. Jean-Louis Debré, Ministre de l'Intérieur, sur le renforcement des mesures de lutte contre l'immigration clandestine et le séjour irrégulier d'étrangers en France*. Paris, Ministère de l'Intérieur, 6 mars.

Dench, Janet. (2001). "Controlling the borders: C-31 and interdiction." *Refuge – Canada's Periodical on Refugees* 19(4): 34–40.

Dench, Janet and François Crépeau. (2003). "Introduction. Interdiction at the expense of human rights: A long-term containment strategy." *Refuge – Canada's Periodical on Refugees* 21(4): 2–5.

Dent, John A. (2002). "No right of appeal: Bill C-11, criminality, and the human rights of permanent residents facing deportation." *Queen's Law Journal* 27: 749–84.

Devetak, Richard. (2004). "In fear of refugees: The politics of border protection in Australia." *International Journal of Human Rights* 8(1): 101–9.

DFAIT. (1995). *Canada in the World. Government Statement*. Ottawa, Department of Foreign Affairs and International Trade, Government of Canada.

DFAIT. (2001). "The Smart Border Declaration: Building a smart border for the 21st century on the foundation of a North American Zone of Confidence", Ottawa, December 12. Available online at http://www.international.gc.ca/anti-terrorism/declaration-en.asp (last accessed November 18, 2010).

Dillon, Michael. (1996). *Politics of Security: Towards a Political Philosophy of Continental Thought*. London, Routledge.

Direction de la population et des migrations (DPM). (2005). *Rapport Annuel 2004*. Paris, République Française.

Dirks, Gerald E. (1995). *Controversy and Complexity: Canadian Immigration Policy during the 1980s*. Montreal, Buffalo, McGill-Queen's University Press.

DND. (1994). *White Paper on Defence*. Ottawa, Department of National Defence, Government of Canada.

DND. (2005). *Canada's International Policy Statement. A Role of Pride and Influence in the World: Defence*. Ottawa, Department of National Defence, Government of Canada.

Doty, Roxanne Lynn. (1998). "Immigration and the politics of security." *Security Studies* 8(2): 71–93.

Doty, Roxanne Lynn. (2007). "States of exception on the Mexico–U.S. border: Security, "decisions," and civilian border patrols." *International Political Sociology* 1(2): 113–37.

Doucet, Marc and Miguel de Larrinaga, eds. (2010). *Security and Global Governmentality: Globalization, Governance, and the State*. London, Routledge.

Douste-Blazy, Philippe. (2005). *Déclaration de M. Philippe Douste-Blazy, Ministre des Affaires Étrangères, sur les priorités de la politique étrangère et de l'action diplomatique de la France au regard de l'état actuel du monde*. Paris, Ministère des Affaires Étrangères, 30 août.

Dublin Convention. (1990). *Convention Implementing the Schengen Agreement of 14 June 1985 between the Governments of the States of Benelux Economic Union, the Federal Republic of Germany and the French Republic on the Gradual Abolition of Checks at their Common Borders*, Reprinted in 2001, *The Schengen Acquis: Integrated into the European Union*. Luxembourg, Office for Official Publications of the European Communities.

Dubuc, Alain (1992a). "Éditorial." *La Presse*, 2 mars: B2.

Dubuc, Alain. (1992b). "La pression des groupes de pression." *La Presse*, 19 mars: B3.

Dubuc, Alain (1993). "Éditorial." *La Presse*, 4 novembre: B2.

Dubuc, Alain (1994). "Éditorial." *La Presse*, 29 octobre: B2.

Dubuc, Alain (1999). "Éditorial." *La Presse*, 2 octobre: B2.

Edelman, Murray. (2001). *The Politics of Misinformation*. Cambridge, Cambridge University Press.

Eisenhower Institute. (2004). *Space Security Index*. Washington DC, Eisenhower Institute and Canada's Department of Foreign Affairs.

Elbe, Stefan. (2005). "HIV/AIDS: The international security dimensions." In *New Actors and New Issues in International Security*, edited by Elke Krahmann, pp. 111–30. London, Palgrave.

Emmers, Ralf. (2003). "ASEAN and the securitization of transnational crime in Southeast Asia." *Pacific Review* 16(3): 419–38.

Enloe, Cyntia. (1989). *Bananas, Beaches and Bases: Making Feminist Sense of International Politics*. London, Pandora.

Eriksson, J. (1999). "Observers or advocates?: On the political role of security analysis." *Cooperation and Conflict* 34(3): 310–30.

EU High Representative for the Common Foreign and Security Policy. (2003). *A Secure Europe in a Better World. European Security Strategy*. Brussels, European Union.

European Union. (1997) "The Treaty of Amsterdam. Amending the Treaty on European Union, the Treaties establishing the European Communities and certain related acts", Amsterdam, 2 October. Available at http://www.eurotreaties.com/amsterdamtreaty.pdf (last accessed November 18, 2010).

Faist, Thomas. (2004). *The Migration–Security Nexus. International Migration and Security Before and After 9/11*, Willy Brandt Working Papers in International Migration and Ethnic Relations, No.4/03. Malmö, Sweden, Malmö University, School of International Migration and Ethnic Relations.

Favell, Adrian and Randall Hansen. (2002). "Markets against politics: Migrants, EU enlargement and the idea of Europe." *Journal of Ethnic and Migration Studies* 28(4): 581–601.

Fearon, James D. and Alexander Wendt. (2002). "Rationalism v. constructivism: A skeptical view." In *Handbook of International Relations*, edited by Walter Carlsnaes, Thomas Risse and Beth A Simmons, pp. 52–72. London, Sage.

Feldblum, Miriam. (1999). *Reconstructing Citizenship: The Politics of Nationality Reform and Immigration in Contemporary France*. Albany, State University of New York Press.

Finnemore, Martha. (1996). *National Interests in International Society*. Ithaca, NY, Cornell University Press.

Finnemore, Martha and Kathryn Sikkink. (1998). "International norm dynamics and political change." *International Organization* 52(4): 887–917.

Floyd, Rita. (2007). "Towards a consequentialist evaluation of security: Bringing together the Copenhagen and Welsh Schools of security studies." *Review of International Studies* 33: 327–50.

Freedman, Jane. (2004). *Immigration and Insecurity in France*. Aldershot, Ashgate.

Freeman, Gary. (1995). "Modes of immigration politics in liberal democratic states." *International Migration Review* 29(4): 881–913.

Freeman, Gary. (2002). "Winners and losers: Politics and the costs and benefits of migration." In *Western European Immigration and Immigration Policy in the New Century*, edited by Anthony M Messina, pp. 77–96. Westport, Praeger.

Freeman, Gary. (2006). "National models, policy types, and the politics of immigration in liberal democracies." *West European Politics* 29(2): 227–47.

Gagnon, Katia (2001). "Éditorial." *La Presse*, 14 septembre: A14.

Gagnon, Katia. (2003a). "Éditorial." *La Presse*, 4 avril: A12.

Gagnon, Katia (2003b). "Éditorial." *La Presse*, 9 août: A12.

Galloway, Donald. (1997). *Immigration Law*. Toronto, Irwin Law.

Gallup. (2005). "Huddled masses welcome in Canada." The Gallup Organization. Accessed through Lexis-Nexis, June 21.

Geddes, Andrew. (2003). *The Politics of Migration and Immigration in Europe*. London, Sage.

Gibney, Matthew J. (2004). *The Ethics and Politics of Asylum: Liberal Democracy and the Response to Refugees*. Cambridge, Cambridge University Press.

Giesbert, Franz-Olivier. (1990a). "Éditorial." *Le Figaro*, 2 avril: 1.

Giesbert, Franz-Olivier. (1990b). "Éditorial." *Le Figaro*, 29 mai: 1.

Giesbert, Franz-Olivier. (1991a). "Éditorial." *Le Figaro*, 26 mars: 1.

Giesbert, Franz-Olivier. (1991b). "Éditorial." *Le Figaro*, 9 juillet: 1.

Gruda, Agnès. (1993a). "Éditorial." *La Presse*, 19 août: B2.

Gruda, Agnès. (1993b). Éditorial. *La Presse*, 11 décembre: B2.

Gruda, Agnès. (1996). "Éditorial." *La Presse*, 9 mai: B2.

Gruda, Agnès. (1999). "Éditorial." *La Presse*, 24 février: B2.

Gruda, Agnès. (2001). "Éditorial." *La Presse*, 23 février: A10.

Guild, Elspeth and Joanne van Selm, eds. (2005). *International Migration and Security: Immigrants as an Asset or a Threat?* New York, Routledge.

Guiraudon, Virginie. (1998). "Citizenship rights for non-citizens: France, Germany, and the Netherlands." In *Challenge to the Nation-State*, edited by Christian Joppke, pp. 272–318. Oxford, Oxford University Press.

Guiraudon, Virginie. (2000a). *Les Politiques d'Immigration en Europe. Allemagne, France, Pays-Bas*. Paris, Harmattan.

Guiraudon, Virginie. (2000b). "The Marshallian triptych reordered. The role of courts and bureaucracies in furthering migrant's social rights." In *Immigration and Welfare: Challenging the Borders of the Welfare State*, edited by Michael Bommes and Andrew Geddes, pp. 71–88. London, Routledge.

Guiraudon, Virginie. (2002). "Logiques et pratiques de l'Etat délégateur: Les compagnies de transport dans le contrôle migratoire à distance." *Cultures & Conflits* 45(1): 51–79.

Guiraudon, Virginie and Christian Joppke. (2001). *Controlling a New Migration World*. London, Routledge.

Guiraudon, Virginie and Gallya Lahav. (2000). "A reappraisal of the state sovereignty debate: The case of migration control." *Comparative Political Studies* 33(2): 163–95.

Guzzini, Stefano. (2000). "A reconstruction of constructivism in international relations." *European Journal of International Relations* 6(2): 147–82.

Hall, Rodney Bruce. (1999). *National Collective Identity: Social Constructs and International Systems*. New York, Columbia University Press.

Hall, Stuart. (1990). "Culture, identity, and diaspora." In *Identity, Community, Culture, Difference*, edited by J. Rutherford, pp. 223–37. London, Lawrence & Wishart.

Hansen, Lene. (2000). "The Little Mermaid's silent security dilemma and the absence of gender in the Copenhagen School." *Millennium: Journal of International Studies* 29(2): 285–306.

Hargreaves, Alec G. (2001). "Ethnic relations in Britain and France." In *Media and Migration: Construction of Mobility and Difference*, edited by Nancy Wood and Russell King, pp. 23–37. London, Routledge.

Hawkins, Freda. (1988). *Canada and Immigration: Public Policy and Public Concern*. Toronto, McGill-Queen's University Press.

Heisler, Martin O. (2006). *The Migration–Security Nexus after 9/11: Regional Migration and Security in North America in Comparative Perspective*. Paper Presented at the 47th annual meeting of the International Studies Association, San Diego, March 22–25.

Hier, Sean and Joshua Greenberg. (2002). "Constructing a discursive crisis: Risk, problematization and illegal Chinese in Canada." *Ethnic and Racial Studies* 25(3): 490–513.

Higashino, Atsuko. (2004). "For the sake of 'peace and security'? The role of security in the European Union enlargement eastwards." *Cooperation and Conflict* 39(4): 347–68.

Hollifield, James F. (1992). *Immigrants, Markets, and States: The Political Economy of Postwar Europe*. Cambridge, Harvard University Press.

Hollifield, James F. (2000). "The politics of international migration." In *Migration Theory. Talking across Disciplines*, edited by Caroline Brettell and James F. Hollifield, pp. 137–86. New York: Routledge.

Hollifield, James F. (2004). "France: Republicanism and the limits of immigration control." In *Controlling Immigration: A Global Perspective*, edited by Wayne A. Cornelius, Philip L. Martin, and James F. Hollifield, pp. 183–214. Stanford, Stanford University Press.

Homer Dixon, Thomas. (1991). "On the threshold: Environmental changes as causes of acute conflict." *International Security* 16(2): 76–116.

Huntington, Samuel P. (2004). "The Hispanic challenge." *Foreign Policy* March/April: 30–45.

Huysmans, Jef. (1993). "Migrants as a security problem: Dangers of 'securitizing' societal issues." In *Migration and European Integration: The Dynamics of Inclusion and Exclusion*, edited by R. Mailes and D Thanhardt, pp. 53–72. London: Pinter.

Huysmans, Jef. (1998). "Revisiting Copenhagen: Or, on the creative development of a security studies agenda in Europe." *European Journal of International Relations* 4(4): 479–505.

Huysmans, Jef. (2006). *The Politics of Insecurity. Fear, Migration and Asylum in the EU*. London, Routledge.

Ibrahim, Maggie. (2005). "The securitization of migration: A racial discourse." *International Migration* 43(5): 163–87.

INSEE (2005). *Les immigrés en France*. Paris, Institut national de la statistique et des études économiques.

Inter-American Commission on Human Rights. (2000). *Report of the Situation of Human Rights of Asylum Seekers within the Canadian Refugee Determination System*. Washington, Inter-American Commission on Human Rights.

Ipsos-MORI. (2006). *Ipsos Global Citizens Monitor May 2006*, London, Ipsos-MORI, International Social Trends Unit.

Ipsos-Reid. (2006). *Annual Tracking Survey Winter 2006. Research Findings submitted to CIC*. Ottawa, Ipsos-Reid Corporation.

Ireland, Patrick. (2004). *Becoming Europe. Immigration, Integration and the Welfare State*. Pittsburgh, University of Pittsburgh Press.

Jackson, Nicole. (2006). "International Organizations, security dichotomies and the trafficking of persons and narcotics in post-Soviet Central Asia: A critique of the securitization framework." *Security Dialogue* 37(3): 299–317.

Jackson, Peter. (2008). "Pierre Bourdieu, the "cultural turn" and the practice of international history." *Review of International Studies* 34(1): 155–81.

Jacobson, David. (1997). *Rights Across Borders: Immigration and the Decline of Citizenship*. Baltimore, John Hopkins University Press.

Jedwab, Jack. (2006). *Keep on Tracking: Immigration and Public Opinion in Canada?* Paper presented at the conference of the Association for Canadian Studies, Metropolis Canada, Vancouver.

Job, Brian. (2003). "Track 2 diplomacy. Ideational contribution to the evolving Asia security order." In *Asian Security Order. Instrumental and Normative Features*, edited by Muthiah Alagappa, pp. 241–79. Stanford: Stanford University Press.

Joppke, Christian. (1998). "Why liberal states accept unwanted immigration." *World Politics* 50(2): 266–93.

Joppke, Christian. (2001). "The legal-domestic sources of immigrants rights: The United States, Germany, and the European Union." *Comparative Political Studies* 34(4): 339–66.

Joppke, Christian. (2005). *Selecting by Origin: Ethnic Migration in the Liberal State.* Cambridge, Harvard University Press.

Joppke, Christian and Ewa T. Morawska, eds. (2003). *Toward Assimilation and Citizenship: Immigrants in Liberal Nation-States.* New York, Palgrave Macmillan.

Jospin, Lionel. (1998). *Discours de M. Lionel Jospin, Premier Ministre, lors du dîner du Conseil Représentatif des Institutions Juives de France.* Paris, Bureau du Premier Ministre, 28 novembre.

Jospin, Lionel. (2001). *Discours relatif à la situation consécutive aux attentats du 11 septembre 2001.* Paris, Bureau du Premier Minister, 3 octobre.

Kaplan, Robert. (1994). "The coming anarchy." *Atlantic Monthly* February: 44–76.

Katzenstein, Peter J., ed. (1996). *The Culture of National Security: Norms and Identity in World Politics.* New York, Columbia University Press.

Keely, Charles B. and Sharon Stanton Russell. (1994). "Responses of industrial countries to asylum-seekers." *Journal of International Affairs* 47(2): 399–418.

Kelley, Ninette and Michael J. Trebilcock. (1998). *The Making of the Mosaic: A History of Canadian Immigration Policy.* Toronto, University of Toronto Press.

Kennedy-Pipe, Caroline. (2004). "Whose security? State-building and the emancipation of women in Central Asia." *International Relations* 18(1): 91–107.

Kenyon Lischer, Sarah. (2005). *Dangerous Sanctuaries. Refugee Camps, Civil War, and the Dilemmas of Humanitarian Aid.* Ithaca, Cornell University Press.

Klein, Bradley S. (1998). "Politics by design: Remapping security landscapes." *European Journal of International Relations* 4(3): 327–45.

Koopmans, Ruud, Paul Statham, Marco Giugni and Florence Passy. (2005). *Contested Citizenship: Immigration and Cultural Diversity in Europe.* Minneapolis, University of Minnesota Press.

Koslowski, Rey. (1999). "A constructivist approach to understanding the European Union as a federal polity." *Journal of European Public Policy* 6(4): 561–78.

Krause, Keith and Michael C. Williams. (1997). *Critical Security Studies: Concepts and Cases.* Minneapolis, University of Minnesota Press.

Kruger, Erin, Marlene Mulder and Bojan Korenic. (2004). "Canada after 11 September: Security measures and 'preferred' immigrants." *Mediterranean Quarterly* Fall: 72–87.

Laffey, Mark and Jutta Weldes. (1997). "Beyond belief: Ideas and symbolic technologies in the study of international relations." *European Journal of International Relations* 3(2): 193–238.

Lambroschini, Charles (1992). "Éditorial." *Le Figaro*, 23 avril: 1.

Landau, Loren B. (2006). "Immigration and the state of exception: Security and sovereignty in East and Southern Africa." *Millennium: Journal of International Studies* 34(2): 325–48.

Latour, Bruno. (1993). *We Have Never Been Modern*. Cambridge, MA, Harvard University Press.

Le Front National. (2002). *Pour un avenir français. Le programme de gouvernement du Front National*. Nanterre, Front National.

Le Monde. (1991). "L'image des réfugiés politiques est meilleure que celle des immigrés." 21 septembre: 8.

Le Monde. (1993). "Éditorial." 8 novembre: 18.

Le Monde. (1995). "Éditorial." 2 mai: 20.

Le Monde. (1996). "Éditorial." 21 decembre: 18.

Le Monde. (1997) "Éditorial." 24 février: 13.

Le Monde. (2001a). "Éditorial." 6 novembre: 21.

Le Monde. (2001b). "Éditorial." 22 février: 16.

Le Monde. (2002). "Éditorial." 11 décembre: 20.

Le Monde. (2003). "Éditorial." 8 novembre: 16.

Le Monde. (2004). "Éditorial." 14 février: 17.

Le Monde. (2005). "Éditorial." 8 octobre: 18.

Liotta, P.H. (2002). "Boomerang effect: The convergence of national and human security." *Security Dialogue* 33(4): 473–88.

Loescher, Gil. (1992). *Refugee Movements and International Security*. Adelphi Paper 268. London, International Institute for Strategic Studies.

Loescher, Gil and Laila Monahan. (1989). *Refugees and International Relations*. Oxford, Oxford University Press.

Lohrmann, Reinhard. (2000). "Migrants, refugees, and insecurity. Current threat to peace?" *International Migration* 38(4): 3–22.

Lowry, Michelle. (2002). "Creating human insecurity: The national security focus in Canada's immigration system." *Refuge – Canada's Periodical on Refugees* 21(1): 28–39.

Lynch, James P. and Rita J. Simon. (1999). "A comparative assessment of criminal involvement among immigrants and natives acrosss seven nations." *International Criminal Justice Review* 9: 1–17.

Lynch, James P. and Rita J. Simon. (2003). *Immigration the World Over: Statutes, Policies, and Practices*. Lanham, Rowan & Littlefield Publishers.

Lyon, David. (2006). "Airport screening, surveillance, and social sorting: Canadian responses to 9/11 in context." *Canadian Journal of Criminology and Criminal Justice* 48(3): 397–411.

Mack, Andrew. (2002). *Report on the Feasibility of Creating an Annual Human Security Report*. Cambridge, MA, Program on Humanitarian Policy and Conflict Research, Harvard University.

Malarek, Victor. (1990). "Into the 1990's Canada to stay favored immigrant destination, study says." *The Globe and Mail*, January 4.

Manley, John. (2000). *Notes for an Address by the Honourable John Manley, Minister of Foreign Affairs, to the Third Annual Diplomatic Forum on the Subject of Canada's Foreign Policy Agenda and Priorities*. Ottawa, Department of Foreign Affairs, October 20.

Manley, John. (2001a). *Notes for an Address by the Honourable John Manley, Minister of Foreign Affairs, to the 56th Session of the United Nations General Assembly*. New York, Department of Foreign Affairs, November 10.

Manley, John. (2001b). *Notes for an Address by the Honourable John Manley, Minister of Foreign Affairs, to the Conseil des Relations Internationales de Montreal*. Montreal, Department of Foreign Affairs, October 11.

Manley, John. (2002). *Notes for an Address by the Honourable John Manley, Minister of Foreign Affairs, to the Canadian Council of Chief Executives*. Ottawa, Department of Foreign Affairs, January 15.

Marchand, Philippe. (1991). *Discours de Philippe Marchand, Ministre de l'Intérieur, "Un projet global pour la securite interieure."* Paris, Ministère de l'Intérieur, 20 novembre.

Marchetti, Xavier. (1990). "Éditorial." *Le Figaro*, 11 mai: 1.

Marchetti, Xavier. (1993). "Éditorial." *Le Figaro*, 1 avril: 1.

Marchetti, Xavier. (1995). "Éditorial." *Le Figaro*, 25 mars: 1.

Matthews, Jessica T. (1989). "Redefining security." *Foreign Affairs* 68: 162–77.

McDonald, Matt. (2008). "Securitization and the construction of security." *European Journal of International Relations* 14(4): 563–87.

McDougall, Barbara. (1991). *Notes for an Address by the Honourable Barbara McDougall, Minister of Foreign Affairs, to the Conference Commemorating the 60th Anniversary of the Statute of Westminster*. Ottawa, Department of Foreign Affairs, December 10.

McDougall, Barbara. (1992a). *Notes for an Address by the Honourable Barbara McDougall, Minister of Foreign Affairs, to the Council of Ministers of the Conference on Security and Cooperation in Europe*. Ottawa, Department of Foreign Affairs, January 30.

McDougall, Barbara. (1992b). *Notes for an Address by the Honourable Barbara McDougall, Minister of Foreign Affairs, to the Official Opening of the Canadian Foreign Service Institute*. Ottawa, Department of Foreign Affairs, October 1.

McSweeney, Bill. (1996). "Identity and security: Buzan and the Copenhagen School." *Review of International Studies* 22(1): 81–93.

Migration Dialogue. (2002). *Migration News* 9(1).

Migration Dialogue. (2003). *Migration News* 10(2).

Migration Dialogue. (2005). *Migration News* 12(1).

Migration Dialogue. (2007). *Migration News* 14(1).

Miller, Mark J. (1997). "International migration and security: Towards transatlantic convergence?" In *Immigration into Western Societies. Problems and Policies*, edited by Emek M. Ucarer and Donald James Puchala, pp. 255–66. London, Pinter.

Miller, Mark J. (1998). "International migration and global security." In *Redefining Security: Population Movements and National Security*, edited by Nana Poku and David Graham, pp. 15–28. London: Praeger.

Milliken, Jennifer. (1999). "The study of discourse in international relations: A critique of research and methods." *European Journal of International Relations* 5(2): 225–54.

Ministère de la Défense. (1994). *Livre Blanc sur la Défense*. Paris, République Française.

Ministère de l'Intérieur et du Développement Régional. (2009). "Missions." Paris, République Française. Available at http://www.interieur.gouv.fr/sections/a_l_interieur/le_ministere/missions (last accessed November 18, 2010).

Mitterand, François. (1988). *Lettre à tous les Français*. Paris, Présidence de la République, 7 avril.

Mitterand, François. (1994a). *Discours de M. François Mitterrand, Président de la République, sur le bilan de trente années d'aide au développement, les propositions françaises pour améliorer son efficacité et celle des organisations internationales et sur l'annonce d'une intervention militaire au Rwanda*. Paris, Présidence de la République, 18 juin.

Mitterand, François. (1994b). *Discours de M. François Mitterrand, Président de la République, sur la démocratisation de l'Afrique, la proposition de créer une force d'intervention interafricaine pour la prévention des conflits et l'organisation du développement et de la croissance du continent.* Paris, Présidence de la République, 8 novembre.

Morice, Alain and Claire Rodier. (2005). "Classer-trier migrants et réfugiés: des distinctions qui font mal." *Hommes et Libertés – Revue de la Ligue des Droits de l'Homme* 129(mars): 58–61.

Morier, Roger. (1990). " 'They should all go back where they belong'. Racism in France." *The Globe and Mail*, April 7: D1.

Morris, Jessica C. (2003). "The spaces in between: American and Australian interdiction policies and their Implications for the refugee protection regime." *Refuge – Canada's Periodical on Refugees* 21(4): 51–62.

Mutimer, David. (1997). "Beyond strategy: Critical thinking and the new security studies." In *Contemporary Security and Strategy*, edited by Craig Snyder, pp. 77–101. New York, Routledge.

Newman, Edward and Joanne van Selm. (2003). *Refugees and Forced Displacement: International Security, Human Vulnerability, and the State.* Tokyo, United Nations University Press.

Nirascou, Gérard. (1997). "Éditorial." *Le Figaro*, 14 juillet: 1.

Nirascou, Gérard. (2000). "Éditorial." *Le Figaro*, 14 juillet: 1.

Noiriel, Gerard. (2006). *Le creuset français: Histoire de l'immigration, XIXe-XXe siècle. Deuxième édition.* Paris, Seuil.

OECD. (2004). *International Migration Outlook 2004.* Paris, OECD.

OECD (2005). *Trends in International Migration: SOPEMI – 2004 Edition.* Paris, OECD.

OECD. (2010). *International Migration Outlook 2010.* Paris, OECD.

Ong, Aihwa and Donald Nonini. (1996). *Ungrounded Empires: The Cultural Politics of Modern Chinese Transnationalism.* London, Routledge.

Ouellet, André. (1994). *Notes for an Address by the Honourable André Ouellet, Minister of Foreign Affairs, to the International Institute for Strategic Studies.* Ottawa, Department of Foreign Affairs, September 8.

Pasqua, Charles. (1993a). *Intervention de M. Charles Pasqua, Ministre de l'Intérieur, à l'Institut des Hautes Études de Sécurité Intérieure.* Paris, Ministère de l'Intérieur, 15 septembre.

Pasqua, Charles. (1993b). *Intervention de M. Charles Pasqua, Ministre de l'Intérieur, à l'université d'été des jeunes RPR.* Paris, Ministère de l'Intérieur, 4 septembre.

Pasqua, Charles. (1993c). *Discours de M. Charles Pasqua, Ministre de l'Intérieur, devant les Commissaires de Police.* Paris, Ministère de l'Intérieur, 10 mai.

Pasqua, Charles. (1994). *Discours de M. Charles Pasqua, Ministre de l'Intérieur, devant les Préfets.* Paris, Ministère de l'Intérieur, 26 avril.

PCO. (2004). *Securing an Open Society: Canada's National Security Policy.* Ottawa, Privy Council Office, Government of Canada.

Pierson, Paul. (2004). *Politics in Time. History, Institutions, and Social Analysis.* Princeton, Princeton University Press.

Pouliot, Vincent. (2008). "The logic of practicality: A theory of practice of security communities." *International Organization* 62(2): 257–88.

Pratt, Anna. (2005). *Securing Borders: Detention and Deportation in Canada.* Vancouver, University of British Columbia Press.

Price, Richard. (1997). *The Chemical Weapons Taboo*. Ithaca, Cornell University Press.

Price, Richard and Christian Reus-Smit. (1998). "Dangerous liaisons?: Critical international theory and constructivism." *European Journal of International Relations* 4(3): 259–94.

Quilès, Paul, (1992). *Discours de M. Paul Quilès, Ministre de l'Intérieur à la réunion des chefs de service de la direction centrale de la police judiciaire*. Paris, Ministère de l'Intérieur, 19 mai.

Raffarin, Jean-Pierre. (2003a). *Discours de M. Jean-Pierre Raffarin, Premier Ministre, devant l'Assemblée nationale*. Paris, Bureau du Premier Ministre, 2 juillet.

Raffarin, Jean-Pierre. (2003b). *Discours de M. Jean-Pierre Raffarin, Premier Ministre, devant les gendarmes et policiers d'Ile-de-France*. Paris, Bureau du Premier Ministre, 24 septembre.

Rebois, Charles. (1991). "Éditorial." *Le Figaro*, 7 novembre: 1

Rebois, Charles. (1993). "Éditorial." *Le Figaro*, 16 août: 1.

Rebois, Charles. (1996). "Éditorial." *Le Figaro*, 23 août: 1.

Reitz, Jeffrey G. (2004). "Canada: Immigration and nation-building in the transition to a knowledge economy." In *Controlling Immigration: A Global Perspective*, edited by Wayne A. Cornelius, Philip L. Martin, and James F. Hollifield, pp. 97–133. Stanford, Stanford University Press.

Reuter. (1990). "Arabs, Jews targets of racism in France." *The Globe and Mail*, March 29: A9.

Rioufol, Ivan. (1996). "Éditorial." *Le Figaro*, 19 août: 1.

Risse, Thomas. (2000). " 'Let's argue!': Communicative action in world politics." *International Organization* 54(1): 1–39.

Roberts, Adam. (1998). "More refugees, less asylum: A regime in transformation." *Journal of Refugee Studies* 11(4): 375–95.

Robillard, Lucienne. (1998). *Speaking Notes of the Honourable Lucienne Robillard, Minister of Citizenship and Immigration, for the Standing Committee on Citizenship and Immigration Concerning the Main Estimates*. Ottawa, Department of Citizenship and Immigration, March 18.

Robinson, Vaughan. (1998). "Security, migration, and refugees." In *Redefining Security. Population Movements and National Security*, edited by David Graham, pp. 67–90. London, Praeger.

Rocard, Michel. (1989). *Déclaration de M. Michel Rocard, Premier Ministre, sur les enjeux de la construction européenne*. Paris, Bureau du Premier Ministre, 15 juin.

Rocard, Michel. (1990). *Déclaration de M. Michel Rocard, Premier Ministre, sur l'intégration des immigrés et des Français d'origine étrangère*. Paris, Bureau du Premier Ministre, 7 janvier.

Rodier, Claire. (2006). *Analyse de la dimension externe des politiques d'asile et d'immigration de l'UE. Synthèse et recommandations pour le Parlement européen*. Bruxelles, Parlement Européen. Direction générale pour les politiques externers de l'Union.

Roe, Paul. (2004). "Securitization and minority rights: Conditions of desecuritization." *Security Dialogue* 35(3): 279–94.

Rudolph, Christopher. (2003). "Security and the political economy of international migration." *American Political Science Review* 97(4): 603–20.

Rudolph, Christopher. (2006). *National Security and Immigration: Policy Development in the United States and Western Europe since 1945*. Stanford, Stanford University Press.

Ruggie, John Gerard. (1998). "What makes the world hang together? Neo-utilitarianism and the social constructivist challenge (in constructivist approaches)." *International Organization* 52(4): 855–85.

Salehyan, Idean and Kristian Skrede Gleditsch. (2006). "Refugees and the spread of civil war." *International Organization* 60(2): 335–66.

Salter, Mark B. (2008). "Securitization and desecuritization: Dramaturgical analysis and the Canadian Aviation Transport Security Authority." *Journal of International Relations and Development* 11(4): 321–49.

Sarkozy, Nicolas. (2002a). *Déclaration de M. Nicolas Sarkozy, Ministre de l'Intérieur, sur la mise en oeuvre de la loi d'orientation et de programmation sur la sécurité intérieure (LOPSI), les missions du Service de coopération technique internationale de la police (SCTIP) et le développement du réseau des attachés de sécurité intérieure à l'étranger.* Paris, Ministère de l'Intérieur, 2 septembre.

Sarkozy, Nicolas. (2002b). *Déclaration de M. Nicolas Sarkozy, Ministre de l'Intérieur, de la sécurité intérieure et des libertés locales, sur la fusion du RPR au sein de l'UMP et sur les engagements électoraux de la majorité issue des élections présidentielles et législatives de 2002.* Villepinte, Ministère de l'Intérieur, 21 septembre.

Sarkozy, Nicolas. (2003). *Déclaration de M. Nicolas Sarkozy, Ministre de l'Intérieur, de la sécurité intérieure et des libertés locales, sur les principales mesures prises dans le cadre du plan Vigipirate renforcé.* Paris, Ministère de l'Intérieur, 20 mars.

Sasse, Gwendolyn. (2005). "Securitisation or securing rights? Exploring the conceptual foundations of policies towards migrants and minorities in Europe." *Journal of Common Market Studies* 43(4): 673–93.

Sassen, Saskia. (1996). *Losing Control?: Sovereignty in an Age of Globalization.* New York, Columbia University Press.

Schmitt, Carl. (1985 [1922]). *Political Theology.* Cambridge, MA, MIT Press.

Schmitt, Carl. (1996 [1932]). *The Concept of the Political.* Trans. G. Schwab. Chicago, University of Chicago Press.

Shain, Yossi. (1995). "Multicultural foreign policy." *Foreign Policy Analysis* 100: 69–87.

Shain, Yossi and Aharon Barth Barth. (2003). "Diaspora and international relations theory." *International Organization* 57(3): 449–79.

Sheffer, Gabriel. (1986). *Modern Diasporas in International Politics.* New York, St. Martin's Press.

Siegel, Arthur. (1996). *Politics and the Media in Canada*, 2nd edition. Toronto, McGraw-Hill Ryerson.

Smith, Steve. (1999). "Social constructivism and European studies: A reflectivist critique." *Journal of European Public Policy* 6(4): 682–91.

Smith, Steve. (2005). "The contested concept of security." In *Critical Security Studies and World Politics*, edited by Ken Booth, pp. 27–62. London, Routledge.

Sofres. (1996). *L'etat de l'opinion.* Paris, Seuil.

Sofres. (1998). *L'etat de l'opinion.* Paris, Seuil.

Soysal, Yasemine. (1994). *Limits of Citizenship.* Chicago, Chicago University Press.

Statham, Paul and Andrew Geddes. (2006). "Elites and the 'organized public': Who drives British immigration politics and in which directions?" *West European Politics* 29(2): 248–69.

Stritzel, Holger. (2007). "Towards a theory of securitization: Copenhagen and beyond." *European Journal of International Relations* 13(3): 357–83.

Suffert, Georges. (1997). "Éditorial." *Le Figaro*, 4 décembre: 1.

Taureck, Rita. (2006). "Securitization theory and securitization studies." *Journal of International Relations and Development* 9(1): 53–69.

The Globe and Mail. (1989). "Editorial." February 17: A6.

The Globe and Mail. (1991). "63 per cent like multiracial Canada." November 5: A15.

The Globe and Mail. (1993). "Editorial." March 11: A24.

The Globe and Mail. (1994). "Editorial." November 3: A28.

The Globe and Mail. (1997). "Editorial." November 6: A26.

The Globe and Mail. (1998). "Editorial." June 9: A16.

The Globe and Mail. (1999). "Editorial." September 16: A18.

The Globe and Mail. (2000). "Editorial." January 31: A14.

The Globe and Mail. (2001a). "Editorial." April 2: A12.

The Globe and Mail (2001b). "Editorial." September 19: A14.

The Globe and Mail. (2001c). "Editorial." September 22: A14.

The Globe and Mail. (2001d). "Editorial." September 29: A16.

The Globe and Mail (2001e). "Editorial." December 4: A22.

The Globe and Mail. (2002). "Editorial." January 12: A14.

The Globe and Mail. (2004). "Editorial." May 31: A12.

The Globe and Mail. (2005). "Editorial." October 19: A20.

The Liberal Party of Canada. (1984). *Liberal Federal Campaign Committee, Issues Sheet.* Ottawa, Liberal Party of Canada.

The Liberal Party of Canada. (1993). *Creating Opportunity: The Liberal Plan for Canada.* Ottawa, Liberal Party of Canada Page.

The Reform Party of Canada. (1993). *Blue Sheet, Principles, Policies and Election Platform.* Ottawa, Reform Party of Canada.

Thierry, Xavier. (2000). "Les entrées d'étrangers en France: Évolutions statistiques et bilan de l'opération de régularisation exceptionnelle de 1997." *Population* 55(3): 562–90

Thierry, Xavier. (2004). "Évolution récente de l'immigration en France et elements de comparaison avec le Royaume-Uni." *Population* 59(5): 725–64.

Thréard, Yves. (2005). "Editorial." *Le Figaro*, 15 janvier: 1.

Tickner, J. Ann. (1992). *Gender in International Relations: Feminist Perspectives on Achieving Global Security.* New York, Columbia University Press.

Tickner, J. Ann. (1995). "Re-visioning security." In *International Relations Theory Today*, edited by Ken Booth and Steve Smith, pp. 175–97. Oxford, Oxford University Press.

Tirman, John, ed. (2004). *The Maze of Fear: Security and Migration after 9/11.* New York, New Press.

TNS-Sofres. (2006). *L'etat de l'opinion.* Paris, Seuil.

Tsoukala, Anastassia. (2005). "Looking at migrants as enemies." In *Controlling Frontiers. Free Movement Into and Within Europe*, edited by Didier Bigo and Elspeth Guild, pp. 161–92. London. Ashgate.

Ullman, Richard. (1983). "Redefining security." *International Security* 8(1): 129–53.

United Nations. (2000). *Replacement Migration: Is it a Solution to Declining and Ageing Populations?* New York, United Nations, Department of Economic and Social Affairs, Population Division.

United Nations High Commissioner for Refugees. (2006). *Statistical Yearbook 2004. Trends in Displacement, Protection and Solutions.* Geneva, United Nations

US Department of Justice. (2000). *Federal Law Enforcement Officers 2000.* Washington, U.S. Department of Justice, Bureau of Justice Statistics.

Vaillant, Daniel. (2001). *Déclaration de M. Daniel Vaillant, Ministre de l'Intérieur, sur le renforcement de la coopération policière au niveau européen pour lutter contre l'immigration clandestine.* Paris, Ministère de l'Intérieur, 28 août.

Valcourt, Bernard. (1992). *Notes for an Address by Bernard Valcourt, Minister of Employment and Immigration to the Legislative Committee Studying Bill C-86*. Ottawa, Department of Employment and Immigration, July 27.

van Munster, Rens. (2009). *Securitizing Migration. The Politics of Risk in the EU*. Basingstoke, Palgrave.

Van Selm, Joanne, ed. (2000). *Kosovo's Refugees in the European Union*. London, Pinter.

Van Selm, Joanne. (2003). "Refugee protection policies and security studies." In *Refugees and Forced Displacement: International Security, Human Vulnerability, and the State*, edited by Edward Newman and Joanne van Selm, pp. 66–92. Tokyo, United Nations University Press.

Vennat, Pierre (1989). "Éditorial." *La Presse*, 27 octobre: B2.

Vukov, Tamara. (2003). "Imagining communities through immigration policies: Governmental regulation, media spectacles and the affective politics of national borders." *International Journal of Cultural Studies* 6(3): 335–53.

Wæver, Ole. (1995). "Securitization and desecuritization." In *On Security*, edited by Ronnie D. Lipschultz, pp. 46–86. New York, Columbia University Press.

Wæver, Ole. (2000). "The EU as a security actor. Reflections from a pessimistic constructivist on post-sovereign security orders." In *International Relations Theory and the Politics of European Integration. Power Security and Community*, edited by Morten Kelstrup and Michael C Williams, pp. 250–94. London, Routledge.

Wæver, Ole. (2009). "What exactly makes a continuous existential threat existential – and how is it discontinued?" In *Existential Threats and Civil-Security Relations*, edited by Oren Barak and Gabriel Sheffer, pp. 19–36. New York: Lexington Books.

Wæver, Ole, Barry Buzan and Jaap de Wilde, eds. (1993). *Identity, Migration, and the New Security Agenda in Europe*. New York, St. Martin's Press.

Wahnich, Sophie. (1997). *L'impossible citoyen. L'étranger dans le discours de la révolution française*. Paris, Albin Michel.

Waldman, Lorne. (2005). *Immigration Law and Practice*. Markham, Lexis-Nexis.

Walt, Stephen M. (1991). "The renaissance of security studies." *International Studies Quarterly* 35(2): 211–39.

Walt, Stephen M. (2002). "The enduring relevance of the realist tradition." In *Political Science: The State of the Discipline*, edited by Ira Katznelson and Helen V. Miller, pp. 197–234. New York, Norton.

Walters, William. (2002). "Deportation, expulsion, and the international police of aliens." *Citizenship Studies* 6(3): 265–92.

Weil, Patrick. (1997). *Rapports au Premier Ministre sur les legislations de la nationalite et de l'immigration*. Paris, La Documentation Francaise.

Weil, Patrick. (2005). *La France et ses étrangers: L'aventure d'une politique de l'immigration de 1938 à nos jours*. Paris, Gallimard.

Weiner, Myron. (1993). *International Migration and Security*. Boulder, CO, Westview Press.

Weiner, Myron. (1995). *The Global Migration Crisis: Challenge to States and to Human Rights*. New York, HarperCollins College Publishers.

Welch, Michael and Liza Schuster. (2005). "Detention of asylum seekers in the US, UK, France, Germany, and Italy. A critical view of the globalizing culture of control." *Criminal Justice* 5(4): 331–55.

Whitaker, Reginald. (1998). "Refugees: The security factor." *Citizenship Studies* 2(3): 413–34.

Wight, Colin. (1999). "They shoot dead horses don't they?: Locating agency in the agent-structure problematique." *European Journal of International Relations* 5(1): 109–42.

Wihtol de Wenden, Catherine. (1987). *Citoyennete, nationalité et immigration.* Paris, Arcantáere.

Wilkinson, Claire. (2007). "The Copenhagen School on tour in Kyrgyzstan: Is securitization theory useable outside Europe?" *Security Dialogue* 38(1): 5–25.

Williams, Michael C. (2003). "Words, images, enemies: Securitization and international politics." *International Studies Quarterly* 47(4): 511–31.

Williams, Michael C. (2007). *Culture and Security. Symbolic Power and the Politics of International Security.* London, Routledge.

Wimmer, Andreas and Nina Glick Schiller. (2003). "Methodological Nationalism, the social sciences, and the study of migration: An essay in historical epistemology." *International Migration Review* 37(3): 576–610.

Wyn Jones, Richard. (2005). "On emancipation: Necessity, capacity, and concret utopias." In *Criticial Security Studies and World Politics*, edited by Ken Booth, pp. 215–36. London, Lynne Rienner.

Zolberg, Aristide R. (1992). "Labour migration and international economic regimes: Bretton Woods and after." In *International Migration Systems: A Global Approach*, edited by Mary M. Kritz, Lin Lean Lim, and Hania Zlotnik, pp. 315–34. Oxford, Clarendon Press.

Index

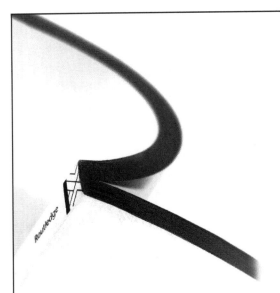

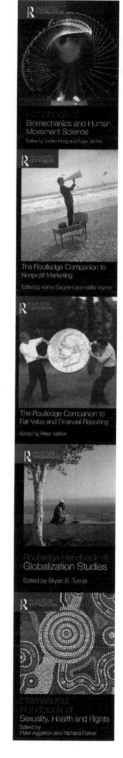

An environmentally friendly book printed and bound in England by www.printondemand-worldwide.com

PEFC Certified

This product is
from sustainably
managed forests
and controlled
sources

www.pefc.org

PEFC/16-33-415

MIX
Paper from
responsible sources

FSC
www.fsc.org

FSC® C004959

This book is made entirely of sustainable materials; FSC paper for the cover and PEFC paper for the text pages.

#0043 - 010914 - C0 - 234/156/10 - PB